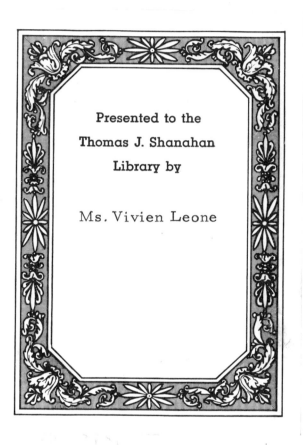

TAKING IT LIKE A WOMAN

TAKING IT LIKE A
WOMAN

ANN OAKLEY

RANDOM HOUSE   NEW YORK

For A

Library of Congress Cataloging in Publication Data

Oakley, Ann.
Taking it like a woman.

1. Oakley, Ann. 2. Feminists—Great Britain—Biography.
I. Title.
HQ1595.034   1984   305.4′2′0924   83-43192
ISBN 0-394-53642-8

Manufactured in the United States of America
98765432
First Edition

'All the world is a stage, thought I; and few are there in it who do not play the part they have learned by rote; and those who do not seem marks set up to be pelted at by fortune; or rather as signposts, which point out the road to others, whilst forced to stand still themselves amidst the mud and dust.'

Mary Wollstonecraft, *Letters Written during a Short Residence in Sweden, Norway and Denmark*, 1796

Contents

Author's Note

Some of the characters in this book are real, and some aren't. I would not like anyone to be hurt by anything they believe I have said about them here. Any sins of omission or commission that may be read into these pages are not intended on my part.

The publisher and I would like to thank the copyright holders of material appearing in the book as follows: on p. 157 the extract from 'East Coker' is reprinted by permission of Faber & Faber Ltd from *Four Quartets* by T.S. Eliot and on pp. 176–7 the extracts from Sylvia Plath's 'Sheep in the Fog' and 'Paralytic' appear by permission of Olwyn Hughes. The words to the song 'Dona, Dona', reproduced on p. 194, by Sheldon Secunda, Teddi Schwartz and Arthur Kevess are copyright © 1940/56 Mills Music Inc., New York and are reprinted by kind permission of Belwin Mills Music Ltd, 250 Purley Way, Croydon, Surrey, England.

A Lake in a London Park, 1975

It is the end of a summer that had no proper middle or beginning. It is late afternoon; the sun with its last strength shines kindly. Around the edges of the lake people sit in deckchairs reading. In the middle of the lake a boat holds a man and a woman. They are almost middle-aged, but quite good-looking still; probably professional people, middle class, not suffering from any obvious kind of deprivation.

What is most striking about them is their vitality. Everything about them is alive—their faces, their eloquent gestures towards the water, their bare toes (they have removed their shoes—perhaps they are not so middle-aged after all?) He touches her: she touches him. They are clearly experienced, but their behaviour is somehow adolescent. She is a little awkward, self-conscious. He is more brazen, but almost his every action is accompanied by laughter, although there is really nothing funny about the situation. She strokes his golden face. He reaches beneath her blouse for her breasts. They care and do not care about their audience; the people in their chairs, a black swan sticking its neck over the edge of the boat, men who may know them walking with briefcases and raincoats behind the trees.

It must be difficult for them to come to terms with passion. There is little passion in professional suburban circles in the 1970s. The mood of the moment is therefore out of place, out of time, stolen, invaluable, a death-bed memory; it is a world away from academic papers and investigations, house improvements

and clean laundry. Visions are for solitary figures in supermarkets, lonely travellers, tired husbands and wives. They are
not for public consumption. And they are not intended to make
real hearts bleed.

Love creates in people more than a bleeding heart. Love takes
us back to all the things we knew and did not know before we
crept out into the world.

None of us can hope to solve our basic problems: why we are
alive, how we should be born, behave, think, love, labour, die.
But, on the other hand, women now more than ever cannot
afford to disregard the task of understanding themselves. 'Re-
vision—the act of looking back, of seeing with fresh eyes, of
entering an old text from a new critical direction—is for women
more than a chapter in cultural history: it is an act of survival.
Until we can understand the assumptions in which we are
drenched we cannot know ourselves.'[1] But such a drive to self-
knowledge is more than the dilatory self-interested pastime of
the so-called liberated woman. It is a serious human enterprise.
It is a protest against the dehumanization of society made by
women on behalf of everyone, because it is women who find
themselves most discomforted by the gap between who they are
and what they are supposed to be. This contradiction signals
others. In particular, it signals the dominant presence within our
culture of a destructive impulse, an impulse that denies the
eccentric authenticity of the individual and insists instead on
concentric conformity to a pre-defined standard. According to
this standard, human welfare is measured in terms of competitive
power and status, by the aggregation of wealth, and in the
statistics of purely physical survival.

This book is about my life, but it is also about others—for it
would be arrogant to suppose I'm unique; I'm not. In those
passages in the book where I write about myself I have no drive
salaciously to exhibit a purely private history. On the contrary,
this has been a most painful and difficult book to write, and it
goes against the grain of a basically shy and retiring nature to see
myself in print in this way. The book has taken far longer to
write than any other book I have written, because, I think, the
chief obstacle to describing oneself as an individual located in a
particular manner in a particular culture is the need *not* to be

honest with oneself, to conceal the person one is from oneself and, indeed, from everybody else. But I have persevered in this task precisely because I know I am living and writing about something which is recognizable to others. I have thus tried self-consciously to draw together in this book some of the connecting threads between my life and the lives of others, between the issues that concern me and those that are of general concern.

The questions I had in my mind when I started to write it included the following:

1 What makes someone into a feminist?

2 What sort of person is a feminist?

3 How can a feminist be part of a society organized in terms of sexual difference and 'the family'?

4 What is the nature of the love between men and women?

5 How do we deal with the fact that we're not going to live for ever?

My own realization that I'm not going to live for ever was one of the motives that led me to begin writing this book. The other was a great tiredness with the representation of feminism in our culture—or not so much with the representation of feminism as with that of the women who, in calling themselves feminists, apparently call forth in others a repertoire of hostility and muddleheadedness that has to be heard (or read) to be believed.

To ask these questions from these motives and to begin to look for answers has one implication above all others: and that is the reclamation of conflict. It's not original to say that conflict and contradiction are part of being alive; we may choose to pretend we've got it all worked out, but we haven't. In Aldous Huxley's *Brave New World* emotions are controlled, temptations are abolished, and divisions excised before they happen. There are no big or little wars. 'The greatest care is taken to prevent you from loving anyone too much. There's no such thing as divided allegiance; you're so conditioned that you can't help doing what you ought to do.' Nothing is inconvenient and everything is comfortable. But the savage from the old world protests that he doesn't want comfort:

'. . . I want poetry, I want real danger, I want freedom, I want goodness. I want sin.'

'In fact,' said Mustapha Mond [from the new world],

'you're claiming the right to be unhappy.

'Not to mention the right to grow old and ugly and impotent; the right to have syphilis and cancer; the right to have little to eat; the right to be lousy; the right to live in constant apprehension of what may happen tomorrow; the right to catch typhoid; the right to be tortured by unspeakable pains of every kind.'

There was a long silence.

'I claim them all,' said the Savage at last.

Mustapha Mond shrugged his shoulders. 'You're welcome,' he said.[2]

We must claim the right to pain and passion. In order to do this, we have to begin by examining our own history.

CHRONOLOGY 0–18

I was born in 1944, although I was imagined and planned long before that. My mother and father married in 1937, at the ages of thirty-four and thirty respectively. She came from a solid middle-class family in South London; her father, Thomas Miller, had a relatively prestigious job as a cutlery salesman. The house in which she grew up and to which I was taken as a child was itself impeccably respectable. The rooms were dark and smelt of polish and the paint was brown. A lace mat occupied the centre of the dining table, and on it stood a green glass bowl containing a china goldfish; tea was served in delicate white cups and good manners were expected. Thomas Miller's mother was the daughter of a Scottish sea captain and she grew up, shoeless, on the island of Rum, so my mother's background was a little more chequered than it appeared. Her own mother, Katie Louisa Miller, Thomas's wife, was the daughter of a Norfolk wheelwright and an Irish woman with a fiery temper, a combination that produced a woman with a dainty, mild-mannered appearance concealing a will of iron. 'Gran', as I knew her, wore stiff white blouses with round cameo brooches at the neck. She had a prim mouth, and only her luminous dark eyes gave one a glimpse of the unbuttoned person inside.

My father, on the other hand, came from a farming family in Bedfordshire that fell victim to the post-First World War depression. In the early 1920s the family left Bedfordshire and moved to the London suburb of Hendon, where Morris Titmuss set up an unsuccessful haulage business and then unexpectedly died. They took his body back to the little churchyard at Lilley, to his ancestors, where his grave, now layered with grass and weeds, proclaims that 'The Face of Death is Towards the Sun of Life'.

Morris Titmuss's death left nineteen-year-old Richard in charge of an elder sister, a younger brother, and a desolate, incapable widow. His sister made a difficult marriage and developed cardiac disease, and his mother remained desolate and incapable until her death in 1972, one year before Richard's own. My father's family always communicated an air of tragedy to me—tragedy with none of that romantic edge that has made it such an appealing cultural theme.

No family is conventional when you take a hard look at it, but my parents, each in their own way, were definitely unconventional products. After an unsatisfactory period spent being a leisured daughter at home according to the fashion of the time, my mother took a secretarial-administrative job at the Royal Colonial Institute (later the Royal Commonwealth Society) in London. After a number of years in this job she realized its limitations, and at the same time met a charismatic congregational minister who came eventually to see in my mother the saviour of the unemployed. She performed this role with enormous verve and enthusiasm for years, often returning to South London on the 1.30 am 'printers' train' from St Paul's. (Social work attracted many independent, original women in those days and was, indeed, a pioneering occupation.)

My father's career started at fourteen when he became an office boy in Standard Telephones. When his father died he moved to the County Fire Insurance Office, where by thirty-two he had risen to the glorified rank of inspector. But his heart was not in insurance, and after he met my mother on a holiday in Welsh youth hostels in 1934 an embryonic interest in the social and political issues of the day began to develop. This led eventually to the publication of several books, *Poverty and Population* (1938), *Our Food Problem* (1939) and *Birth, Poverty and Wealth* (1943), the last of these written in the strutted basement of a London house during the bomb-littered winter of 1940–1. These works fostered a reputation that earned him a post as official historian to the War Cabinet, responsible for a volume called *Problems of Social Policy*, after which his career as an academic pundit and social critic never looked back.

His work was always difficult to classify (a fact of which he himself was obstinately proud), and, since he had no professional academic training, he persisted in calling himself a student of society. He always began with a problem and worked outwards to an analysis of it. He wasn't famous, but he was well known in a certain circle which had a habit of widening throughout his career.

In the early days of my parents' courtship they worked together in my mother's bedroom in her parents' musty house on a poignant unpublished manuscript. This manuscript, bound in black and tied with a purple ribbon, is called *Crime and Tragedy* and is dedicated to 'those who laid down their lives that others might uphold the Divine Right to use Bombing Planes'. It reminds one that the passionate idealism of youth is neither new nor, depressingly, lasting. *Crime and Tragedy* summed up the sense of moral outrage my parents and their friends felt as the country was plunged into another world war. 'How long, O Race of Mankind,' my father asks with a turn of phrase that he fortunately learnt to tame in his later work, 'will you persist in sacrificing the sweetness of life on this bloody altar... Today, old man, I am asked to accept a world of tomahawks and tomtoms, largely the creation of Conservative obscurantists. Tomorrow, you old fool, I shall be asked to die for it.'

The war interrupted a lot of family planning, including that of my parents. The only book they wrote together is called *Parents' Revolt*,[1] and it puts their personal predicament in a general setting—the fall in the birth rate accelerated by the war, due, they thought, to men and women's reluctance to bring children into a world not fitted for them. Their own reluctance was beaten by the constraint of biology. On consulting Aleck Bourne (an eminent gynaecologist who defended the abortion of a teenage girl's fetus conceived in a military rape), my mother was told that busyness in women may prevent conception. So she put her duty to the future first, grew her one and only child, and never worked outside the home again. (The late 1940s marked a period of retrenchment for women's position in the labour force. 'Good' mothers then and in the 1950s simply didn't work outside the home.)

On January 17, 1944, some two weeks ahead of the proper date, and three days before my mother's forty-first birthday, I was

born in the Lindo wing of St Mary's Hospital, Paddington, a
place now famous for the births of royal babies. My mother was
not conscious when I was born, and she breastfed me for four
days only. These are both facts I did not know until recently, and
I find them slightly shocking—although naturally, or rather
culturally, quite understandable in terms of the obstetric and
paediatric habits then prevailing. A nurse brought her little girl
to her bedside, having first brushed her hair up into a feminine
curl at the front. My father, who was not there, later brought me
a teddy bear. A bomb fell next to the hospital and that put the
lid on any prospect of breastmilk, the doctors adding insult to
injury by malevolently declaring lactation inadequate anyway.

My father's work in insurance meant that he did not have to
do active service in the war, but watched for bombs from the
dome of St Paul's Cathedral. My mother and I spent much of the
war evading it in an attic room on a farm in Bedfordshire. I have
some notes my mother made during this period of my achievements, and these say that on a visit to the nearest town, people
described me as 'a beautiful little doll'. I was definitely conscious
even at this early age of the approbation that was forthcoming
when I conformed to this image. Photographs taken at the time
show me as a small, neat child with short, light brown hair
wearing pale dresses and white socks. I walked alone at eleven
months and by two years was saying 'sorry' a lot. Apparently I
was toilet-trained (like many of my generation) very early; our
personalities must have been affected by this, even if researchers
are still struggling to prove it.

I went to school at the age of four, to a small private
establishment with the grand title of Oxford College. We said
our prayers with our eyes oddly raised to the skies of Chiswick,
and I lived in fear that I wouldn't get anything right. A powerful
memory is of an arithmetic test I did one day at the age of five.
The sums were written on the blackboard—perhaps thirty of
them, numbered clearly. I looked at them and thought I would
do the difficult ones first. But the consequence was that halfway
through I couldn't remember which ones I had done and which I
hadn't. I got into a terrible muddle and cried, convinced that I
would come bottom of the class and ruin my academic career for
ever. When I returned after lunch I found I was the only child
who had not only done all the sums but who had got them all

right. My prize was a purple silk purse with a pink flower on it and a bar of Cadbury's milk chocolate inside. The lesson of that experience was for me that following the conventional pattern may be safer, but it is unlikely to be the route to the highest achievement of all.

We went for our holidays to the farm in Bedfordshire where my mother and I had taken refuge in the war. The grandmother's husband had been the brother of my father's mother—it was one of those complex kinship connections with which a small child in our culture (but not in others) is unconcerned. The farmhouse was divided into two: in the right-hand half lived the grandmother, in the left, her son, his wife, and three daughters. (Such disjunction, the one half dark and musty, the other bright and modern, and nothing invisible about the dividing line between.) All the holidays we had in that place have coalesced into a composite memory: the sun is always shining, the roses are always blooming, and the grass is always faintly wet with early morning dew lit like diamonds for miles across the fields. We picked flat black mushrooms and found warm brown eggs. We walked down a dusty flowered lane to a place called Happy Valley, where in the autumn children helped brown-faced workers make hay. We fed the dozens of farm cats on great bowls of bread and milk; we darted in and out of tall whispering trees at the end of the garden in which rooks cawed, a magic forest that could only be reached through an archway of blood-red blossoms.

The family in the left-hand half of the house fascinated me. The farmer's wife was beautiful: tall, blonde, feminine. The three daughters two years apart, the eldest just two years younger than me, were all beautiful too; each was composed of a different but equally successful combination of the blue eyes, fair hair, pink cheeks formula. At night they slept in what was impressively called a nursery: a large pink room with three pink beds in a row as in the Beatrix Potter children's books. Just outside it in an enormous airing cupboard were stored piles of sweet-smelling pink and white clothes. The scene as a whole represented my idea of a normal family life such as I did not have. Each child had others to play with. The mother put curlers in the children's silver hair and bought them impractical white leather shoes. The father had chosen his wife for her beauty.

Our visits to the house stopped eventually because the appearance of normality crumbled to reveal a skeleton of terrors beneath. The farmer did not love his wife, but a much harsher, brown-haired lady on a neighbouring farm whom he then married. The wife found a man who made her happy, had a hysterectomy, and took up painting. Much later the eldest daughter married the son of her father's new wife, had three blonde children and divorced her husband. By then I knew intellectually that no family is normal, and that cycles of deprivation have a disturbing tendency to be passed on from one generation to another. But what one knows in the head and what one feels are two different things. I felt and still feel an enormous nostalgia for the rural masculine-feminine idyll of my childhood. Such a nostalgia perhaps inhabits, in one way or another, the minds of all urban twentieth-century people, since it stands for the successful merging of the human with the natural environment, for roses round the unmortgaged door and space around the peaceful self, for the idealized and unhurried dalliance of those whose currency is seemingly not money nor acts of violence of any kind.[2]

At six I went to a new school, a Girls' Public School, in a new neighbourhood. It was always held against my father, who for most of his life was an ardent socialist (in 1950 he had become the first Professor of Social Administration in Britain, at the London School of Economics, a place with an erroneously radical reputation), that he never sent me to a state school. My strongest memories of these years are not, however, of the unsocialist nature of my education, but of being a social outcast. I was not an attractive child. Thin, with thin brown hair in straggly plaits, I had a bad squint and wore NHS glasses, for a time with a black patch over the 'good' eye so that the 'lazy' eye would come to its senses. The glasses made me look like an undersized pirate. My feeling of being different from everyone else was accentuated by my looks and by the horrendous teasing I received from other children. My name (Titmuss, alias Titmouse) didn't help. I had no real friends and led a solitary existence wrapped up in numerous entirely private terrors—of getting stuck in lifts or underground trains, of being lost in shops, of ghosts in the dark, of the strange smell possessed by other people's homes, of school and people in authority, or simply of other people. (Many of these terrors are with me still.)

The school I went to was typical of many late-nineteenth-century educational constructions—a massive structure of dark brown corridors and wind-filled classrooms. Its centre was a large hall with a polished wooden floor on which we kneeled and sat twice daily for assembly, receiving into our green serge tunics and bare knees endless vicious splinters. At one end was a raised platform on which stood an organ, a piano and the headmistress, an ageless clergyman's daughter by the name of Miss E.G. Harold. With her grey hair cut severely in a line level with her ears and held in place with two hair-grips either side of a central parting (the same two hair-grips, apparently, for years and years), she was a suitably austere figure. When she got up from kneeling at assembly sometimes her hand would catch in the hem of her skirt to reveal long pink woollen knickers; six hundred and fifty girls carefully watched each day for this amazing sight.

Perhaps the entire staff of the school were rabid feminists but if so we did not know, and we certainly weren't. We saw them as objects of pity. Most of them were unmarried—those that married rapidly left the school—and they gave off an air of frustration and disappointment (or did we imagine this, hoping for better things ourselves?) Many had hair on their upper lip, a rigid approach to teaching, whatever the subject, and most could not cope with the mock-innocent questions about 'life' that were put to them from time to time by provocative pupils. When we were eleven a girl called Marion, who later became a teacher herself, asked in a Scripture lesson what circumcision was. The teacher blushed and said 'a ceremonious ritual'.

Although I found the school increasingly suffocating, I did well academically, dutifully writing essays on such topics as 'The Men of the Stone Age' who 'lived in caves and ate wild animals and shellfish . . . Bows and arrows were used for shooting . . . They learnt to polish the rough edges of tools, and they kept sheep and goats. They wove linen with the flax plants. When they died they were buried in barrows. We know all these things because of excavations.' Where were the women? In an all-female environment this, clearly, was a question that failed to occur to me.

The motto of the school was 'serve and obey'. From the point

of view of the games field, a place I detested, I adapted this to
conform to the line from Milton's sonnet 'On His Blindness':
'they also serve who only stand and wait'. This I resolutely did,
with Rowntree's gums up my knickers, as lacrosse balls and sticks
flew round me. But the school motto did seem to me deeply
significant as a summary of its philosophy and that of the
education it provided. 'Serve and obey' signalled that knowledge
was something passively created and received: that ours was not
to reason why; that uncritical obedience was good in itself. But it
surely could not be good to accept the world as it was, and it
must be better to meet it with a continual curiosity. Undoubtedly my father helped to foster this attitude in me, since it was
his own. Yet I also had the more general feeling described by Liv
Ullman in her autobiography: 'I realise that I was brought up to
be the person others wanted me to be, so that they would like me
and not be bothered by my presence.

'That person is not me.'[3]

Even in those years I led a double life. Publicly I was a good
middle-class girl, neat in appearance, punctual, polite, serious
and intellectually inclined. Privately I was a mess. My head,
which could pour out respectable accounts of physics experi-
ments and the correct declensions of Latin verbs, was crowded
with powerful invisible imaginings of other worlds, with an
unformed elliptic intuition that the real human world as it was
presented to me was not a world in which I would find it at all
easy to live.

'I think we know quite a lot on a sociological level about the
kinds of women creative women are, and what it is about their
lives that enables them to break out of the routine treadmill of
female existence. Of prime importance is the existence of an
adult model with whom they, as children, can identify, and who
sets them a powerful example of involvement in the non-
domestic world. Henning and Jardim (1978) in one representative study of women enrolled in the Harvard Business School in
the mid-1960s found that all had experienced extremely close
relationships with their fathers as children . . . Equally effective
as a close father-daughter relationship was a daughter's identification with the example of an employed mother. It has been
reported that daughters of employed mothers have less rigid

conceptions of gender roles than daughters of nonemployed mothers (Morantz and Mansfield, 1977; Hansson *et al.*, 1977). They have less "feminine" identities, stressing such masculine qualities as independence and self-reliance (Hoffman and Nye, 1974).'[4]

Mother, father, child. A happy family. Two loving adults, a wanted child. I don't know, and would not presume to guess, how it was for the adults, but as the child I felt the situation was not what it seemed, was a conundrum, paradoxical, a web of contradictions. It is easy to say, and I would not be the first person to say it, but it is the case that, although I loved both my parents, I identified with my father and felt ambivalent towards my mother. In that sense my relationship with my father has been the most powerful influence of my life. The particular family structure and interior from which I came created a particular kind of woman. But when I set about analysing what accounted for my different relationships with my parents, I only come up with half answers. My father seemed wholly 'good' to me. This was an impression he gave to others; it was his public face. In fact, he was not 'good' at expressing negative emotions—anger, irritation, hatred, resentment. This fooled people into thinking he had no such emotions. But he did. By contrast, my mother spilt out the moods inside her with that well-recognized feminine incapacity to keep the floodgates closed, and with that common feminine response to a constraining and frustrating all-domestic environment. Thus my mother seemed to my childish eyes less remarkable and more ordinary than my father. No moral passion bound me to her as it did to my father. Yet I loved her and needed her: she loved me and needed me. I suspect that what my mother and I had was a 'normal' (I mean statistically average) mother-daughter relationship for this culture, whereas the extraordinariness of my father's personality and life overlaid the ordinary relationship of father and only daughter with an extra element of difficulty.

The strongest recollection of my relationships with my parents in my childhood is of an alignment of opposites: my mother angry and reluctant to comfort, my father with open arms and a gentle patience. When I locked myself in my room or cried for hours about some childish incident, it was my father who refused to leave me in my state of bitter alienation. Undoubtedly it is easier for fathers, who come home refreshed for the domestic battle by their work outside, to be patient than it is for mothers. My father's greater patience should not be allowed to count against my mother in her mothering of me—and that is something I am to be heard saying about my own reputation as a devoted, but at times impatient, mother.

Family relationships are part of a culture, and this culture is one dominated by men. One result, as Nancy Chodorow and others have shown,[5] is competition between women. Although women 'in fact' may be essential for the future of society in a way that men are not (men actually threaten its survival with their predilection for weaponry and ideologies of nationalism), the much higher prestige of masculine activities ensures that women battle with one another to be the favoured object in their men's eyes. And so my mother and I were often surreptitiously at war with one another. She thought she had first claim on my father's love; and I thought I had first claim. Even now he's dead, our differences over him survive. He was not the same person for each of us. We cannot, through rational discussion, bring the two pictures to merge. We have to disagree. I hope she does not find this too hurtful.

The difference in age between my parents; my father's 'feminine' gentleness and my mother's 'masculine' anger; my father's lack of education and my mother's middle-class origins; these factors added up to an unusual marriage. It was in fact a marriage that nearly didn't happen. My father's mother, whom I can only describe as a fat, self-indulgent, hypochondriacal woman with cow-like brown eyes and limitless demands, occupied his emotions to the end of her life. When she came to stay in our house she brought with her a thick odour of ancient skin and resentment. The smell, mixed with that of the many bottles of medicine that always accompanied her and had to be specially accommodated on a tray in her room, penetrated the whole house. She imposed routines: supper at six, a hot-water bottle full of not-quite-boiling water at nine o'clock. Cheese, she said, keeps you awake. Once the three of us watched a small caterpillar wriggle cosily on a lettuce leaf she was about to eat and said nothing. The caterpillar would give her protein, and removing it would give us the benefit of her hysterics for many weeks to come. (In that sense as a family the three of us could feel ourselves to be an alliance—a positive feature of our life together I am too ready to forget.)

It was because of his mother that my father wouldn't arrange a date for his marriage to my mother: my mother told me that she threatened to throw her engagement ring into the Thames if he didn't reform his behaviour. He did, but only made the wedding by leaving his mother's home early in the morning and drinking many unwanted cups of tea in Lyons Corner House as a rite of transition between sonhood and husbandhood. The rite was not entirely successful. He was never free of his mother. Though he used to hold his weekly telephone conversations with her while reading papers or writing letters (her monologue of complaint requiring only the occasional thoughtless punctuation of a 'hmmmm' from him), there was no release from the jealousy she felt for the woman he married.

The sense of my own uniqueness I had as a very young child had something to do with the unique relationship I judged my parents to have. Perhaps all children feel that, especially only children. I felt I was a symbol of the contradictory forces and attitudes that made up the interaction between my parents; I was the human representation of their incoherence, their struggle for coherence. But because I was human I was not only a symbol but a witness. And, witnessing, I was a voyeur, a stranger who hovered in doorways, on the edges of streams of light, poised on the margins of relationships. Simply, I was in the way. In the house where I spent most of my childhood, a late Edwardian monstrosity in Acton, there was a chair on either side of the fireplace. Because of the temperature in that room it was necessary most of the year to sit by the fireplace which harboured either a 'real' fire or an imitation of one. If I wanted to sit there with my parents I had to draw up an extra chair. But then I could not see to read because the only two lamps in the room were beside their chairs. Probably unfairly, but with some justification, I thought they felt me to be an intruder in their relationship. (In much the same way my own children take this view now, but whereas they are all in it together, I had to fight my own battle.)

Maybe this was one reason why I couldn't wait to grow up. On the one hand I couldn't wait, but, on the other, I couldn't bear the thought of putting childish things behind me: my eighteen dolls lined up round the room with their unchanging faces and imaginatively bestowed personalities; socks rather than nylon stockings and the awful machinery of suspender belts; sleeping with a squashed teddy bear called Brownie, not a man. Physically I was slow to mature. On my thirteenth birthday I had hardly any breasts or signs of menstruation and I was the shortest girl in the class. I had just about acquired the facts of life—those facts which are hardly sufficient in themselves—but I have no recollection of my mother being the person responsible for giving me this information. I do know from my own children how information conveyed when it has not been strictly asked for tends to go in one ear and out the other, so perhaps that is what happened. I learnt about periods first from the usual illicitly acquired booklet about the birds and the bees. My mother was fifty-four so I couldn't learn directly from her as my own daughters have done, the fourteen-year-old with an extensive knowledge of physiology, hormonal fluctuations and technical equipment, the five-year-old unwrapping a Tampax out of my handbag during her developmental assessment at the GP's surgery one day. One by one my classmates 'started', and you could see from the tell-tale bulge in their navy blue knickers that womanhood was upon them. My day came on September 15, 1957. I was tremendously happy and excited, having no inherited theory about the pain and nuisance of menstruation. But when I told my mother she curiously confined me to bed and brought me breakfast on a tray. I wanted to tell my father and she said I mustn't. Inchoately I thought, if being a woman is a good thing, then why isn't there a public celebration of this biological event that is happening to me? If it's my destiny to bear children, if the womb is a precious vessel and women are assets of the nation, then someone ought to give me a medal or at least shake my hand and congratulate me on the state of grace my body has achieved.

The mechanics of reproduction left me, at thirteen, extremely hazy. It was a subject my best friend, Clare, and I discussed often, and one day walking round the school playground I committed myself in the form of a bet to a neat account I had invented for myself. I told Clare with absolute conviction that when a man and woman got married and shared a bed God made the seed of a baby pass between them. Nonsense, said Clare, who was a much more down-to-earth girl, and proceeded to list for me the details of the physical engineering involved. I didn't believe her. It sounded altogether too practical an arrangement. Was the whole world really based on such a crude, animal act? Did love really not work wonders?

One of the deficiencies of my life as a privileged middle-class girl was that I knew no boys. I had no brother and I went to an all-girls' school. I had actually never spoken to a boy my age. This, of course, is quite extraordinary. However, other women who lack brothers and whose education was single-sex have reported to me the same feeling of segregation from the entire male sex. It does, I think, account for a certain difficulty in accepting men as fully human, and must, in that sense, be regarded as an important precursor of feminism.

It is surprising, then, that at fourteen I managed to fall in love. The boy was eighteen months older than I, the son of a social worker friend of my parents. He had a firm muscular body and a halo of golden curls round a masculine face. The fact that he also had artificial legs was entirely irrelevant to me. James and I led up to our first kiss with grasped hands under the Monopoly board—he came for tea on Saturday afternoons with his mother and younger brother. The kiss occurred when I went out to the kitchen to empty the teapot. He came in awkwardly after me, down the two steps. 'I wanted . . . ' he began clumsily, and then his arms were around me and our eager mouths met. It was an apocalyptic event: a five minutes that transformed my life, much more important to my sexual development than the time I lost (as the well-worn phrase has it) my virginity; in all the important ways I lost my virginity that January evening in 1959.

James and I conducted an intense but strictly unconsummated love affair for three years. His first letter to me, written some two weeks later, was my first love letter. It is fourteen pages long on soft blue paper with blurred ink demonstrating the ravages of time—and usage, for I wore it under my school tunic for several weeks. It told me that he would be proud of me if I did well in my exams. 'I do like your parents,' he noted, 'they are so kind and sensible—rather like you (which is nonsense, because, of course, it is really you who are like them).' Later he saw me through glandular fever at a distance, wrote, despairingly, 'Ann, shall we ever be able to do anything to save the Labour Party? Do you

care?' and sent me a booklet called 'Practical Family Planning'.
He also sent me extensive poems in Russian and German (the
Russian ones were accompanied by translations). Goethe: 'O du
loses, leidigliebes Madchen, /Sag mir an: womit hab ichs
verschuldet . . . ?' Then there was the famous 'Studentenlied'
with whose sentiments I entirely agreed: 'Unser's Lebens schnel-
le Flucht/Leidet keinem zugel . . . Zeit und Jahre flieh'n
davon . . . ' and (strangely) an extremely morbid poem by one
Johann Gunther (1695–1723) called 'Am Abend' and expressing the view that each day was another plank in the coffin and
another step towards the grave—which was undoubtedly true,
but hardly cheering.

Our affair, from the notes I have of it in the diary I kept, was
really one between children—as perhaps all such first love affairs
are bound to be. I filled this diary with observations in easily
broken code about 'psychological difficulties' and told myself that
it was impossible for me to know what to do for the best. I noted
that when he paid for me to go to the cinema (*Date with Disaster*
and *Carleton-Browne, F.O.*), 'I didn't really mind because both
of us have enough money, and it makes the boy feel responsible
and grown up to take the girl . . . ' I don't know how I knew that.
Almost everything I wrote about the relationship smacks of an
uneasy simulation of adulthood. But it is very significant that my
dog-eared copy of Simone de Beauvoir's *The Second Sex* is
inscribed 'Ann, with love from James'—a present on my
sixteenth birthday that wasn't read for many years.

I was a very self-centred adolescent, constantly reflecting on
the state of my own emotions and continually attempting to
assess other people's perceptions of me. But I suppose that in this
state of self-absorption I was not all that different from my peers.
I was obsessed with The Meaning of Life and also, of course, with
what I personally was Going to Do with My Life. I wrote
dramatically in September 1959, at the age of fifteen and three-
quarters, about an evening walk I had taken. I was emotionally
(and somewhat oddly) impressed by a car, an ordinary small car,
in the street, that suddenly seemed to me intensely fragile,
'small, very human in its insignificance'. It made me ask, 'Why
are we here, why have this and other worlds been created, what
is their ultimate aim and destiny? . . . Will there ever be an
answer? Perhaps next autumn or perhaps not until 1,000,000

years after my death,' I concluded, darkly. The next passage, almost illegible and written at great speed, concerns my school. 'Today I realized that my school is designed to suppress individualism and create mass-produced human beings. This is neat and economic,' I granted, 'but not what I require of my education. From now on my aim will be to live as a person in my own right and not as a textbook of antiquated ideas. I know that there are certain feelings inside me which today find inadequate expression. I am afraid these may disappear unless I take steps to preserve them. *This is very important. . .* ' (It was, and is.)

Observing that life ought to have a meaning and that the objectives of education are narrow and conformist are common adolescent preoccupations. They were aided in my own case by the political character of life in my parents' home. If the meaning of life wasn't directly debated, the meaning of education certainly was. In the 1960s my father formally adopted the role of adviser on Labour Party policy. He was on a number of committees that developed Government policy in a variety of fields, and our house was always full of political discussions and people. Richard Crossman once gave me a history lesson, the young Peter Shore before he became an MP often came to the house (accompanied by his medical wife who always seemed to bring her knitting). We knew such individuals as (Professor) Peter Townsend and (Lord) John Vaizey well—I was mistakenly in love with the latter after he gave me a beautiful Irish shawl one Christmas and told me that women had to suffer in order to be beautiful (he was referring to the tight-waisted adolescent fashions of the time). The historian R.H. Tawney slept cosily by our fire after Christmas dinner, and woke up to make entirely non-senile remarks and blow his yellow coltsfoot tobacco all over my mother's clean carpet. He gave me a white lace handkerchief, 'To Miss Titmuss, with kind regards'. I remember well how my father, Brian Abel-Smith and Peter Townsend, in their work demolishing the notion of Britain as a post-war haven of class equality, were known irreverently as the 'Holy Trinity'. They were God the Son and God the Holy Ghost; he was God the Father.

My own energies did not turn overtly to politics until I liberated myself from the constraints of schoolgirlhood. At the age of fifteen I became an openly disobedient pupil, flaunting the school motto I had long despised. Not only would I not tidy my desk to order, but I once performed the revolutionary act of leaving school in the middle of the day. I walked past a bush of magnolia blossoms and their heavy honeyed scent confirmed my suspicion that considerable pleasures were to be had outside and beyond my schooldays. I wanted my freedom.

I got it, by moving into the more liberal atmosphere of a polytechnic in West London where I worked for four A-levels, discarding my school uniform to leap into another—sloppy jerseys and skirts, blue duffle coat and CND badge. It was terribly shocking to find myself in the company of men all the time; but clearly something I had wanted. Eugene, who wore silk cravats and had a squint, pronounced Chaucer beautifully and held hands with a pale-faced long-nailed witch (self-styled) under the desk. A handsome youth called Malden threw my shoes out of the window during a history lesson. Bill, an asthmatic thirty-year-old, gave off an air of decayed gentleness and lived in a book-crowded flat in Shepherd's Bush with a cameraman called Ron. Bill was friendly with John, a gigantic ex-pharmacist with aspirations—now achieved—to join the academic elite and live near Hampstead Heath.

It was good to have such a mixture of friends—female as well as male. From sixteen to eighteen I cried less and thought more than before; mostly I thought about love and socialism in that order, though I claimed in an ingenuous piece called 'Socialism and Me' published in the *Chiswick Polytechnic Bulletin* in 1961 that the two were the same. I said I was a socialist because I loved people. Loving people appeared to mean comprehensive education, public ownership of industry, nuclear disarmament, the abolition of capital punishment and the resources of the NHS being available to foreigners. I ended up quoting Peter Shore in *Conviction*: 'I want a society which shapes its institutions so that men may become self-determining, their own masters.'[6]

The mastery of men is something which I find less interesting now. Indeed, even then I had dimly begun to feel that history as it was taught was not history as it took place. The achievements and tribulations of great men were not those of great women, but neither, more significantly, were they those of the 'ordinary' people who wrote their own history by living and dying in such a way that the destiny of nations did not appear to be affected. As

Sheila Rowbotham has said,[7] the language that makes people invisible to 'history' is no coincidence: it is part of their real situation.

Joining political movements doesn't necessarily make one more visible to history, but it can help. Along with thousands of other teenagers I joined the National Campaign for the Abolition of Capital Punishment and the Campaign for Nuclear Disarmament. In the latter capacity I went on the Easter marches from Aldermaston to London with blistered feet and an uplifted heart. We sang

> Don't you hear the H-bombs' thunder
> Echo like the crack of doom?
> While they rend the skies asunder
> Fall-out makes the earth a tomb.
> Do you want your homes to tumble,
> Rise in smoke towards the sky?
> Will you let your cities crumble?
> Will you see your children die?
> Men and women stand together.
> Do not heed the men of war.
> Make your minds up, now or never,
> Ban the bomb for evermore.

—and meant it. In a notebook I wrote:

> 'US Secretary of Defence in 1958 estimated that in a nuclear war between NATO and the powers of the Warsaw Pact, 160 million Americans would die, 200 million Russians and everybody in Western Europe and Britain. Communism is infinitely preferable to death.'

The Aldermaston marches were, as an *Observer* account put it several years later, occasions of 'primal innocence and gaiety' with a 'sense of involvement in a modern Canterbury tale'—that is, with an underlying deep moral purpose. As the *Observer* account remarked: 'The success of Aldermaston roughly coincided with the appearance of the "teenage thing"—a new-found adolescent self-consciousness and independence...'[8] Teenagers were unmistakably 'the most radical element in CND... Everywhere, it seemed to be the teenagers who tried hardest and did the most. It was the teenagers who sold newspapers and gave leaflets on the sidewalks, started the singing, shouted the slogans, organized the baggage, handled the rations, collected the garbage . . .'[9]

When CND gestated the Committee of 100, a non-militant organization that took non-violent civil disobedience as its strategy, I joined this too. I was not arrested in the great demonstration of September 17, 1961 (1,314 people were), but in the April demonstration I got my picture in the *Observer*—sitting next to my fellow student John and reading Bindoff's *Tudor England*—with a story about the two policemen who picked me up to put me in their van and then jokingly said I was too heavy (I was not) and put me down.

My parents watched all this adolescent politicization with amusement and a certain pride, being political creatures themselves. However, when I began to relax my limbs in Whitehall, they grew horrified instead. My mother told me that if I got arrested she had no intention of bailing me out of prison. I thought this cruel; after all, who had set me the example of political commitment, and what were my actions if not the logical extension of this?

Politics and sex were the main topics of conversation in the circle in which I moved. Both involved issues of responsibility. For women-to-be in those days, as in most others, being without a boyfriend signified a certain physical and moral unattractiveness, whereas the state of being without a girlfriend had no such implications for men-to-be. After James came a series of romantic entanglements. It was a tiring, strangely enervating practice. Often these affairs made us far from happy, though the amount of time and energy we put into them suggested we thought they should. I remember endlessly dressing up to go to parties—the discomfort of high heels and lacquered hair, the assignations that developed and were not what one wanted, those that were wanted and didn't. I remember the tears and the headaches; the occasional unbounded joy and optimism for the future that made it temporarily worth while.

When Esther Greenwood in Sylvia Plath's *The Bell Jar* finally meets Irwin on the steps of the Widener Library in Cambridge,

Massachusetts, and decides that he is intelligent enough to be the first man she will sleep with ('Irwin was a full professor at twenty-six and had the pale, hairless skin of a boy genius') she feels enormously relieved to have got rid of her virginity at last. She describes it as having 'weighed like a millstone around my neck. It had been of such enormous importance to me for so long that my habit was to defend it at all costs. I had been defending it for five years and I was sick of it.'[10] I, and my friends, felt rather the same way. Statistically speaking we were not yet into the era of sexual permissiveness: heavy petting was okay, 'going all the way' was not; apparently only 12 per cent of us did do so (and most of us found it a disappointing activity at first).[11] As Michael Schofield points out in *The Sexual Behaviour of Young People*, for girls, as opposed to boys, to become sexually experienced in middle adolescence in the early 1960s required a much greater repudiation of the family and striving for personal independence. Sex was, I think, much less important to us than the media supposed it was. We (by which I mean women-to-be) had enough respect for ourselves and enough scorn for the double standard not to feel we would be devalued by the act of sex. Fear of pregnancy put us off a little but was regarded as solvable; and certainly not a barrier to the breaking of rules (or hymens). VD wasn't mentioned at all. There were two compelling reasons for having intercourse: first, curiosity, and second, the value of experience. Those of us who were most curious in general *did* ask why the boundary between permissible sexual activity and non-permissible sexual activity should be drawn at one particular place. We did not believe that marriages are made in heaven and therefore shouldn't be anticipated in the pleasures of the flesh. It merely seemed useful to find out one's sexual capabilities ahead of the time when one would promise lifelong fidelity to one man, which is, most significantly, what we all imagined we would one day do.

Martin was twenty-three when I was seventeen. Since leaving school, he had done a number of different jobs and joined the navy for a while. He was tall and thin with curly hair, a lean face and a wicked smile; he wrote good poetry and made me laugh. He looked as though he took a lot of risks with life and always won; as an insurance policy he retained the Catholicism of his upbringing, but he was an extremely bad Catholic, constantly

committing sins and having to confess them and weekly almost
missing Sunday mass. He had a habit of diving into the nearest
church wherever we were to savour that bit of the service which
was essential; he explained to me once which bit it was and why
it didn't matter if he missed the rest, but what impressed me most
was that he always got the timing right.

The religious aspect worried me. Aesthetically the church
appealed, and still does: incense, candles, singing, stained glass
and peace. Yet intellectually any religious ideology seems
literally incredible. I exchanged a series of letters with the
Catholic Information Centre in London during my affair with
Martin in an attempt to sort it out; this was obviously the bit I
had to get right first, just as Esther Greenwood had to wait for
the requisite degree of intelligence. I wrote to the Catholic
Information Centre on the subjects of nuclear war, sin, and birth
control. I have no copies of my letters, and only one of theirs to
me has survived. It was written by a Reverend Ripley and began
'My dear Ann . . . you must realize that to answer your questions
adequately would require several books. You will find most of
them answered by my own *This is the Faith*. Perhaps you will be
able to borrow it from the public library?' The Reverend Ripley
spelt out for me the difference between mortal and venial sin
(tiny lies come in the second category, murder in the first) and
the circumstances under which a 'just war' might be waged ('Our
Lord never condemned soldiers'). On birth control, he observed
that marriage is a sacrament and that it must be 'used according
to the cardinal virtue of prudence'. He told me that artificial
birth prevention 'is simply mutual masturbation'.

I didn't find these answers satisfactory, and not only because I
didn't feel prudent. For this and other reasons it was predictable
that eventually I would commit the ultimate sin. Afterwards,
like Esther Greenwood, I felt relief that the rite of passage had
been accomplished; and Martin went to confession. That, but
nothing else about our affair, made me feel somewhat unclean
(as no doubt it is meant to). My parents, I thought, had no idea
of what had happened to me and I felt sad that I couldn't tell
them. They were still the people I loved most in the world, and I
told them, especially my father, everything of significance that
happened to me.

I heard a story the other day of a mother whose seventeen-year-old daughter had just slept with her boyfriend for the first time. Mother and daughter had a good relationship, and the mother had taken the daughter to the birth control clinic and discussed the whole thing with her. Then the daughter came home at 1 am one night full of excitement and woke up her mother to tell her the deed had been done, and to describe in detail all that had transpired. When telling the story afterwards, the mother complained that she didn't mind her daughter·telling her, but she resented being woken up in the middle of the night to hear it. What she really meant was that she was delighted. That is how I think it should be.

SCENE 2

A Hotel Bedroom, Undated

Laughing, they come into the room. Two beds, of which they will only occupy one: a lamp already streaking its pale light over jumbled papers. A cool, kind night outside, in which they found a restaurant with red-checked tables, flowers, flute music and a glowing spit, and nobody in it but themselves. They drank champagne and tried not to think about the future.

They take off their clothes and lie on the bed. She is exhausted with going to bed, her own bed, late, and getting up early to see her daughter before joining him again. In fact, what with the lack of sleep and the champagne and a bout of crying earlier in a pub at the futility of it all, she cannot remember ever feeling so tired before. He is resolute in the face of her tiredness. This is their last chance this time to lie together like this, and who knows if there'll be another? He loves her, an amazing enough fact on its own, for love is a concept that does not come easily to him. He is going to make the best of the situation, adopting a pragmatic male attitude which is designed to cover up the real profundity of his feelings about this mess into which they have got themselves—or, rather, it could be said, into which he has got them.

And so he anoints her with every part of him, seeing and feeling her to be a whole body, a length of amazing and precious silk, a velvet flower of iron strength—no simple assemblage of separate parts to be worked separately: press this button for that effect, that one for this. He has said that this occasion is for her; others in other cities and other seasons if they have a future will be for him. He has a concentrated look upon his face: making love to this woman is no mere animal exercise. And so, despite her exhaustion, she responds. She feels his fingers everywhere inside her oiling every orifice; she cries out knowing that he has penetrated the centre of her being, offered her a connectedness that few human beings ever achieve in a lifetime. How can she refuse? Worst or best of all even in this prostrated condition she knows that the physical act is in the end merely a token. What counts is the emotional capture. Again and again she cries out. She says she is going to die, knowing that what she means is that she has never felt so alive. As she nearly loses consciousness he complains that the manager of the hotel will shortly be knocking on the door to comment on the noise she is making.

In the weeks to come she is to make her complaint to him that he should never have done this to her because she can't live with its memory. In stiff boardrooms looking at the earnest faces of white-collared gentlemen, on crowded underground trains, during bureaucratic mundane telephone conversations, she feels like an iron flower again. Timelessly, the event, his act, continues to occupy her. But more seriously she is disturbed by it. What is she doing being made love to, being loved, by this man in this overweening manner? Was this affair of her own choosing? Did he ever ask her if she wanted to love him? Did he ever ask her if she wanted to cry out in that way, whether it would embarrass her, bring out into the open things about her that were perhaps better hidden? The answer to these questions is plainly no. So, is she simply being swept along, as most women are, by the tide of male events? She, who has struggled for so many years to understand and control the malevolent forces in herself that lead her to enjoy dependence and compliance where a more politically appropriate active independence is what she would prefer? Something seems to have gone wrong.

He says he loves her for her contradictions. She does not love herself for them.

Family: reflections

Dream, October 1, 1962:
'I was helping in a shop, in some kind of seaside town. A woman appeared from the back of the shop and asked me what I was doing. When she was talking to me, we both heard noises behind us. She went to investigate and it turned out to be a nurse about two feet high, dressed like Florence Nightingale. Martin arrived on the scene. A friend of my father's rang up. She had given Martin a birthday present, and he thanked her for it, but without speaking directly into the receiver. I also remember . . . putting on some kind of white windcheater and saying mass. My mother was standing next to me and urged me not to. She was frightened I was going to become a Catholic.

'Next, I was sitting in a dirty café with several old men trying to order something to eat. The middle-aged woman sitting opposite me cried because she couldn't have a cream cornet. Then I went down to the harbour with some pirates. They got back on their ship.

'I also played the harp with an orchestra and two other harpists. It was definitely a harp, though I remember blowing through it. I could play it properly, but I felt much happier when I peeped over the second harpist's shoulder and saw the fingering for B flat, which was the second and fourth fingers on the right hand. The conductor of the orchestra was the geography mistress from school.'

The ability to produce vivid, clearly remembered dreams is a well-recognized part of psychoanalysis. Some classic motifs in this one can be picked out: cream cornets, flutes, the telephone receiver. Other parts (my mother's fear, the tyranny of the geography mistress) are more literal. Yet others—the pirates— are simply obscure.[1]

Amongst the events of my personal life in 1962 was something that resembled what is popularly called a nervous breakdown. I can't reconstruct the details now, and what I say about it is partly based on the knowledge of myself gained since. Its symptoms were uncontrollable hysteria and unmanageable weeping. I told my parents I needed some help. My mother could see that I was right. My father couldn't accept my insistence that any help he was able to give me was not enough. Eventually I gave up and took to my bed, refusing to eat or get up unless something was done. Against his better judgment, my father telephoned a friend of his, the child analyst Donald Winnicott, and arranged for me to see him. The idea was that Donald would work out whether analysis or some other form of psychotherapy would be helpful and refer me to the right person. I got out of bed and went to see him. Evidently he was most used to dealing with small children, but I felt like a child at the time. Gently he asked me what it was like being the daughter of a 'famous' man. It was the right question to ask.

Subsequently, Winnicott referred me to an up-and-coming analyst of slightly unorthodox persuasions who bore an uncanny resemblance to my father. I went to see him several times a week until I began my undergraduate career in Oxford in the autumn of 1962, thereafter less frequently until the day before my twentieth birthday in January 1964.

Sceptical as I am of the value and underlying assumptions of psychoanalysis, I have to admit that my own provided a much needed safety valve. Without it and the lessons it provided I doubt whether I would have survived emotionally the subsequent twenty years. My parents and my friends loved me and cared about me, but they could not distance themselves sufficiently from my situation (of which they were a part) to see how deeply troubled I was. It did not seem credible that someone like me should be in such distress: I had had a relatively privileged upbringing materially and emotionally, was short of nothing. I was intelligent, even quite gifted. Physically I wasn't beautiful, though the straggly plaits and the squint had given way to an appearance that in conventional terms was reasonably attractive. I had no obvious blemishes. The blemishes were all beneath the surface.

What I learnt from my encounters with Dr Lomas will come, by now, as a surprise to nobody. However, it did surprise me at the time; I had read no Freud, and the early 1960s in Britain were not years in which analysis or any kind of psychotherapy for the troubled professional classes were yet fashionable. (Indeed, I concealed my trips to Harley Street from most of my friends. Those whom I did tell thought them rather reprehensible, like visits to a VD clinic.) What was the cause of my hysteria, my constant emotional lability, and lack of certainty about my place in the world? Being an only child, having a (relatively) well-known father, being born of, and reared by, parents who appeared to confuse the personalities of their genders—these were some of the factors. But these were superficial explanations. The real dilemma was that of being born female in a man's world. I did not put it like this at the time, and neither did Dr Lomas, but this, I see now, is what both of us were saying.

Feminine or masculine: child or adult: whore or housewife? My dreams during the period of my analysis expressed these paired alternatives so neatly as to be virtually unbelievable: was there a Freud, a designer of dreams in heaven? Sleeping with Martin signalled my birth as a fully sexual person and thus sealed off for ever the retreat into childhood. No more could I legitimately protest that I wasn't responsible for myself. I had entered adulthood without knowing in what guise I had done so. Was I to be a dedicated, if irascible, wife, housewife and mother, like my mother? Was I to be the kind of person who found a valid personal domain of labour and then relinquished it for the domain of the household? Would I, like her, in the years to come search for a glory reflected off the polished table-tops and in the achievements of my husband, whilst uneasily suspecting that I had failed to qualify for this role—I hadn't and couldn't make the necessary act of self-sacrifice? Were housewives sexual creatures? As Philip Slater has observed,[2] the position of the housewife-mother in Euro-American culture is desexualized: the sexy woman and the tidy, devoted housewife are two different models representing opposed strands in the patriarchal ideology of womanhood. We are men's mothers and their mistresses.

Rarely can we be both at the same time—even supposing that that is what we want to be.

The adult women I knew as I was growing up were of two sorts. There were the housewives and mothers like my mother, women who did not have full-time careers or jobs, and who, to a certain extent, lived vicariously through their husbands. Then there were the women who did not have children (or, often, husbands), whose role was much more masculine: the career or job was the centre of their lives. When my father went to the London School of Economics in 1950 he found a department staffed with women of this latter kind, and he met many others in the course of his work. I met them too. They seemed to me well-rounded and happy in a way that my mother and mothers like her were not. I have to say here what my mother once said to me, that when I was eleven she took on a voluntary job in education which meant that occasionally she wasn't there when I came home. Apparently I protested so much that she gave it up. I have no memory of her strike for freedom nor of my reaction to it, which must be significant. Most significantly, I remember the scene I came home to each day: a brightly lit room, the kettle boiling, 'Mrs Dale's Diary' on the radio, and my mother ironing white sheets, a cigarette burning between her lips. In a document dated 1959 I wrote, almost completely under the influence of prevailing ideologies of femininity and at the advanced age of fifteen, that, 'More important than being human . . . is the need to be a woman, and be true to instincts of loving and childbearing and feminine tenderness . . . Women who deny their womanliness are not being true to themselves.' Despite the fact that so-called career women seemed generally more attractive to me as role models, I was aware that this model of womanhood was not popular at the time. I recall as well my father's almost vitriolic attacks on working mothers.

So I didn't know which sort of woman I was, and I didn't know how sexuality combined with either. The core of my uncertainty lay in not knowing who I was if I wasn't my father's daughter. In 1961 (at seventeen) I contacted a lawyer to see if I could change my name; this, of course, would not have solved the problem. Did I really believe what my father believed? Was everything about my life derivative, secondhand? I might have written articles about 'Love and Socialism' in the Chiswick Polytechnic

Bulletin, but he had said in a letter to me that love and socialism always got mixed up in his mind. I might have decided to go to Oxford because it was the oldest university in the land, but you didn't have to be a detective to discern my father's concealed adulation of certain unsocialist institutions. I might have slept with Martin because my virginity was a burden, but why was he tall and thin, brown-haired and brown-eyed with hollow cheeks like my father? My father didn't write poetry himself, but in 1962 he found a poem that expressed aspects of what I meant to him. It was called 'Song of a Growing Girl':

> In spring I found the beauty of the world too much to bear;
> All that breaking into fruit and all the new perfumes in the
> air,
> I was trapped, astonished, yet frightened at this wonder.
> So much alone amid this struggle into life,
> This fired clay of newborn colour.
> I could not hold the pain of such arrivings,
> I felt my soul as dark and fruitless in that springtime air.
> The eyes around me could not see that I was filled with first
> despair,
> Till in a moment at the end of spring flamed out inside
> myself
> Some thorny rose, coming with such wounding joy
> That in its bursting miracle of blood, I did become the
> spring.[3]

I was always conscious even as a very young child of how much my father's hopes for the future centred on me. I felt he had a spiritual yearning to make amends through me for those parts of himself and his life of which he was not proud. His feeling would perhaps have been the same had I been a boy. Yet the fact I was a girl was important. His relationships with women were always difficult, and always had a ring of ambivalence about them, while his relationships with men had an unconsummated air. In me, as a pre-woman, he could vest all his desires for perfection. I could not therefore afford to let him down.

The anguish of being my father's daughter belied the generic problem: to what extent was I like men? Did I want a career? Did I want to dominate? I came to this general intellectual confrontation with the problem from the specific emotional one: in my relationships with men—my father, Martin—I did dominate; that is, I could get them to do practically anything I wanted, except, significantly, show anger towards me. (At the age of five I bit a thermometer in half in order to make my father angry. I didn't succeed; he reacted only with concern.) Such manipulation is, of course, not usually described as domination, since it is a process normally engineered by feminine 'wiles' of one kind or another. These wiles are common psychological techniques used by underprivileged social groups for exerting control. I was not happy unless I had control, but, at the same time, having achieved it, I lost respect for those I controlled. What did this mean? Should I seek to adjust to a more comfortably feminine mode of existence in which I was happy to be controlled by men? *Was* there such a mode of existence? Or ought I to recognize my pleasure in power and find a career that would make use of it and thus satisfy me?

My childhood feelings of aloneness and specialness, which had their origins in the quite ordinary situation of being an only child, had, by the time I was eighteen, mutated into a conviction that I had some kind of extraordinary contribution to make in the world. I 'knew' that inside me was a 'great' personage trying to get out—a great writer, a great politician, a great courtesan. I could not accept that there were many people like me with similar problems and potentials. I can now; and that, perhaps, is the major advance of the second half of my life. Feminism enabled me to make it.

But feminism was a long way off in 1962. Dr Lomas at the time employed classical analytic strategies to force the dawn of self-knowledge in me. He sat almost motionless in his chair throughout the fifty minutes assigned to each of my encounters, his legs crossed, his face passionless. He hardly ever initiated a conversation. He rarely made any direct or authoritative statement about what I had said or was, except towards the end of our acquaintance when, as I now know, his views of the psychoanalytic relationship began to change.[4] Imperviously, he waited for my organized exterior to crumble and reveal the seam faults of my personality, waited for re-enactments of anger, resentment, hatred, love, anxiety, self-doubt. Between September 1963 and January 1964 I took extensive notes on our encounters. I couldn't tell anyone about these encounters, and I calculated that they cost 1s 3d (about 6p) a minute. This seemed to me (and was) an enormous sum. I was determined to derive the maximum benefit possible from its expenditure by recording for the future such claims as:

26.9.63 Blocks to emotional development due to position of only child in family, and unresolved relationships with parents when a child... Emotional outbursts largely those of a child against father (father=authority)... Cannot take criticism, as a child will not take criticism from parents. Compulsive need to be thought lovable in all situations... Cannot organize my love-hate relationships properly. Fall in love, seeing only good qualities, and suppressing acknowledgment of bad ones.

7.1.64 'Unless you give me everything I ask for, you can have nothing'—attitude to males. From the particular to the general: why do I need to be in control of the situation? As a child I wanted my father to be masterful and dominating. But he wasn't. I consequently gave up, and my complaint that 'nobody has ever learnt to control me' is partly due to the fact that when they try, I turn round and say 'It's no use now, it's too late'.

My parents were reasonable with me too young.

8.1.64 Strange atmosphere, partly because it was late, and the curtains were drawn, with a small light on, and his face, which looked much older and rather tired. I cried, and he saw the tears down my face. He said, 'You're depressed about something aren't you?' and then that it wasn't at all clear what I was depressed about. I said I had been depressed for weeks, because I felt my life lacked purpose. He said he had felt all along that I don't believe I have a right to lead a happy and normal life, that I am strangely masochistic. I said this was true; that I would rather enjoy a tormented kind of life because it is more productive and creative. He suggested that this was nonsense. He said also that I didn't feel I had a right to psychoanalysis—that there were others worthier than I. I explained that there is no more money to go on; he suggested it was because I didn't want to hurt my father emotionally (any more) by going on...I asked what would happen if I didn't come for analysis any longer. He said that the problem was not now on the 'nervous breakdown' level, but on the level of being able to realize my potential. I said, 'What is my potential?' He said, 'You have never accepted the fact of being "ordinary" in its most important sense, that you are just another person, just another human being.'

I knew very little about the theoretical underpinnings of psychoanalysis in 1962 but a great deal more by 1964. Dr Lomas and I had long conversations about Freudian constructions of women and Karen Horney's revisionism—about what I thought of as her revisionism until I made the discovery many years later that some of her thoughts on the matter pre-dated Freud's.[5] I constantly tried to prove that Dr Lomas was imposing unwarranted theories on me. I quoted Jung at him, to the effect that the patient is there to be treated and not to prove a theory, and that the patient's resistance to therapy should not automatically be regarded as unjustified. On the contrary, the resistance could well point to the false assumptions underlying the treatment. I argued about penis envy and what it really meant, i.e., what women wanted was not men's genitals but their social privileges. I got nowhere in this putative debate, since Dr Lomas agreed with me. We parted amicably, me thanking him for what he had done for me, him suggesting that the profession of psychoanalysis needed women like me (although I was introverted, I was also observant about others). He ventured the opinion that if life treated me gently in ensuing years I would have no further major problems. It did not, and I did.

In any case, I gradually came to understand that the problems of being a woman in this culture are quite insoluble, even without the particular family structure and upbringing I had.

CHRONOLOGY 18–23
MINUS TWO WEEKS

In October 1962 I went to Somerville College, Oxford, to take a three year degree course in politics, philosophy and economics.

Dining in hall with the other inmates of Somerville College that first night took me back to the fake sorority of my girls' school. I wept with loneliness into my already diluted tomato soup. In the early weeks I rang my parents frequently, always reversing the charges, and wrote long, falsely bright letters home every other day. In my first (11.10.62) I recounted my adventures trying to buy a bicycle in a fish and chip shop, opening an account at Blackwell's bookshop, and attending the Freshers' Fair, where I joined the Socialist Group, Amnesty, the Film Society, the Oxford branch of CND and the Oxford University Ensemble Orchestra. I said home had acquired 'all sorts of virtues which it never has when I am actually there . . . M [Mum] can shout at me as much as she likes after December 8th [the end of term].' In the next letter I had met Hugh Gaitskell's second daughter, Cressida, also at Somerville, agreed to become a college representative for the Labour Club, and begun to grapple uncomprehendingly with economic theory. I described the outlines of the talk given to newcomers by the principal of Somerville, Dame Janet Vaughan. Somerville had produced, she said, some of the most influential people in the world (viz, rather oddly, Eleanor Rathbone, Hannah Stanton and a host of minor novelists), and you are, therefore, the world's future. This I found quite inspiring. It wasn't an overtly feminist talk, and I certainly wasn't a feminist, but it was actually the first time I had heard the public value of women being publicly extolled. It made me feel stronger to hear this, even if Somerville never subsequently lived up to the promise of those words. (As far as I'm concerned, it didn't. Indeed, having recently been asked to write for the annual Somerville College Report a potted story of my life since leaving Oxford, including 'both your successes and your failures', I am impressed by the fact that they have left out my own reported successes entirely.)

Our first task as newcomers to Oxford was to learn how to be proper undergraduates. Being female, we had to make our way in a man's world. The sex ratio was about eight to one, which meant that any reasonable-looking female was pursued by men. I had seventy or so invitations of one kind or another from men in my first term, and I can't say I didn't enjoy it. But such attention, given the statistics, was not really flattering. It was soon boring. This was largely because most of the men were boring intrinsically, and in the eager persistence with which they pursued women. Sometimes I was quite unable to fend them off, and so arranged for them all to call on me in my room at the same time; I left the door unlocked and went out myself so what they met was each other.

Secondly, we had to accommodate ourselves to Oxford in a narrower educational sense. The tutorial system, together with the particular philosophy of education then current in the women's colleges, meant hard work. I wrote two essays and had two one-hour tutorials a week for most of the three years—apart, that is, from a full quota of lectures to be attended. I had never before found myself in the company of so many obviously very clever people. I use the word 'clever' in a specific sense, for what Oxford specialized in was a kind of mental quickness and brightness that left the question of a more thorough and thoughtful intelligence completely open.

Another reason I had to exert myself so much mentally was the degree I had selected, a taxing and unrelated collection of topics. I attacked the logic and economics of the first two terms with gusto, while only half believing in their value. I tried to mould myself into a caricature of an Oxford undergraduate. The happiest times were spent in the antique comfort of the Radcliffe Camera. I liked to work there in the evenings when, approaching the building on my bicycle fortified by the diluted tomato soup, I could admire the golden arched windows against the black sky. Inside it I read the *Confessions* of Saint Augustine ('To Carthage I came, where there sang all around me in my ears a cauldron of unholy loves . . .') and the thoughts of Marcus Aurelius Antoninus, whose attitudes to life I found very appealing. The idea that my entire future was ordained, and that it was my task merely to 'love wholeheartedly' everything that happened to me had a nicely philistine ring about it. Also, I sensed that Marcus Aurelius was right when he told himself to live in the present, and reminded himself of the physical fragility of human beings: 'Now is the time to learn at last what is the nature of the universe whereof thou art part . . . Forget not there is a boundary set to thy time, and that if thou use it not to uncloud thy soul it will anon be gone, and thou with it . . . ' As his mentor Epictetus said, a man (or woman) is only a little soul burdened with a corpse.[1]

But my enthusiasm for being a 'real' Oxford undergraduate with all the rich history such a label implies, was not sufficient to bear me over the sea of moribund linguistic-philosophical debate in which Oxford at the time was drenched. I arrived in the era of what was known as the Foot–Hare controversy, most of whose details now escape me. But I received a strong impression of the dryness of the individuals who engaged in philosophical debate, and was put off by the fact that the empirical illustrations in the philosophers' arguments were cameos of upper-class life. Of course one should distinguish between the social origins of philosophy and its practitioners and the actual usefulness of philosophy itself; but at the time, in my mind, the two were mixed. For my first public examination at Oxford in 1963 I had to answer such questions as 'Why is England not the meaning of "England"?' and 'Which of the expressions in the following sentences would be used referringly if these sentences were used to make statements? (i) Peter is not the only person who was there. (ii) A weasel is a carnivorous animal. (iii) A man came to see me this morning.' I didn't feel very enlightened by getting the answers right. Most of what philosophers were doing seemed to consist of putting the structure of language under a microscope and ignoring the social world that gave birth and meaning to the language in the first place. Hare, of the Foot–Hare controversy, worked in a caravan in his front garden, had town planning as his hobby, and believed that most of the evils of the world were due to unclear thinking. His philosophical views were formed as a prisoner of war in Singapore and Thailand, where he decided that moral values are born with the individual. Foot was a woman, one of three who opposed themselves to Hare's belief in an instinctive morality. The other two women were Iris Murdoch, the novelist, whom I never met, and Elizabeth Anscombe, translator of Wittgenstein, who, for a short while, gave me tutorials in her littered house near Somerville. She had a lot of little children who used to pull the lavatory chain noisily during her tutorials, and was a robust and forbidding figure wearing baggy trousers, a scholastic gown and a constantly bemused look.

By my third Oxford year I had come round to the view that good philosophy was sociology and bad philosophy was not worth having, since it really didn't amount to anything more than linguistic quibbles. An Indian named Ved Mehta wrote a book called *Fly and the Fly Bottle* which was published in Britain in 1963 and which I found consoling, since it confirmed my own conclusions.[2] Subtitled 'Encounters with British Intellectuals' it began with a tour of Oxford philosophy. This tour took in Ernest Gellner in London SW15, because Gellner, a sociologist at the London School of Economics, had attacked Oxford philosophy for its character as an arid inquiry into the rules of language rather than what philosophy ought to be—an investigation of the universe. ('There are more things in heaven and earth, Horatio, than are dreamt of in your philosophy.') Ved Mehta reported Gellner as saying that to understand Oxford philosophy one had to practise sociology, that only by understanding the social milieu and political stances of people like Foot and Hare could one really evaluate what they were doing.

I had similar problems with economics. It was clear immediately that economics had little to do with the real world. In addition, I was suspicious from the start of the doctrine of 'economic man' who makes rational choices based on price in order to maximize his economic happiness, apparently unaffected by all other considerations. (Not being a feminist did not prevent me from noticing that the discussion presumed male rationality in economic behaviour but in fact cited endless incidences of housewives buying peas for the Sunday dinner.) 'Principles of Economics' and 'Economic Organization', the two subsections of the economics taught for PPE, appeared to contradict one another. In the former one was presented with a model of the capitalist economy marked by 'perfect' competition: this state of perfection was said to obtain when a large number of firms all produced closely similar products, where there were no restrictions on entry into the industry, where individual pro- ducers couldn't affect by their own actions the ruling market price and where consumers only exercised control because their 'rational' demands for a commodity were a function of price. In 'economic organization', on the other hand, one was told that reality was far from perfect. The tendency for industry to develop pockets of monopolistic control reduces some producers and all consumers to mere puppets.

I wasn't interested in big business and found it difficult to sympathize with the plight of corporations which couldn't maximize their profits. Welfare economists such as Marshall, Pigou and Pareto seemed more democratically minded, since they were concerned about how the consumer fared. But why did we not discuss the ethics of capitalism itself? Why did no one incite us to read Marx? There was no sense of excitement or challenge in what we did. The only challenge was to ingest and regurgitate an accepted body of doctrines—'knowledge' so- called. In 'Theory and Working of Political Institutions' and 'British Political and Constitutional History since 1865', the two elements of the politics syllabus, the resemblance to earlier parts of my education was even stronger. To listen to the women who tutored us at Somerville was to discover that history was a series of static, monochrome pictures and that politics was dead. In our second and third years we were 'farmed out' to more exciting intellects in other colleges. These were always men, which surprised me not at all at the time, though now I wonder why Somerville, which claimed a reputation as nursery of a female future, should have harboured such mediocrity.

As soon as I left Oxford I wrote a piece called 'On the Disadvantages of an Oxford Education' which I sent to the *Guardian* (they rejected it). My main complaint was that an Oxford education was too specialized; you didn't learn how society works. I listed as more specific problems with PPE too rigid demarcation lines between subjects, and resistance among those who teach to new ideas. This was proved, I said, in the fate

of sociology, which, in 1964, became for the first time an option
on the PPE syllabus. Its introduction was opposed most strongly
by the philosophers, who did not recognize the implications of
Wittgenstein's dictum that 'language is a form of life'.

I leapt at the chance of doing sociology. It was like seeing
the light at the end of the tunnel. Sociology was about *people*.
Even if it engaged in a certain amount of theorizing about
social processes and relations, this did not seem irrelevant to
'real' issues such as 'What is equality?', 'Why do people
behave themselves (or not)?' and 'What is education?' My two
sociology tutors were located at opposite ends of the Oxford
social spectrum. Bryan Wilson was unmarried, lived in the
hothouse world of All Souls College, wore severe suits, once
cancelled a tutorial when the more important social engagement of wine-tasting presented itself, and cultivated a generally inscrutable, humourless façade of middle-class convention.
He was said not to see the double meaning in the pronuncia-
tion of the title of his book *Sects and Society*. He called me
'Miss Titmuss' and when I married in my third year he moved
effortlessly to 'Mrs Oakley' which sounded equally peculiar to
me. I enjoyed the rarefied atmosphere of an All Souls tutorial,
and it was quite proper that Bryan Wilson taught me sociological theory rather than the more prosaic 'modern social
institutions'—there was nothing modern about either him or
the setting.

My other sociology tutor was a more practical man with a
working-class background that showed. He wore pale blue jerseys
and yellow ties and called me by my first name. He was a
socialist, a friend of my father's. He introduced me to Marx, to
Weber, and, indeed, gave me the intellectual means to get
outside the society I lived in and see for the first time the stuff of
which it was made. The first essay I wrote for A.H. Halsey was
an appreciation of Ralf Dahrendorf's *Class and Class Conflict in
Industrial Society*. Imagine the impact of that on someone who
has been grappling for two years with 'Can ethical naturalism be
shown to be mistaken in principle?', 'How far does the Fifth
Republic differ from the constitution?' and 'What is the balance
of payments?'

What I wanted to understand was not the minute workings of
this or that political party or the benefits and hazards of this or

that philosophical or economic orthodoxy; I wanted to understand how the society I lived in came to be, as a totality, the way it was, and how individuals like me were constructed in a certain format. For I had already appreciated how far the accident of my birth—to those people in that time in that place—had moulded me in a particular way. My genetic inheritance could not explain my psychology, my conflicts, my incapacities; only my social inheritance could do that. By extension, I felt that nothing could be understood without reducing (or rather, elevating) individual actors to the status of social products and participants.

Although the work had its problems, Oxford as a place inspired me at times to a manic happiness, even during the snows of the second winter, the coldest England had seen for a hundred years. The colleges and quadrangles and parks and rivers lost even their surface deformities to a luscious sheen of crisp, flawless white. The cold didn't really penetrate us: we glowed inside whatever the weather. We were lit by the fire of youthful omnipotence—we could do anything, be anything, the world was an open book. But it was the Oxford summers I remember best. 'Instantly something like a vision shines out of the valley,' says James Morris, later Jan, describing Oxford as a female city with ecstatic moods. 'The towers, spires and pinnacles of the city, honey-gold and tightly packed, leap suddenly from the shadows as though they are floodlit. All is sudden etched intricacy—chiselled, elaborate, vertical—a cluster of golden objects picked out in theatrical silhouette . . . it leaves you with a shame-faced mystical feeling—as though you have enjoyed a moment of second sight.'[3] We were out from early in the morning to late at night, only some of the time doing what we were supposed to be doing. We walked and we sat and we talked and wherever it was we were drowned in beauty. Mayflies danced; flowers bloomed; the wind blew purely warm on our faces. On the Cherwell punters happily fell in the water, and couples entwined themselves with books and each other in the stagnant but oddly sweet-smelling bottoms of boats. One day when the American tourists unloaded themselves into Turl Street as they were wont to do, we took off our shoes and for their benefit walked giggling and barefoot on the cobbled stones so they could take 'authentic' pictures of us. We ate huge meals in cheap Indian restaurants and repaired to country pubs whenever someone had the means of transport, particularly to The Trout at Godstow, where a married man on a motorbike once told me my eyes were bottomless like trout pools (I took the remark as a compliment at the time).

By this stage Martin and I were drifting apart. He was a mature student at Leicester University. He came to Oxford for weekends and I went to Leicester, but I became increasingly inconsistent in my affections. I had a vision at one point, based on the film of *Look Back in Anger* which I had seen in Aberystwyth in 1960 while my father was taking an honorary degree there, in which Martin and I lived in one room with a squalling baby and Martin, an unsuccessful poet, was always drunk while I was always in my dressing gown trying to do the ironing. (Another film popular at the time was *Woman in a Dressing Gown*.) In other words, I finally came face to face with the fact that the relationship had no future. That is, it could not have the future I had been brought up to believe girls like me should look forward to. I did not want to leave Oxford without at least the prospect of getting married. Was this unusual? I think not. Even today, there are few girls who envisage an entirely marriageless future.[4] Mary Ingham, in *Now We Are Thirty*, writes: 'I ought to be able to say at this point that we were all fiercely self determining, but in 1968 I wrote in my diary: "Oh God, why am I not married and happy with two kids? Why am I aimlessly wasting away?" I had automatically assumed I would be bound to meet someone [at university] in whose shadow I could follow.'[5] I, myself, didn't think of marriage as a primary goal; rather of a degree as an empty achievement without a husband to go with it. My school and my parents had both made it plain that girls should get married. If they could fit in a career as well, that was fine. Nobody pointed out to us that in this situation there was a certain conflict to be resolved. We had to find that out for ourselves.

I first saw Robin at a seminar on Marxism and social anthropology at Nuffield College on May 18, 1964. I was recovering from a passion that finally killed the long-drawn-out affair with Martin—a brief and intensely self-wounding passion, in which two people were so overimpressed by each other's social status and attractiveness that they pledged eternal love within three days of their first meeting. To this day (and unlike most other events and episodes in my life) I don't understand how it happened; but we both quite obviously saw perfection where there was none. The delusion foundered. For the first time in my life I was manless. The perfect human being who turned out not to be so perfect after all married my best friend, divorced her and is now a Labour MP with a growing propensity to appear on the front pages of newspapers. No doubt he will be Prime Minister one day.

Robin, whom I have loved and to whom I have been married and indebted for eighteen years, is another kind of person altogether. I find it very difficult to write about him. The other relationships I have had can be summarized, albeit with difficulty, in words. But not this one, the one that has been and remains the central support of my life in sickness and in health, in poverty and (relative) wealth, in femininity and in feminism.

Robin gave that day a good paper that was well received. I decided on the spot that I would marry him, because he looked as though he would make a good husband and father. This sounds extremely calculating. It was, and I make no apologies for it. Men chalk up such calculations about women all the time. In any case, my defence is that I was right.

The problem was to get to know him. I didn't have the temerity to walk up to him and introduce myself, but I did know a few people who knew him. To one of these I offered twenty cigarettes for an introduction. The introduction was duly effected and I was not ashamed of the means, only, subsequently, of the reward. Robin was cautious. He didn't take my hand at the cinema and he assumed I would pay for myself at the cheap Chinese restaurant where we ate our first meal together. He said, as we parted, 'Well, you know where to find me.' He lived in a smelly six-foot-square room in a crooked street from whence he could only be lured by a call or a stone thrown at the window, since there was no front door bell. He subsisted entirely on pork pies, beer and yoghurt and rarely washed his clothes or himself. A few days after we met he retired to an isolation hospital with 'pyrexia of unknown origin', i.e., a high temperature, due, I thought, to his poor diet. I visited him, resented being told to wait outside as the nurses washed his (as yet to me unknown) body, and met a previous girlfriend also visiting called Melanie who bore a melon. The quality of surrealism mounted when

Robin sat up in bed one day, still with his PUO, and said, 'You don't want to get married in church, do you?' I didn't even know he liked me.

When he came out of hospital we had a few days' holiday in a rented blue Mini. We sat on the horse's back on Whitehorse Hill, and searched for the ideal sleepy Cotswold village made of grey stone and roses for our first night together, finding instead a rather ugly village called Corsham; the setting turned out not to matter. Robin was shocked that I came to bed wearing a diaphragm I had acquired from a lady doctor in Oxford who had six children under five and did family planning in her bathroom. (I did doubt at first that it would work.) We visited a series of Saxon churches lit with sun and timelessness, and sat by slow-moving rivers in Burford, Swinbrook and the ruins of Minster Lovell Hall. I wrote, as a reflex, a 'Love Poem' which ended

if I were to write about you
the books of the world
could not contain
what I should write
for words are not enough—
words and moments—
only us
whole and now.

Carefully, Robin explained to me that he had arranged to travel in Europe that summer with a group of archaeological friends (he had once been a budding archaeologist himself), particularly in a loose affiliation with a girl called Judy. I was not to worry. He bought me the Beatles' record of 'A Hard Day's Night', and I retired to my bedroom in Acton and wrote, to the music of 'If I fell in love with you, would you promise to be true', a long sociological essay on 'The Family and Industrialization' which won the Somerville College PPE prize that year. Many letters and telegrams passed between us; one of mine went to Skopje in Yugoslavia, where the earthquake got it before Robin did. In August I flew to Athens to meet him. We stayed in someone's flat on a hill called Kleomenous above the city and worked together in the library of the Ionian Bank, where I read A.J. Ayer's *Language, Truth and Logic*, and wrote in my diary, 'I

have no role or status which is not based on being in love with
R.' We went on a boat to Skopelos, a then unknown island, in a
terrible storm which made me throw up continuously and from
which we were rescued by fishermen. It was on Skopelos on a
deserted beach under the proverbial blue sky with our feet on the
proverbial white sand that I pointed out to Robin that he had
not 'asked' me to marry him, as men were supposed to do. He
went down on his knees and proposed, laughing. He later sought
my father's permission to marry me, though what we would have
done had this been refused is not clear.

Of all my so-called boyfriends, Robin was the one who most
pleased my parents. He looked the epitome of the sensible young
man that all middle-class parents want their daughters to marry.
His father had been a chartered accountant and the family had
lived in a large farmhouse in the wealthy commuter country of
Kent. The four children were all sent to private schools and in
childhood they had a nanny. It was a distinctly upper-class set-
up. Despite the fact that after Robin's father's death from cancer
of the spine at the early age of forty-nine, relative poverty set in
and the family was forced to retire to the gardener's cottage,
niceties such as linen table napkins and freshly polished silver
were preserved at all costs. I felt that Robin was coming down in
the world by marrying me, though according to the Registrar-
General, chartered accountants and university professors'
families both belong to social class I.

When I met him, Robin was doing a postgraduate diploma in
social anthropology at Oxford. He had previously completed an
economics degree at Cambridge and subsequently was to register
for an Oxford D.Phil. He confessed two leading ambitions: to
live and work in Greece and to marry and have two children. I
was much happier about the second ambition than the first
(although I always wanted three). In Greece that summer we
went to the Athenian suburb where his research was to take
place, an evil-smelling district called Nea Ionia, and I confessed
in turn that I did not think I wanted to live there and speak
Greek; and, anyway, what would *I* do? We agreed on a
compromise. Robin would study the immigration of Greek
Cypriots to Britain instead, and we would live in Islington,
North London, an important settlement area. We did not make
any such decision on the basis of my future work. But there was

no doubt in our minds that we wanted children. Was this why we got married? Neither of us questioned the ethics, sexual or otherwise, of marriage. It merely seemed the right thing to do, like brushing your teeth in the morning or buying new clothes when your old ones wore out. Most people, whatever the particular moral climate, enter the institution of marriage in this way: blindfolded and naively hopeful.

It was a gentleman called Barry Digweed, who had performed the same office for one of the Beatles, who married us on December 17, 1964, at 3.45 pm in Caxton Hall Registry Office for a cost of 11s 3d. I had needed not only the permission of my parents (being under twenty-one) but also that of the governors of Somerville College in order to get married. The latter was, strictly, permission to continue studying after marriage, and the criterion was whether marriage would help or hinder my academic work. The consensus was that it would help by 'settling me down' (an interestingly false idea). We moved into a damp basement flat in North Oxford, our first home together. It cost £4 a week and consisted of a coconut-matted kitchen with fungoid cupboards and a temperamental fuel stove, a sitting room, bedroom and bath. There was also a narrow slit of a room, about three feet wide and six feet long, which I used for my work. It, too, grew violently coloured fungi on the walls unless preventive measures were taken. I kept a paraffin heater in there and studied for my final exams with a paraffin-induced headache.

In those months after marriage and before the end of my undergraduate career I met the housewife-career woman conflict head on without recognizing it. I had never done any housework and, when told by my mother to take responsibility for washing my own clothes at the age of fifteen, I adopted the foul habit of having my Friday night bath surrounded by them. I couldn't cook at all, and even the instructions on frozen food packets defeated me. I learnt how to burn beefburgers and disguise all sorts of disasters with garlic and cheap wine. My greatest problem was the stove in the kitchen which that winter was absolutely necessary as it was our only form of heating. It drove me to distraction almost daily and I ended up in tears at my failure to be a good and provident housewife. However, I did manage (usually) to make the bed in the mornings before going off to lectures, and I brought my Somerville friends back to admire my

marital abode. I felt superior to them, that I had achieved
something immeasurably more valuable than their freedom
persistently to engage in trivial love affairs. I think I really
thought I had solved the whole thing. Here was I, a wife at the
age of twenty, sitting in my tiny study constructing a card index
of aides memoires for my final examinations: 'Growth and the
Trade Cycle', 'The Keynesian System', 'Liberty and Punishment', 'Good and Bad Acts', 'Pressure Groups', 'Social Stratifica-
tion', 'Durkheim and Merton on Anomie'. I had it all sewn up.
But if someone had asked me which had priority, self-develop-
ment or wifehood, what would I have said? I didn't question that
mine was the domestic function. I didn't expect Robin to lift a
finger in the house (except in the direction of the stove).
Equally, I knew I would be terribly upset if I didn't get a good
degree. And I still didn't know what I wanted to do with my life.

On learning that I had 'only' got a second-class degree I wrote
on the back of an old envelope which I've kept, 'People who
don't get firsts have babies.' In the first sixteen months after
leaving Oxford I wrote two novels, fourteen short stories, six
non-fiction articles, started and decided not to finish a children's
history textbook and completed four different bits of research. In
the second sixteen months I had two children. These periods
divide absolutely; the first feels continuous with my life now, the
second not. In the first period my energies were focused on the
two novels. The first, *Eyelight*, takes as its theme the university
career of a girl who ends up as a happily married housewife and
mother. 'I want it to be', said the heroine, a thinly disguised me,
'the biography of my generation: it is my aim to document,
through the experience of one person, the distinctive way of life,
beliefs and opinions, thoughts and activities of this generation of
youth to which I belong.' This was serious stuff.

There was a lot of myself in that book, and its rejection by
publishers was especially hard because it wasn't really rejection.
The readers' reports kindly passed on to me by various eminent
publishing gentlemen noted that the book was very obviously a
first novel, but said it was 'one of the few really readable first
novels, that have any memorable quality about them . . . one
thinks back on it with pleasure as something well accomplished';
that it would have more appeal if it were straight autobiography,
and that 'There is no "fine writing" and an absence of

overstressing and purple passages which I find—since this is the first book by a young writer—very encouraging indeed.' It isn't clear from the correspondence I have filed away why *Eyelight* wasn't published: indeed, I think it would have been had I persevered and made the cuts that were recommended. (And then my life might have taken an altogether different turn.) What apparently sealed its fate was the 'delivery' of the second book, *The Unborn Child*, a totally different exercise in which a married woman called Martha went mad in St Albans as a consequence of discovering that, although she wanted to, she couldn't have children, while her sister-in-law, who didn't want to, could. I wrote this book speedily as a rejoinder to the statements that appeared in readers' reports on the first that I might be a 'one novel' person. In my view *The Unborn Child* proved that I wasn't, but in retrospect I can see that the marked disjunction between the structure and tone of the two novels must have been disconcerting to publishers used to identifying writers as belonging to one school or another. Versatility of talent wasn't appreciated—or at least that is the interpretation I favour.

The final rejection letter came from a man called Raleigh Trevelyan at Michael Joseph. He said he wouldn't publish *The Unborn Child* and enclosed a reader's report on it which annoyed me so much that I threw it away. Nor would he, he said, on second thoughts, publish *Eyelight*. He added that he thought I wrote extremely well and he and his advisers could well have made an utterly wrong decision: he would always be enormously interested in seeing anything else that I wrote. I got the letter on Christmas Eve, 1966. I was supposed to give birth the next day. Unsurprisingly in the circumstances I decided my salvation lay in motherhood.

South of the Baltic Sea

The morning spent waiting for him was perhaps the best time. (She would not like him to misunderstand this.) She walked in the snow for hours; down to the harbour, with its big ships and its little ships selling fish, the market with its flower and leather stalls. She stood with shoppers in the busy department stores, studying them as much as the wares they were buying. She found the monuments and the parks, white wastes by frozen water; she listened to the music of a language she did not understand. And all the time she knew she was waiting for him.

The minute he arrives she realizes that their time together is again beginning to be over. He stands there and seems both a stranger and her intimate lover. He is euphoric: the conference was good, better because he knew she was there at the end of it. He smells of the conference, of other people: of which other people? What are the two of them doing together? What do they mean to each other? Is it all worth it?

The hours are crowded with experiences, not just of the two of them together (though that would, of course, suffice) but of this place, its ambience, its difference from the cultures they know best. They get lost together in the rain, they stand together in a church and kiss. They sit, listening to mournful music in the minor key, in warm restaurants where everything is submerged in vodka. They walk through the hotel and shock the management, although the management does its best not to show it. He acquires an orange from a bemused waitress in the hotel restaurant because he wants to eat fruit as part of an act of love. Authoritatively, he demands that she discard her underwear so his hands can have an interesting time under the starched white tablecloth while they meditate out loud on the sexual predilections of the men and women around them. He insists on testing her fitness by climbing eight flights of stairs with her. They cannot find the stairs, and the woman behind the label that says 'information' doesn't know where the stairs are. In the end, she passes the test (just). They look at the city at night from the panoramic windows of the sauna which turns out thoroughly to justify its stereotyped reputation as a sexual adventure playground. They lie together and wake together, or rather once he wakes first and once she does. She studies his form in the darkness, so neatly folded, so unmoving, so separate from her; but her strongest feeling through it all is that each sight must be imprinted on her mind, each word recorded, each act added to all those past acts which comprise her knowledge of him and the history of their relationship.

She looks at him and his face is the world; its texture, its contours, the message in his recessed green eyes, his smile. His voice with its foreign edges, words slightly mispronounced, nuances unintended, is her delight. His body is her pleasure, her plaything. It gives her some of the greatest pleasure she has ever had. His fingers are sexual organs. They caress and explore and insinuate themselves everywhere; now they know, because their owner has learnt so quickly, what to do. His mouth has a personality and will of its own; she never knew what mouths could do before she met his. Her response incites him to new heights: she wonders if he is a true lover of women (he says no such person exists; much later in their relationship, she realizes how very wrong she was).

When he enters her their half-open eyes are also joined. She tells him that he cannot know how incredible he feels inside her, but he does know. She really feels she has lost her identity. She really feels as though she cannot, does not, exist apart from him. She really, for those moments, does not care why he wants her and what he sees in her. He could be the original Viking pillager for all she cares. All she knows is the moment. This is the unpremeditated ecstasy of the biological accident of life: not what we live for, but its serendipity; the peak that rises above the plain, the force that powers the waves, the wind, the lava flows and the cold bright stars.

Among the things he says in scenes 3, 4 and 5 are the following:

1 I love you.

2 The problem for men is that the only way to secure a stake in children is to marry, but marriage is a problem.

3 I have given up drink because it makes me kiss girls at parties.

4 Why do you mind when I use the word 'girl' in this context?

5 You mustn't kill yourself for four reasons, in this order: the contribution you can make to society; your child; your husband; me.

6 I want to meet you in the desert with only a fur coat on.

7 If it's like this in nine months we must decide to end it.

8 I love you.

She can't remember what she said. Perhaps he could record it for her? She is hurt by some of the things he says. Mostly this is because she asks for honesty, gets it and can't take it. Why doesn't he say she is beautiful? Why doesn't he say he loves her incredibly, more than he has ever loved anyone, and for ever; that he wants to spend his life with her; that she is everything to him? Why doesn't he buy her red roses and swim the sea with chocolates? She wouldn't believe it if he did (although in fact there is to come a day of warm rain in another city when he says, and does, all these things—save for actually personally swimming the sea). She distrusts romantic chivalric gestures in men. It means they are treating women as sex objects. So why does she want it? Why is she hurt by his pragmatism? The last thing she needs is to live with him, with his self-interest, his self-centred depressions, his magisterial exercise of male power. The last thing she wants is to be like his wife. She knows what she wants: she wants him to love her now, wholeheartedly, to think of no one and nothing else when he makes love to her. She wants him to make sure she doesn't get pregnant (which is a disinterested gesture, it would be her problem, not his) and write her considerate frequent letters. She wants him to look forward to, and mourn the passing of, their times together, with appropriate, reasonably controlled delight and distress. She wants him to think of her fondly at meetings and conferences. She wants him to feel about her as he does about no one else, to be so conscious of her individuality that whether or not he loves another woman does not matter. She definitely does not want him to claim more than his fair share of her.

Such common sense may fill cheerful ordinary daylight hours, but it is not what possesses her the rest of the time, or now. Is it the force of her socialization, the moulding of her feminine personality? Of course it is. If it is, it divides them, for he, being made in the masculine mould, cannot feel the same. He must have a more cavalier attitude. 'Thanks for the nice time we had together. I look forward to seeing you again one day.' And yet she remains convinced that they feel the same. Now, for example, at ten o'clock on the morning after scenes 3, 4 and 5 he is back in his office. It is cold and dark. His wife irritated him this morning. He misses her. He cannot rid himself of the awareness that he misses her. It is a permanent pain. Inside he really is distressed and bereaved. He is as confused as she is by the simultaneous profundity and hopelessness of this affair. What he knows and what he feels are two different matters.

It could be five months before they meet again. Who knows if they will ever make it? And if they do, so what? As the aeroplane bumped its way down through the English clouds she thought: what matters is that we care for each other, not as a man and a woman, but as people.

As she woke this morning instantly depressed, she had another, more practical, thought. She is quite sure they have to bring this affair to an end. It only remains for her to tell him so, and act upon it.

Love: irresolution

The source of such trouble, which is trouble quite a few women find themselves in, is more deep-rooted than a mere love-affair. In 1974 I wrote: 'The other day on a train from Manchester I saw a man plugged into a tape-recorder. He was sitting in splendid isolation in a window seat with a cassette recorder on the table in front of him. Two wires came out of its sides and led into his ears. His face wore the abstracted expression of someone who had contrived to tune out the entire world—as in a sense he had. This sight symbolized acutely what has always been some kind of ruling fantasy in my life.

'To be in the world, yet invulnerable, not bombarded by endless disturbing transmissions, as I am; to be the sphinx with the stony smile, contained and self-contained; to be an island in the midst of water that does not even ripple in response to a pebble; sometimes over the last few years I have felt myself moving nearer this desired (but undesirable) goal. There are fewer occasions now on which I feel myself to be an object, a collection of responses...'

But I have not solved the problem. The problem is feeling too much. Let me analyse it, because it is a female problem and therefore not mine alone: it is, moreover, a problem of love, of all the love stories that happen between men and women. In it is wrapped up the doggedness of dependence, the need for one human being to be affected by another. How can any of us love without dependence, without laying ourselves open to the most horrendous conflicts and disasters?

As a woman, in the first place, my emotions rule my life. From them I derive the pleasure and pain of my existence. My thoughts are directed by them. There is nothing that I do or think which is not inspired by feelings.

In the second place, I take it as my chief duty to study the feelings of others. Their emotional welfare is my responsibility.

In the third place, any attachment that is formed between myself and another becomes, for its duration, my ruling concern. I become inseparable from that person and lose much of my capacity for independent voluntary action. I have given myself up to the other person, whether or not such self-sacrifice was asked for, and I am, indeed, nearly willing to give up everything.

In my head, the calm, organized part of my head, I am aware of the silliness of these characteristics. If love (maternal, heterosexual, or homosexual, marital, filial, or whatever) means that one person absorbs the other, then no real relationship exists any more. Love evaporates; there is nothing left to love. The integrity of self is gone. Like wax, one's borders melt and run away.

I want to know why I am like that. I ask a friend, a psychoanalyst, why women are like that; she doesn't know, but comments that her own two-year-old daughter already is. Women as a category do have this characteristic. Others, besides myself, have said so:

> . . . women stay with, build on, and develop in a context of attachment and affiliation with others. Indeed, women's sense of self [is] very much organized around being able to make and then to maintain affiliations and relationships. Eventually, for many women the threat of disruption of an affiliation is perceived not as just a loss of a relationship but as something closer to a total loss of self . . . [1]

> . . . although both sexes are capable of performing both the instrumental and the supportive functions, there has tended to be in most cultures throughout the world a specialization of women in the supportive or stroking function. In fact, this assignment of the supportive or stroking function to women can be traced in all their roles throughout the social structure, in the family, at work, at play, and in social life generally. There are few feminine

wiles better documented than the willingness of young
women to build up the male ego by underplaying their own
talents . . . A century of guidebooks for working girls has
emphasized the importance of ego-support for male employers. Girls are admonished not to win at tennis or other
sports . . . Indeed, the behaviours that constitute stroking
. . . add up to a description of the ideal-typical woman
wherever she is found.[2]

The attachment and other-supporting behaviour of women is
variously characterized as pre- or post-social; at any rate, there is
no doubt that in terms of the reproduction of the labour force, it
is a useful quality. By virtue of their sensitivity to others, women
are led to want to procreate. Thereafter, they have the logical, if
personally destructive, desire to guard their fledglings, a necessity
that extends to those definite non-fledglings, big strong adult
men, the rulers of society. Patriarchs are babies in disguise: the
governed are the protectors also; comfort and be damned.

Women, therefore, are non-human. Their existence is a
precondition for all human existence. That this is not a fact of
biology but a fact about the cultural interpretation of biology we
may discern from other cultures. There is, anyway, no such
contradiction as Nature versus Culture. The one mediates the
other so absolutely that the question itself is absurd. Who, then,
are the oppressors of women? Obviously, their mothers and their
mothers before them. But this does not get us (them) very far.

It should be said that the capacity to love others to the point
of self-annihilation is not, when properly constituted, a weakness but a strength. Society is founded on countless female
labours of love. My sisters gestate and nurture babies both young
and old, and facilitate with inconspicuous nourishment the
flowering of multiple talents and achievements. 'Behind every
great man there is a little woman.' 'For men must work and
women must weep.' Without this there is no society, only
insentient disorder. Hence, 'We might say that one of the major
issues before us as a human community is the question of how to
create a way of life that includes serving others without being
subservient . . . women today have a highly developed basis for
this social advance.'[3]

It is certainly the issue before me, in all my relationships. I am beset all the time with feelings of engulfment and hence an enervated stasis of self. My mother saw me as part of her. I saw myself as part of my father. The triad made no sense to me, but the dyads, which did, conflicted and added to my confusion. I never am sure in any so-called face-to-face relationship which one of us is me. A 'good' relationship is 'good' by virtue of the merging that occurs.

Let me mention one further element, remarked on by the existential psychiatrist David Cooper:

> The appearance of love is subversive to any good social ordering of our lives. Far more than being statistically abnormal, love is dangerous, it might even spread through the aseptic shield that we get each other to erect around us. What we are socially conditioned to need and expect is not love but security. Security means the full and repeatedly reinforced affirmation of the family.[4]

David Cooper is a man, and so are half the characters in the fairy tales of love. Women who create the 'security of the family' knowing that they are creating their own prison, ultimately can do without it. 'You begin by sinking into his arms and end up with your arms in his sink.' Another major issue before us as a human community is, in other words, the creation of lasting, loving, reproductive relationships which bestow freedom instead of confinement.

I reject the drama of the romantic heroine who, on discovering she is not everything to a man, throws him over for another with whom she repeats the same fugue. I reject the repertoire of grand gestures altogether. I want to surpass my femininity. This, after all, is what I have been trying to do for a long time.

CHRONOLOGY 23–29

I saw myself as a Technicolor Madonna, lactating and serene. My serenity was untroubled by the principal actor missing his cue and failing to materialize on the twenty-fifth. No one suggested inducing labour (obstetric customs were different then); I went for nightly walks round Chiswick and scrubbed the floor instead. It wasn't until January 2, 1967, that I woke late, having missed my appointment at the antenatal clinic, and went into labour.

I couldn't wait for the baby to be born. Curiosity had been my main motive for wanting a baby; I had a tremendous desire to find out if I could conceive, how I would look and feel when pregnant, whether birth was female self-fulfilment, what a child of mine and Robin's would look like, whether breastfeeding was all it was made out to be. In the event I discovered that conception was easy, pregnancy made you fat and tired but was a miracle of invisible humanity, limbs poking and heaving at your underclothes in the supermarket, infant hiccoughs causing rhythmic shifts in a monumental abdomen. Before I was pregnant, I had assumed that the pregnant abdomen was somehow soft, like a sack full of grain; it would yield when you pressed it. I was amazed to discover how hard it really is, not only because it contains bones, but because of its own fibres supporting the weight of the baby, fluid and accoutrements. I was both fascinated and horrified by my body when pregnant. I thought it beautiful, that mound of glistening flesh, but also obscene—a tumour of some kind. Indeed, one had no control over its growth. And one's breasts grew too, heavy, changing their angles, striped with blue veins, ready to be, it seemed, the world's dairy.

I had a 'show' (whose emotional impact reminded me of my first menstruation) at 12.30 while making macaroni cheese for lunch. Thereafter I had contractions at three-minute intervals for thirteen hours. Robin and I ate lunch, but he washed up in the middle of the night. I lay on the sofa in my homemade maternity dress and breathed as the books said, ordering music to distract me (it didn't) and sips of water. Why, I said, were the contractions only three minutes apart? And why did they hurt so much? Was I about to give birth? The horror that I might be and that I might not be were both too much to bear. I had attended no preparation classes (out of laziness only) but firmly believed that childbirth was a natural process and if you weren't anxious and behaved in the right way it would be no more than a passing pain. I confidently expected a marvellous experience.

At half past three I went into hospital by ambulance because I was beginning to cry at home: more and more my body seemed possessed by some demoniacal drama of its own and I, the person who had humanly willed this event, was nowhere to be found. In hospital an army of strange unsympathetic faces added to my sense of alienation. The atmosphere was white and cold, not at all a celebration of a human birthday; I didn't find it surprising that Jesus had chosen to be born in a stable. Robin was taken from me to the 'Fathers' room'; I can see the look of silent protest on his face now as if it were yesterday. I needed him. We needed to cling together not for any comfort he particularly could give me, but because we were in this together. This was our baby. But the Board of Governors of the hospital discouraged such a belief. Women had babies on their own. Husbands fainted in the delivery room, broke their skulls on wash-basins, sued the hospital for interfering sexually with their wives, or, at the very least, were so appalled by all the blood and mess of birth that further sexual connection with their wives was rendered impossible.

I was given an enema, and a bath, and had my pubic hair shaved. My clothes were enumerated on a piece of paper and I was asked to sign it in the middle of a contraction. All these procedures were uncomfortable and impersonal: I was in no doubt now that I was just a body, a baby-producing machine, and not a very good one at that, for why else did I need all these adjustments? I had never been in hospital before and had never therefore experienced that process of institutionalization, which, as Goffman has described it,[1] is designed to remove individuality altogether. In a hospital gown, bereft of my pubic hair and my faeces and bathed in disinfectant, I was apparently suitably anonymous for birth, that most personal of acts. No single nurse or midwife or doctor was especially unkind, but none gave me to understand that it would be in order for me to be myself. The doctor described me in my case notes as a healthy primigravida at forty-one weeks with an uneventful pregnancy now five centimetres dilated with bulging membranes, or words to that effect. That summed me up.

I lay for eight hours in a room with several other women, separated from them by curtains. Most of them were screaming 'Help me, nurse,' or 'I'm going to die.' Midwives appeared periodically not to monitor, or to minister to, these women in distress but to listen to unborn hearts and measure the pressure of blood in our arteries. They made various offhand remarks to the noisy women about how much discomfort they were causing the silent ones (it could have been the other way round). If the noise became insupportably loud they came with syringes full of pethidine like the well-equipped insensitive vanguard of an army on the battlefront. For a war it was. Between them and us—the so-called providers of maternity care and its so-called users—and between us and them—mothers-to-be and the babies fighting their way out of tight wombs through narrow pink passages into an unhappy world.

For much of the time Robin stood or sat next to my bed holding my hand or rubbing my back or reminding me that the answer to the pain of childbirth lay in the correct adjustment of one's lungs. I couldn't understand how I had ever believed this to be the case. But I did concentrate on my breathing simply because it was something other than the evident unrelieved pain around and inside me to focus on—just as effective or ineffective as counting sheep jumping over a fence. Robin complained that I was tense. With an unexpected surge of bitterness I told him to shut up. The woman opposite me was wheeled away and when the nurse told me an hour later that she had had her baby I felt a slight sense of purpose: so there was to be a baby at the end of this after all? Once I felt a sharp pain in my buttock and turned to see a retreating midwife with a syringe. 'What's that for?' I asked. 'To take the edge off your pain, dear,' she said. Obviously no one had told her that pethidine is hardly the best drug for the relief of pain in childbirth.[2] After that a fog descended. The pain was the same but I had become completely identified with it. I couldn't fight it or overcome it any more but instead drowned in it. Life was oceanic; I was tossed from one gigantic wave to another, each time more and more convinced that when the wave receded I would have been totally swept out to sea by it.

I said I wanted to push. I didn't, but I had read that that was the sign of the second stage and I had had enough of the first. The midwife came in and with an air of nonchalant expertise played around with various tubes and bits of metal in the area in which I had been given to understand birth would occur. Amniotic fluid flooded the bed. She said, 'You're going to have your baby, now.' I marvelled at the precision of her knowledge. Why didn't I know that? I was having the baby, not her. Or was I? I was wheeled to the delivery room, Robin nowhere in sight. The contractions intensified and I shouted, released from the inhibiting cries of the other women. 'Now, now, Mrs Oakley,' they said, 'you mustn't lose control now, you're nearly there.' The midwife said to a young Scandinavian pupil midwife, 'How many deliveries have you done?' 'Three,' she said. 'Right,' the first one said, 'you can do this one on your own.'

On my own was how I felt. I asked how long it would be before my baby was born. 'That depends on how hard you push,' they said. In that case, I'll push bloody hard, I thought. They instructed me to put my hands under my knees and my head on my chest and push with every contraction. The effort was almost too much and I never managed to time the push and the breath with the contraction, so that each time I stopped pushing and felt the continuing agony of the contraction. The pupil midwife kept telling me to push a bit more, only she couldn't quite get the 'sh' sound, so she said 'puss a bit more' instead. I would have laughed had I not felt I was about to die. I was incredibly thirsty but there was no one to give me any water. One of them (by this time the room seemed full of women: there were five or six of them, the rest students) looked at the clock. 'She's been pushing for an hour,' she said. They tried for the thousandth time to listen to the baby's heart and they couldn't find it. They took my pulse and exchanged knowing looks. 'You must', they said, 'get the baby out with the next push or we will have to get the doctor.' In my drained terrified state a small part of my brain still functioned and I deliberated whether to yield myself and my baby up to their not-so-tender mercies completely, or whether to summon up my non-existent reserves of strength. It was an important decision to make. I didn't want a forceps delivery, and I didn't think the baby did, either. So not at the next contraction, or the one after, but the one after that, the head of my child was born with a searing stretching and cutting of flesh that I knew would mutilate me for ever but welcomed for the baby's sake. I heard the sound of my perineum being cut rather than felt it—like a tailor with his scissors and some especially tough cloth. But the birth of the head I certainly felt. 'It's not crying,' I complained. 'It's only the head,' they said. With the next contraction I felt with blissful relief the whole body slip out and this great blue boy landed between my feet, arms and legs thrashing, cord huge and twisted, mouth screaming, eyes wide and blue, a vital anger in every particle of his newly born self.

This separation that I had longed for I found hard to take. Immediately, I couldn't believe that the baby was really mine and had come from my womb, although I had been present and conscious at his coming. I needed to be reunited with him, to be on my own with him. I needed his father, my lover, there to marvel at this act of creation. Instead two students took the baby to a cot in the corner of the room and, giggling, pretended to be counting his fingers and toes. Instantly I was alarmed. Perhaps there was something wrong with him? The students in their white gowns stood with their backs to me and between me and the baby. I could hear him crying but I couldn't see or hold him to acquire the knowledge for myself that he was perfect.

The pupil midwife pulled on the umbilical cord so much that it snapped and she fell against the opposite wall. 'Don't worry,' said the midwife, and pummelled my uterus inside and out, like a cook baking bread, until she triumphantly produced the placenta. After that I was left alone with my screaming baby in the corner of the room for two hours. I became increasingly agitated and unhappy and rang the bell several times asking for Robin, if the baby was all right, for a cup of tea. I had had nothing to eat or drink for fifteen hours, had had (I discovered later) a post-partum haemorrhage. I was covered in a rash which was said to be due to the immense effort I had exerted in defeating the threat of forceps. 'Of course the baby is all right,' they said. 'No, you can't have a cup of tea until you've been stitched and the doctor is busy at the moment.' 'No, you can't have your husband in to see you because you haven't been stitched.' 'And if you press that bell again I'll take it away from you.' She did. Then she took the baby away too and when Robin came to see me at the same time as the tea but before the stitching there was no baby for us to admire together. A nurse had shown him his son in the corridor still crying and with blood on his forehead. The baby had now gone to the nursery. Robin was shocked by my appearance but bravely told me what splendid work I had done. I drank my tea. A doctor came to stitch me painfully three hours after the birth. I was taken up to the ward, where I didn't sleep for what was left of the night. Robin walked home at 4 am with my clothes in a suitcase.

Then you were twenty-one and a half inches long, now you are seventy-two inches, taller than I who bore you. Your voice, which no longer screams, is that of a man. I have trouble recognizing you to be that great blue boy who landed between my feet, that so-beautiful baby (not my perception only but that of the medical staff too) who imposed his will so unscrupulously on the entire ward.

I am quite ashamed of my post-birth feelings about you. I was proud of your weight and your sex and of my refusal to allow you to be dragged out of me with metal blades around your head. The first and the last are understandable, but why the second? It was an enormous thrill to have produced a boy. The first time we were alone together I threw off your nappy to check; such a splendid sight! But these were all facts about you: emotionally I judged you from a distance. I did not, at first, really love you, only admired you from afar as an alien object. In fact you seemed quite threatening. Wherever I turned you were always there with a nappy full of shit or pee, a bed full of sour milk, a wailing mouth and an eternally empty stomach. You made demands that repeated themselves in a tight cycle and I unreasonably felt I would never be able to satisfy you. I offered you my breasts and you emptied them both, took your mouth accusingly off my enlarged red nipples and asked for more. I filled glass bottles with National Dried Milk and emptied them into you, afterwards dropping them in fragments on the floor in my tiredness. You wanted food every four hours day and night for three months. You grew enormously, doubling your weight in less than four months and moving on to vast plates of Robinson's Groats and other similar messes according to the fashion of the time. Indeed, I have to say that when I watch you now filling your plate with cereal in the morning I have no trouble in recognizing the baby of 1967 who always had an open mouth. One day you even found some Green Shield stamps under your pram mattress and ate those as well. I found them in your nappy the next day, washed them, and stuck them into the book (such was our poverty).

Dr Hugh Jolly, self-appointed British paediatric adviser to mothers, says that mothers have to fall in love with their babies or there is no mother-child bond. I am sure he is right. I did fall in love with you, but it took a long time: I would say about five years. During the first five years I was watchful, devoted, admiring, anxious and occasionally extremely angry, but I did not feel an unspoken intimacy, a yearning bottomless fund of unconditional affection for you. You always seemed separate from me in a way my daughters haven't. Is this because of your sex or your position in the family? Was it my ignorance and innocence, my unhelpful projection of my feelings about men, whatever these were? Or your personality and mine mixed, both tense and self-centred? My own research a decade later into the process of becoming a mother has shown me how much it matters that a mother should have seen, and cared for, small children before she has her own. You were my experiment in motherhood. But I am also certain of one thing, and that is of the contribution the management of your birth made to the awkward beginning of our relationship. Again, my work and subsequent experience of childbearing have taught me how what must be preserved at all (or most) costs is the woman's feeling that she is the person who is having the baby both before and after it is born. The people who officiated at your birth did not understand that. I am sure they had no idea of how lonely and lost I, who was having a normal delivery, really felt. More than that, they had no idea of how such isolation and disorientation can mould the mother's perception of her child for a long time. Those other paediatric experts Marshall Klaus and John Kennell are right for not wholly the right reasons when they say

> There is a sensitive period in the first minutes and hours of
> life during which it is necessary that the mother and father
> have close contact with their neonate for later develop-
> ment to be optimal . . . Some early events have long-lasting
> effects. Anxieties about the wellbeing of a baby . . . in the
> first day may result in long-lasting concerns that may cast
> long shadows and adversely shape the development of the
> child.[3]

I am not saying that I would like to sue those students who,
giggling, counted your perfect limbs and shielded them from me,
but it took another birth a decade later fully to reveal my
knowledge of the awful and influential panic this at the time
aroused in me, and therefore, by extension, in you. I never really
believed I could be a good mother to you. My milk dried up when
you were five months old which was at least four months before I
wanted it to. I liked you best asleep, your dark hair poking out of
the top of the blue blanket in the wicker basket on our bedroom
floor. You might say, what mother doesn't like her baby asleep?
But there was a difference in my appreciation of you and your
sisters. Your vitality countermanded mine, whereas theirs was an
extension of it. Whereas when you were awake I worried
anxiously what you were going to do next (and you did do some
truly awful things like mutilate the telephone, consume quantities of zinc and castor oil nappy cream, run a fever of 106
degrees and fall out of a window), I somehow always seemed to
know what they were doing. I still worry about you and I feel you
are unpredictable (perhaps that is a good thing). But now I feel I
am all right as a mother (what is a good mother anyway?); I can
both provide for you and let you go. I think we have reached a
state of mutual affection and respect.

So if I have one single message for you, it is to ask your
forgiveness for the clumsiness of your beginning, however
caused. You did not, as you have sometimes remarked, ask to be
born. It was I who asked you to, and then went on to commit the
further appalling sin of providing you with a sibling close in age,
to be, as I thought, your lifelong companion. As both you and
she told me the other day, the relatively small gap in your ages

has meant a certain competitiveness between you. You would fight daily, and I imagined you doing so in your twenties and thirties, each ringing up to ask how many biscuits the other has had today. It's more of a problem for you than for her because she has never known what it is like to be an only child. You had the undivided attention of your parents for more than a year and have never quite recovered from the shock of having to share it.

I, you see, was the victim of a mythology. The mythology is on the backs of the cereal packets you so love, and it looks out at us from posters, the television screen and the pages of magazines. It is that the only way to be happy is in a properly constituted nuclear family. Mother, father, boy, girl (and dog). I wondered whether the reason I had not been happy as a child was because the nuclear family I came from was not properly constituted. Thus, I determined to restore the balance in the next genera-tion. I was also young (twenty-two when you were born chronologically but about sixteen emotionally) and moved by a desire, the product of insecurity, to follow convention, as if by following convention I would automatically gain happiness. Motherhood, I discovered in 1967, was not a bed of roses and my labours of love were strenuous ones. I thought that if I did not have another child in 1968 I never would.

Emily was born in May 1968, sixteen months after her brother. But what should have been the happiest years of my life (according to the mythology) were not at all.

We had by this time bought a small house in Chiswick with help from our families. I made curtains as good housewives should; on one pair the flowers grew downwards instead of upwards—a dangerous sign, looking back on it, that my heart wasn't in housework. I cleaned the house with a wedding present hoover in which the Chiswick mice relentlessly ate holes, making me wring my hands in housewifely distress. I did the washing, which included a dozen towelling nappies a day for a year and a half, in a malevolent device that masqueraded as helpful automation but flooded me daily with despair and the kitchen with filthy water. Money was difficult. Robin earned £1,000 a year as Assistant Lecturer in the Department of Sociology, Bedford College, University of London. I had a small red book in which I wrote down the cost of every purchase, as though by so doing I would somehow bring about the balancing of income and expenditure. Two months after Adam was born the list included babyfood (1s 6½d), kidneys (2s 6d), coley (4s 0d), peas, beans, butter, fish fingers and eggs (9s 0d). Cotton wool, disinfectant for the nappies, tinned babyfood and catfood were more recurrent items than protein or fresh fruit and vegetables for ourselves; paintbrushes and aspirin cropped up very often. About the same time, I wrote a list of all the things I wanted most in the world but didn't have:

a Mini or eleven hundred (car)
a Hotpoint automatic washing machine
lots of cupboards
two more babies
three pints of cream
two garden chairs
a mincer
a side on my bath
a wig for the baby
some gin
a new bath hat
some white boots for next winter
a pushchair
a cleaning lady
a portable television
some huge meals in posh places

(Perhaps it should be noted that, as is the habit with human beings, most of these ambitions have been achieved, yet I seem to have an infinite capacity to extend the list.)

There is nothing in my diaries for 1967 and 1968 except clinic appointments, the weights of babies, shopping lists and the beginnings and ends of Robin's terms. We had no holidays and we never went out in the evening together. I can't remember what he did, but I watched old films on television or went to sleep. I do remember—and this is important because it is part of the contradiction, one of the biggest unsolved problems—loving my two bright-eyed children intensely. They were the centre and the purpose of my life. My love for the second child was easier than my love for the first. I could not express (and did not begin to understand until much later) my deep happiness at having a daughter. She and I fitted together as effortlessly after birth as we had in the pregnancy whose impact on my life I had hardly noticed. By one week she was smiling at me, at the face beyond the milk-laden breast with which her small mouth bulged. All the early photographs show her eyes locked in a steadfast gaze with mine. I felt I was being watched all the time by a private detective building up a tremendous dossier on me, but with the best motives: the achievement of an eternal and mutually self-regarding love.

But none of this served to make me happy. Passionate love, such as the love I felt for my children, doesn't guarantee happiness. It often prevents it, and that is why such love is a major cultural and personal preoccupation. I didn't know this at the time. I didn't understand my own predicament at all. Other people called it depression. If it was postnatal, nobody ventured an opinion as to whose natality it followed. The point was I was ill. It took five or six white pills to make me sleep. It took combinations of little blue and red pills (stelazine and imipramine—I thought of them as characters in a Shakespearean play) to make me into the mechanical housewife of my daily life. The pills were provided by my GP, a large, energetic, not unkindly man, to whom I took my tears and tales of woe. (Where else could I take them?) He should have given me an analysis of the difference between the experience and the institution of motherhood,[4] and explained how social conditions may provoke distress in women like me, educated for a world outside the home and then confined to life inside it. He should have told me that around four-fifths of women in our society are depressed after birth,[5] about a third most or some of the time.[6] Yet that was (is) too much to expect. Instead, he offered me the traditional remedy of a pharmacological adjustment to my situation, along with weekly appointments in his surgery which did, literally, keep me alive. On March 3, 1969, at his instigation, I was the case-study for BBC television's *Television Doctor* on depression. I sat with Emily on my knee and Adam playing with his matchbox cars on the floor and told some anonymous male television director how I felt.

I was paid ten guineas for this exercise in self-disclosure. I wonder if it helped anybody out there? Another GP, to whom I went somewhat later, took the distinctly less helpful step of referring all four of us to a psychiatric hospital. We attended once, and a psychiatric social worker had a great time interpreting our family life from Adam and Emily's manipulation of the contents of a doll's house, while a psychoanalyst concentrated so completely on the dynamics of our marital relationship that he failed to notice Emily pouring the dolls' bathwater over his feet. We were offered inpatient treatment for a few months, but they wouldn't tell us what was wrong with us. Our reaction was to suppose that if I, or we, weren't already totally mad, we certainly would be so after months of living in one of the hospital 'family' suites (two rooms). I eventually and illicitly read the analyst's report on us when selecting interviewees for my Ph.D. from the GP's case notes. His conclusion was that the children were normal but that Robin and I had problems with our masculine and feminine roles. Don't we all?

However, to say that the medical profession labelled me, along with several million other women, as depressed between 1967 and 1969 is not to explain anything about the way we felt. Personally, I felt exhausted and incapable. I did have every reason to feel exhausted. Two young children have not been one woman's exclusive responsibility and workload throughout most of history. Our own culture's nuclear family arrangement for childrearing is extremely peculiar. My own two children had limitless energy. One of them woke up several times a night for five years. For a total of one year, one or the other had to be fed at night. It was the pills that made me capable of coping with this; at least then I cooked food for the children, washed everyone's clothes and slept for short periods when allowed to do so, even if I had no particular regard for myself. I took the pills self-consciously as a way of coping, and I was not alone in that strategy.[7] I felt that my life, despite its centredness on my beloved children, and a marriage that by anybody's standards was 'good' (few rows, no wife-beating, affection and mutual respect), was simply devoid of meaning. What was it all for? How could I go on?

During this period, I felt that I had lost the sympathy of my parents, who thought I should be able to manage their grandchildren and myself rather better than I did, and who apologized to Robin for what they hoped was a temporary disablement on my part. My father's lack of understanding of my predicament hurt me particularly, in view of our previously close relationship. I suppose he would have said the same the other way around. Robin himself stood by me, loving but bemused. He didn't understand what had happened to me at all. He could see I was unhappy but he knew the births of Adam and Emily had made me very happy and I was the one who, in 1967, had insisted that children wouldn't grow up right unless they had their mothers most of the time. Dimly he felt that my unhappiness had something to do with him, that there was something he wasn't doing right—but he didn't know what. Neither did I. The birth of Emily had meant a change in our division of labour. He took to coming home earlier and doing more. But this was a husbandly reaction to what we both saw as a temporary wifely need. It was definitely not a step towards the liberation of women (and men) from the sexist politics of the household.

If my husband and my parents couldn't understand my distress, nobody could. I had no friends in Chiswick. Indeed, I had no friends anywhere in the same situation as mine. I was the first in my circle to have children: I took the plunge into family life earlier, more deeply and with my eyes more completely closed than anyone else. This was 1967 and 1968 and 1969—the era before the women's movement. There was not even a murmur of feminism in English suburbia at that time; there may have been voices of dissent, but what they were dissenting about was a problem they couldn't name, '. . . a strange stirring, a sense of dissatisfaction, a yearning';[8] guilt, anger, loneliness, frustration, the dehumanization of women, their forfeited selves. Betty Friedan called it *The Feminine Mystique* and she called it that a long time before many of us knew there was anything wrong besides ourselves. Antidepressants, tranquillizers, obscurantist psychoanalysts and busy GPs: these represented techniques of adjustment that appeared reasonable because we thought individual adjustment was just exactly what was needed.

Having said all that I do have to add that some kind of consciousness of the feminine predicament must have been dawning in me then. When five months pregnant with Emily I put an advertisement in the *New Statesman*: 'Graduate mother of 1½ children needs work to do at home. Anything considered.' I disliked my economic dependence and its connotation of secondariness, of belonging to someone else and not to myself (and we did need more money). To be paid for one's labour is an unhappily mechanical solution to this problem, but it is a solution of a kind. My advertisement turned up a quota of obscene phone calls, but some genuine offers as well; a firm called 'Research Writers (Publications)' run by a V. Leff, Dip.Soc., and a G.H. Blunden, B.Comm., Dip. Ed., wanted me to ring up businesses in London's East End using such resources as the Leyton Chamber of Commerce Directory, and excite their interest in advertising in an official guide to the local area which would presumably raise their profits. I got 37p an hour for this work, plus the cost of the telephone calls, though frequently the only way I could do it was by getting inside the playpen with the telephone and giving Adam the run of the house (an arrangement that appeared highly sensible to me perhaps because I felt I was the one who was confined anyway).

After that I moved on to what is the fate of many mothers under capitalism—that activity known as 'market research'. The two surveys I worked on concerned 'Attitudes to Gloss and Emulsion Paints' and 'Foundation Garments'. Market Investigations Ltd, for whom I worked, seemed to have an obsessive interest in the thinnability of paint and women's figures. One of the problems we researchers faced was that we had certain 'quotas' to fill. In the Foundation Garments Survey, for example, I had to interview only married women under sixty, two-thirds of whom had to belong to skilled, semi-skilled or unskilled manual categories or be lower grade clerical or distributive workers. In addition, a certain number had to wear at least a size forty inch bra costing forty shillings or more. I have no idea where these requirements came from, but they were a real pain in practice. In the end, I used to haunt the aisles of supermarkets, and in between the cereals and the dog biscuits spot middle-aged women with enormous breasts and follow them home hopefully to solicit an interview. So far as I remember these poor victims responded well to such questions as 'How satisfied are you with your bust?' and 'Who sees you in your underwear?' The most embarrassing bit was where the interviewer was supposed to ask to see all the bras owned by the interviewee. I myself would have been totally mortified at having to produce in front of a complete stranger my own collection of grey, no-longer-elasticated garments, and I simply couldn't bring myself to ask anyone else to do so. Fortunately, Market Investigations Ltd never found out how badly I did the job, and the experience did at least prepare me for how to treat interviewees properly.[9] The third genuine offer I took up following the *New Statesman* advertisement involved writing scripts for children's television. I have no record of how many of my products ever saw the light of day, but one did, since I still have the script and the contract (fifteen guineas for eleven and a half minutes). It was called 'Nonsense' and included a story about two small people called Wiseman and Bertha who lived in a house made of cheese. Bertha asked Wiseman to go and buy her a grandfather clock because the kitchen kettle wasn't very good at telling the time. He bicycled across the lily pond and then took a camel to Big Ben (Big Ben knew all about grandfather clocks). Quite possibly this script succeeded because its nonsensical sexist content came effortlessly out of my own head.

The years of giving birth and breastfeeding, which should have been years in which I felt fully alive, spelled instead a kind of death. I understand why, now. I did not have the kind of social supports that prevent depression in married women.[10] I had not been prepared properly for the realities of motherhood.[11] I had not been educated for that existence. (What had I been educated for?) I couldn't get away from the fact that by the age of twenty-five I had done the only four things I had wanted to do— viz., get a university degree, a husband, a house and two children. Now I had achieved all this I felt I had achieved nothing except the illness of feeling life over at twenty-five, life meaningless thereafter; no challenge or development anywhere; only the passage of time and the static evolution of the conventional drama of family life.

What happened to change this? Because it *did* change. I puzzle over what made it change, and when I do so I go back to a moment in 1969 when I took a book called *Alienation and Freedom* by Robert Blauner off the shelf in Robin's study. (I must have been looking for something but I can't remember what—or perhaps I was 'just' dusting?) The book was about factory workers and their attitudes to their work. Its author tried to prove in it that the technological and social organization of work deter-mines whether workers feel in control or controlled, a sense of

purpose or not, social connection rather than isolation, fulfil-
ment or discontent. I could see it was a book about men and
their work; there seemed to be a lot of books about that on this
shelf. I looked up 'women' in the index. There were eight
references. These argued that although women in factories have
the most objectively alienated jobs, they don't mind, because
they're wives and mothers; that a valuable aspect of women's
low-status work is that it allows men to feel less alienated because
they can have the better jobs, and that unpleasant work
conditions don't make women workers feel unpleasant because
'successful work is not part of the traditional female role'.[12] I was
outraged. What had I been doing for the past five years if not
working? With some degree of success? And why did having the
housework to do and the children to rear mean that employed
women could be exploited?

Until this point in my life I had not been much of a feminist. I
had chosen to identify with that ethic of gender differences
which makes femininity incompatible with sex equality. That
was my solution to the traumas of female adolescence; it was safer
and morally better to be a housewife. In the years from twenty to
twenty-five I put this ethic into practice and found it difficult.
Now I had come to a turning point. All that 'depression' I had
felt was suddenly transformed into anger. Reading those words of
Blauner's I became angry with the world instead of with myself. I
don't know why it happened then. I suppose the time was right;
the phrase 'women's liberation' had begun to be muttered in
middle-class kitchens. Or had I simply had enough? When I read
Blauner's pronouncements on the nature of women I was
reminded of an event that had moved me deeply. In 1963 when
Betty Friedan published *The Feminine Mystique* a young woman
called Hannah Gavron was interviewing other young women in
North London about their lives. In 1966 *The Captive Wife* was
published. Its author was already dead. She had killed herself.
Although I had only met Hannah once, she was the sister of a
close friend of mine, the daughter of one of my first employers, a
seemingly happy married mother of two children, and she
worked at Bedford College, where Robin lectured. I didn't know
why she had died but I thought it was something to do with the
special difficulties of living out the feminine mystique, of being a
woman in a man's world, of understanding the place of sexual

love in women's lives. I thought then about the misery of two children left motherless; now I think about the tragedy of a life unspent. I don't suppose it's any coincidence that I was to follow in Hannah Gavron's footsteps academically by publishing a study that was in many ways a logical progression from *The Captive Wife* and by doing it as a Ph.D. student at Bedford College.

When I registered for postgraduate work I stopped calling myself depressed and I stopped eating pills. I knew what I wanted to do—a study of women's attitudes to housework as work. But I had to insist on the seriousness of my aim in the face of a lot of patronising jocularity about the academic absurdity of such a topic. The idea of doing a Ph.D. on housework in Britain in 1969 was laughable. The man I finally ended up with as my supervisor tended to think at first that what I was talking about was the harmony or disharmony of the marital bed, or, at the very least, the marvellous things that could be done with the handles of vacuum cleaners. But in the four years that followed he did change his mind a bit.

Along with the forging of my academic credibility I fought a battle for the recognition of childrearing as productive work with the Department of Education, whose rules prevented women like me from receiving a full grant. However, a protracted correspondence with the Secretary of State for Education only produced the revelation that it was in the character of the relationship between a husband and a wife that the husband gave his wife 'pocket money' (the actual phrase used) to finance this sort of thing (the rules were changed some years later).

I couldn't pay a nanny on the £410 per annum I received from the Department of Education, so some change in the marital relationship itself was necessary. Specifically, Robin stayed at home one day a week to look after the children while I went to a library. Generally, the situation forced us both to begin a long process of reconsidering our roles. Once the project outgrew its original conception, and became not only a Ph.D. but also a series of articles and three books, the logic of my personal dissatisfaction with domesticity was reinforced with the logic of hard cash. There are two questions here: one, how did the initial limited idea take on such gigantic proportions; and two, how did the relationship between myself and Robin, which started out on such a traditional footing, become the unrecognizable egalitarian affair it is today? The 'how' of the first question is the 'why' of the second; for as my intellectual work occupied me more and as its link with the personal politics of my, and other women's, situation became clearer, so my relationship with Robin had to change as well or founder completely. There is, after all, no reason why men should renounce the comforts of patriarchy other than that the women to whom they are attached require them to do so. I wouldn't exchange an easy life for a more difficult one without a good reason: would you? So you could say that, while my life became easier—or, rather, more satisfactory—Robin's became more difficult.

Once I started to sit at my desk and formulate questions about housework ('Do you like housework?' 'Would you say you have particular ways of doing things you regularly keep to in doing housework?' etc.), I found myself asking a lot of other questions as well. Why do women do housework? What are the differences (or similarities) between men and women? With my mind on the situation downstairs I also had to ask, what is the relationship between children and their mothers? After perusing the literature, I wrote an article which I called, pretentiously, after John Bowlby's well-known monograph, 'Deprivation of Paternal Care'. In this I complained about men's inattention to their children and talked about the difference between children's needs and the opaque curtain of 'the maternal instinct'. (Amongst other things I pointed out that certain groups of monkeys boasted a 'paternal instinct' as well.) I submitted this article to the magazine New Society and they printed it because they needed something along these lines to publish the week of the first national women's liberation conference in Britain. The cover of the magazine was black, purple and white, suitable suffragette colours; they called the article 'The Myth of Motherhood', and it was my first publication.

In early 1971 I started the interviewing for my housework study. One of the questions I asked in these interviews was 'Have you ever heard of the women's liberation movement?' followed by 'If yes, what do you think of it?' One gentle, pretty mother of three to whom I put this insurgent inquiry laughed and told me to come back next week, because she was about to attend a meeting of the local National Housewives' Register at which there would be a speaker from the women's liberation workshop.

I decided I would go, as a kind of participant observer, with neutral attitudes and a nice blank notebook.

The woman who opened the door wore tight shorts with a bib top and boots. An expensive pram nestled in the hall. The front room, full of Ealing housewives, looked just like a Tupperware party. There were, in fact, two speakers from the workshop, Debbie and Elyse —both Americans. I can't remember exactly what they said (I don't think they quite managed to alter the prevailing atmosphere of the meeting) but I recall feeling an instant identification with them. They gave off an air of independence and assertiveness which seemed just what I needed (and lacked). After the meeting I went to talk to them. They told me they were starting a women's liberation group in Ealing the following week. I said I would join them.

Of course the women's liberation movement is not a movement one 'joins'. 'It exists in your mind, and in the political and personal insights that you can contribute to change and shape and help its growth.'[13] But I did have to join it in a formal sense to find out a lot of things I needed to know and couldn't read in books or discover by myself alone.

What did I learn? What did we all learn? We discovered that we weren't alone. That is by far the most important discovery. If the pathways we each had taken to be the people we were when we came together in that group were different, they were also the same. Certain factors act to mould the cultural product of woman, as Simone de Beauvoir said. Those factors induce responses—difficult daughterhood, ambivalent motherhood, permanent guilt, sexual unhappiness, a trivial self-confidence, the wish to retreat and deny rather than the will to advance and confront—which women individually guard in secret, each believing herself to be unique in them and seeing herself to be the disabled dangerous owner of a deformed personality, instead of the proud possessor of an impossible socialization. It was in this group that I grasped for the first time my ordinariness, not least because I discovered the essential humanity of women, whom previously I had thought of in an entirely sexist way as a sex apart.

The first step was learning that my uncomfortable experiences were not mine alone. Other women had resented their mothers

and loved their fathers and hated themselves for this; other
women had felt such ambivalent passion for their babies that
they wanted them at their breasts for ever and out of the window
in the middle of the night; other women had been reared to the
belief that all women's missions are dependent on the leadership
of men; other women had wanted to find themselves as well as
their husband's socks and children's toys; other women had
wondered how they might acquire the temerity to insist on a
fifty-fifty division of labour in marriage, to insist that marriage
might not be all it is set up to be for women, but rather
something that is set up to satisfy the appetites of men; other
women had more than idly queried why the state of womanhood
is cherished and decried, why motherhood is idolized and
banished to the home, why the power to reproduce, so
inalienably female, is none the less deposited in the hands and
instruments and ideology of a discourteously powerful medical
profession.

'It is impossible to confront a common condition before you
have recognized it . . . You can't begin to find your own power
until you have consciously recognized your nonpower.'[14] To hear
others reciting the depths of your own experience is tremendously liberating as well as comforting. It liberates by releasing
you from the fear of pathology to anger about, and against, the
external social arrangements that bring about this situation. But
to be more than minimally liberating, it requires a radically
reworked version of the nature of women, and that is a process
which is still going on. We, along with many other women,
started it in those first women's liberation groups in the early
1970s. And as we read our weekly newsletter from the women's
liberation workshop or were passed literature from our trans-
atlantic sisters, we knew ourselves to be part of an international
movement and to share in a world-wide confidence that women
collectively could potentially accomplish a revolution for women
from which all would benefit.

On a more practical level than international revolution, what
we did was to organize jumble sales to raise money and
conferences to share thoughts; write 'where we are at' papers and
produce copies of *Shrew*, the aptly named women's liberation
paper. We also 'demystified' our womanhood by looking at our
own and each other's cervices; by learning to locate our wombs

and ovaries and establishing a more friendly relationship with them than we had hitherto managed. We acquired the easy skill of pregnancy-testing, which we offered gratuitously for a short while to the women of Acton, before deciding that our energies would be better spent outside the group and thus disbanding it. We went some very different ways: one of us to an intensely suburban marriage, one of us to supposedly more revolutionary socialist politics, and one to start a group with the neatly confusing title of the 'West London Naked Dancers under Cypress Trees'. For my part, I set up with several others a group of women doing feminist research who faced common problems due to the distinctly sexist academic environment of the time, and our own lack of sureness as to what was (or should be) feminist about our research. The relative triviality of this problem was brought home when one of us, a beautiful and very vital woman called Pauline Marks, was suddenly killed one night. She was on the way to fetch her husband from their house in North London to come to supper in our house, and a car going in the opposite direction crossed the central reservation and hit hers, instantly breaking her neck. There is something especially shocking about unexpected death; and in one so young and full of life. Even now sometimes I have difficulty grasping the fact that Pauline is dead. Such a death has to be a salutary lesson in never really knowing one's chances, in never really being able to count on anything.

In those early women's groups we had problems with the realization of equality: some of us talked more than others, and it wasn't always the truth that was told. But through it all a sense of solidarity was generated and persisted. I won't ever forget the national women's liberation conference of 1972: the first I attended in full. I won't ever forget sitting in the hall with hundreds of other women all clapping and cheering together at something one of us had said, or sitting joined in silence, listening. The women's liberation movement changed my life from what it was to what it only might have been before it, but has, because of it, become.

We meet again, ten years later; not all of us, but most of us. In fact there are eight of us seated round a large table in a Chinese restaurant. What are we all doing now? Going clockwise round the table, this is how it is: one, aged thirty-seven, has just had her first baby by the man with whom she was living ten years ago. She married this man just before their son's birth. It is quite impossible to tell if she is happy or not, because all she can think and talk about is the baby: his weight at birth, his sleeping pattern, his name, his prospects. She holds him bound in a white shawl tightly to her thin breast. Later, I hold him on my lap and he dribbles milk down my skirt. I feel faintly broody. In fact, we all hold this baby, and there is something more than a little bizarre about the way we all pass him round; have different effects on him and reactions to him, this symbol of the patriarchal order we met, a decade ago, to interpret and protest about.

Next to the baby's mother is a Heavy Goods Vehicle driver on the point of emigrating to Canada. She was married ten years ago and still is, though a series of other relationships with both sexes mark her development as a more emancipated person than the rest of us. She still laughs in the same way, however; I wonder if she has really changed, has really found the answer? On her left is a librarian, a vegetarian, an animal-lover who wears plastic boots and has a son of eighteen. Now *she* always seemed to have such a satisfactory relationship with her husband; or was it that I fancied him? (Is it age that brings such cynicism?) At any rate, he has gone. She lives alone with her son and is 'just enjoying a lot of casual relationships'. She always did seem edgy and nervous and she seems so still. The unanswered question about her life is why she is still a librarian.

Next to her is Elyse, my lasting friend from the early days, suntanned and giving me conspiratorial glances as we both try to work out what's going on. The next two arrive late; the gentle duo. One has come from Leamington Spa where she's learning how to be an acupuncturist. The other has taken up making silver jewellery, though when she said she was a silversmith I thought she said she was a conservative. She is the oldest— forty-seven. These two have two sons each and a complex relationship: they live in the same house (an arrangement initiated after the end of the group's life), and I think one of them is having an affair with the other one's husband. Yet they both exude a saccharine calm. With their waved hair and wide-eyed faces, shawls and bangles, they epitomize a seductive femininity without meaning to. The 47-year-old belongs to an older women's group where, she says, 'We're much kinder to each other than we ever were.' Hmmm. Were we unkind? Yes, I suppose we were. She asks me what I'm doing now. I reply, 'It's difficult to answer that. What do you really want to know?' 'Okay, leave it,' she says at once, dismissively. But I didn't know what she wanted to know—was it a question about my shopping habits, my salary, my mothering, my sexuality, my publications, my marriage, my housing situation: what is it that she is inquiring about? We look away from each other. In between us sits a dental receptionist, the mother of three adolescent girls who remain the absolute centre of her life. She never really was a convert to feminism. 'I think of it now as the unhappiest period of my life,' she said to me earlier, when I had a preliminary brandy at her house to quell her nerves. It was I who suggested she enter the group. She felt she had less education than the rest of us and that none of us could match her in maternal love. We felt she had hang-ups that we could help her with: personal items to do with the nature of orgasm and the insertion of internal sanitary protection and the power of children to dictate the content of their mothers' lives. 'None of you really liked me,' she protested earlier to me, thus drawing our attention to the fact that the love of oppressed women for each other may never move out of the realm of a theoretical construct, and that the hardest thing is to realize that it can't always or often do so.

And then there is me. As the meal lingers on and the Chinese waiters despair of our ever removing ourselves from our pots of Chinese tea, I become more and more reluctant to disclose anything about myself. I become profoundly depressed. Is this because retrogressive remarks about unhelpful husbands and the failure of the state's educational system circulate in the air round my head? Or is it because of my own feelings about these women and my intuition of their feelings about me? If my receptionist friend always felt unliked, so perhaps did I. Although it was in this company that I grappled with my first important work, wrote my first book, spoke at my first seminar; and although it was the group that gave me the support to achieve these things, it couldn't solve all my problems, could it? Undoubtedly, I feel alone tonight. In fact I do feel the unsolved problems are all mine. That's where I started. Has any progress been made at all?

Family: a personal declaration

Preface: several moments in the life of a mother and daughter

I have had a bad day, but am too impressed by the badness of my day to notice that yours has been bad too. I am emptying a pot on the middle floor of the house when you come in (your little sister is vomiting and has diarrhoea). In the kitchen we stand and look at each other, pale with exhaustion. You tell me you need a red scarf for school, the mornings are so cold, that you have another A and may get a distinction (four As in a row). You remind me you have a music lesson in twenty-five minutes. We make tea and observe that it is raining. Your little sister pulls crossly at my skirt for the thousandth time that day. The air is tense: I know I am not being a good mother. I drive you to your lesson and promise you a hot drink at the end of your wet walk back. When you return I am on the telephone yet again to a publisher with whom I am discussing the prospect of this book, a plan to write a textbook on 'The Family' and the fate of the book I have just completed. You write me a cryptic note: 'I like that. I thought you were going to make me a hot drink.' I respond by crumpling it up and throwing it in the wastepaper basket.

Later, I try to explain my predicament (a sick child, an Open University Unit to complete, endless telephone calls about two advertisements your father and brother have placed in the local paper, one to sell a disused child's car seat, the other to sell some toy soldiers we no longer need, the latter incorrectly advertised as costing £2,250 not £2.50). You listen, understand, and explain that you don't mind not getting a hot drink, what you mind is a promise that is not fulfilled. I feel humbled by this logic and your charity. Over supper, I try to tell you and your brother about this book I am writing—what might be in it, how it might affect you—because I have always tried to explain my work to you, and I genuinely feel that if this book is a problem for either of you, I won't write it. Adam says he looks forward to reading it and as long as there's nothing too personal about him in it, that's fine. But there you sit, my beloved daughter, crying into your sausages. Of course I knew you would, but I am not sure what in particular upsets you. I follow you into the sitting room and ask you to tell me. You ask me if I have ever slept with anyone else since I married your father, and I pause before saying yes. You say that is disgusting, and cry harder and louder. I have thought about such questions being asked, but am not well prepared for the occasion when it arrives. I don't even know why it arrives now. But I know I want to be open with you and that I must be if I want you to be so with me in the years to come. Yet perhaps you are simply too young and too fragile to bear the weight of this knowledge? Is it right for me to try to explain my values to you—for values of consideration and commitment to you, your father, your brother and your sister I do have: strangely enough, my life is rooted in them.

We sit on your bed and discuss the problem. What is the problem? You say that what comes into your head when you think of me in bed with another man is all those images of painted ladies and passionate men rolling around in crumpled beds with which the television screen these days is littered. You say you will write to the television programme *Points of View* and complain about it. Without this media presentation of extra-marital affairs you would be much more able to grasp the bare fact that very occasionally (and you agree I should not tell you with whom) I have broken a marriage vow I did not make. I say Robin knows, is not unhappy about it, and says he doesn't own me, nor I him. You agree that is right. I talk about the problems of possessiveness and feminine dependence in marriage. You say: I see why you are a feminist, and tell me of conversations with your friends in which, not because of me, but because of the reality of sexism, you have made what are self-consciously feminist statements. I say you must not feel you have to be like me: I will love you, I do love you, whatever you are. You know there is an important sense in which I mean that and another sense in which I don't.

Coming back to the original topic of our conversation you ask me to promise that I will never succumb to the same temptation again. I ask you to think—because such a picture is in my mind—of a time five years hence in which I ask you to promise me not to sleep with a certain male (or female). We agree we cannot ask each other to make promises like that. We move apart, so we can look at each other. Two separate people, once inseparably joined. If you could only know, if I could only find the words to tell you, how much I care about you—you of the unkempt room and melodramatic tempers, of the too-quick retort and hidden Mars bars, you of the shining spirit and vitality. In your face dance all the feelings you have; I can read in it many moments: your unbelieving face when it was born, laughter at four months, a cool psychic regard, 'You know Grandpa's dying, don't you?' at four years; the child who went eagerly to school at three, less eagerly at ten. Your face now and then seems entirely transparent to me. Is that because I am your mother? Or because we are two women together? For you, too, can read me, as they say, like a book.

I feel profoundly sorry for you being my daughter. Undoubtedly it makes your life harder. I am a certain kind of person. I am selfish and self-centred but I am also very loving and very thoughtful. I not only have your best interests at heart, but I know what they are. I would be like this even if I were 'an ordinary housewife' like the mothers of your friends, women whom you half-envy, half-despise. I know part of you at one time wanted me to be like that, waiting daily at the school gates with strips of Elastoplast and Oxo cubes, comforting and solicitous in a soft tweed coat with an apron beneath. But part of you has always responded to the non-maternal side of me that is related to the world.

These thoughts have passed through my mind daily for at least ten years. Now I can share them with you. I want you to remember that my intentions towards you have always been honourable.

Postscript: I read you this and you are happy to hear what I have said, regarding it as an accurate statement of these moments in our life together.

I, who have lived for thirty-six of my thirty-nine years in one of two nuclear families, and protest, in the same breath as is used to cook the Sunday lunch and pay the milkman, that the family as an institution enslaves women and must be destroyed before it destroys us, do, I suppose, have a certain obligation to say what the 'family' is. Moreover, I know that many people do not appreciate the praxis of feminism on this point.

In the newspaper today a woman whose two children were burnt by her common-law husband said, 'I still love him.' They had an argument on the way home from the pub in which he accused her of fancying another man. He hit her and then went home on his own to ignite the sofa and the children with it. The same newspaper discusses two female historians of women's place. One says of the other, and the other agrees, that until she became a mother 'any understanding of the importance of the mother-child relationship was missing from her analysis'.[1]

'Family' is a word that means all things to all people. We all 'know' what it means. It's a word that's bandied around easily in conversation. 'How's the family?' 'Are you going to your family for Christmas?' 'She wants a family.' 'He's left his family for another woman.' Yet coexisting with this shared usage is a sea of evidence that the *experience* of family life is extraordinarily different for different people. It is so on an individual basis, but, more importantly, social and biological classifications are powerful determinants of the personal meaning of that word 'family'.

The family is an unequal place, a place divisive in its secrets. The young child looks up to her mother, who may be recognized as a mirror of herself but is the deity incarnate: the holder and wielder of power, the giver of kisses and bags of sweets, the dealer-out of slaps on the bottom and banishments to the dark well of the stairs. The mother looks at her husband, to whom she vowed perpetual love, and sees him as the container of too much beer and too little money. From him and the child she derives a chain of labours which give her human joy mixed with the unswallowable antidote of the housewife's depression. The housewife's husband sees wife and child as—what? Femininity possessed; masculinity certified; liabilities for ever.

It is in families that our personalities are formed, smooth or scarred, and obeisance to parental power, or its opposite, is with us all our lives. Families on the breadline are not like families on the private schools–detached houses line; the material base dictates a welter of moral and emotional patterns. The mental health of women in families is considerably poorer than the mental health of men. Men have dangerous physical reactions instead. Indeed, it can be said to be dangerous to combine in one amorous economic equation two such different mixtures: her, trained to emotional response and support, to a web of domestic sensitivities; him, reared to be Tarzan in the modern jungle, brash, dry-eyed and immoderate in worldly ambition. That, presumably, is why the developed world's divorce rate is as epidemic as the mutilating infibulation of seventy-four million women in the Third World in the name of domestic femininity.[2]

I am exaggerating, but not much. It has been pointed out to me that I might exaggerate less were it possible for me truly to imagine the actuality of men's attachment to families. I freely admit that my stance on world affairs is filtered through the sieve of my own life: whose isn't? Of all the words in the language, 'family' is for me the most powerful: it excites in me a far greater range and depth of emotional reactions than any other word. It signals both the most loving and the most hating of relationships, both the highest degree of liberation and the basest level of oppression. Some of my best moments have been lived in the family and so have some of my worst.

When I was a child I used to cry myself to sleep at night worrying about how I would exist without my parents—when I had to go away from them or when, unthinkable thought, they died. The next morning I would get up and scream at them about some minor matter and write my mother searing notes of loathing. Now, a typical scene is this: we are sitting together in the kitchen having supper, all five of us. Three of us are talking at the same time: one about scientific research on rice suitable for the Third World, one about her headache, and one about the fact that she only seems to have nine fingers. This one is kneeling on the side of her chair and in ten seconds will fall off into somebody else's soup. The salt has been forgotten: someone rises to fetch it. There is a knife missing and the dishwasher is still churning away like the *Queen Mary* in the corner of the kitchen with the lunch dishes and all our knives (whose fault is that?) The telephone rings: two of us (them) leap up, unbidden, to answer it, assaulting the table in the process. A tissue is needed for Laura's nose, which has passed the point of social

acceptability even to her loving kin. The water jug is empty.
Emily has suddenly and violently remembered she needs fifty
pence for the school magazine. Adam's perennial complaints
about the unsuitability of his black school shoes to his emergent
adolescent self-image again cannot wait. Unwisely, I remark that
the steroid substance the doctor has provided for his dandruff
should not be overused because it can be absorbed into the
bloodstream and affect one's hormones. Adam says he doesn't
want to be gay at fifteen. They both want to know how
homosexuals come to be the way they are, and I do not know,
nor does anybody, which they cannot believe.

Voices rise and fall but mostly rise. Everyone is tired, everyone
has needs. Robin has a look of harassed discontent about him, as
though he did not really choose this when he chose to 'have' a
family. Neither did I—or they, for that matter. We would all
like peace and an army of slaves. What we get is noise and
fragmented attention. For my children this will be a normal part
of family life and of their childhood. I suspect they will
remember it as creative disharmony, for, as someone said,
without conflict life is dead and art is impossible. But for me the
occasion is daily self-destroying. I feel I should satisfy everyone,
remaining always calm and sentient of everyone's spoken and
unspoken needs. (I *know* of course that this is nonsense, but
knowledge is cerebral and no nerves necessarily join it to the
female conscience.) Since I am not perfectly self-denying, my
self is denied and it minds. I cry out at them, at the injustice of
the social system that insists that families are havens of happiness
while denying that they are repositories of problems too. How
does adulthood qualify one for coping with the alchemy of three
different childhoods, as well as with the enormous basic labour
needed to provide shelter, food, clothing, and health, mental
and physical? In our family there is a division of labour: 51 per
cent/49 per cent, but this could merely mean that both adults
feel the strain.

There are times when there is nothing I want more than the
creative disharmony of 'my family'. The noise is joyful: the
animation on their faces what makes life worth while. It is what I
look forward to at the end of a hard day, because the scene of
peace and slippers waiting by the fire is merely enervating: I feel I
need the electrical discharges of these ambivalent people, I

obtain solace from the fact that I can make order out of chaos, and donate to them a peace to end all their little wars. When I said some of my best moments have been lived in the family, I meant it. For example, the total of two and a half years I have spent breastfeeding have given me a satisfaction quite incomparable with any other. There is something so rewarding about sustaining and making happy a child with one's own milk. Each time each child smiled, nuzzled her or his soft head into my neck or even thoughtfully poured the overflow down my blouse, I did feel my productivity and therefore value as a person confirmed. No other work I've done has made me feel quite that way. Oddly, the involuntary physical component doesn't seem to alter the feeling of accomplishment. The endless refilling of the breasts at inopportune moments, as on the bus returning from shopping (where I once looked down to see my green blouse decorated with large circles of a much darker green), seems in some strange way a voluntary intellectual act. For example, too, I think there is nothing so lovely as a sleeping child. I must have spent another total of months, if not years, altogether in my fifteen years of motherhood hanging over my children while they slept, watching those spreadeagled limbs, those smooth cheeks with a slight pink flush on them, those luscious arcs of dark eyelashes spaced out in the bright darkness. Such trust in their posture; such security in their slumber. And in many ways the most remarkable moment of my life was the birth of my first daughter at home, a birth so unlike the first, unhurried and in a domain that was entirely mine. 'Look,' said the midwife, pointing to the psychedelic sight of a baby's head sticking out of my vagina, wet black hair falling into its eyes, pink breathing face and audibly crying mouth, with absolutely none of the rest of the baby in sight. I will never forget that experience of being nearly but not quite two whole people, the mother of a disembodied living head—a truly liminal state.

People have said to me, why do I advocate the destruction of the nuclear family? Why did I write a chapter to this effect at the end of my third book? What on earth could I have meant?

Ann Oakley has been quite slick with the trigger in *Housewife*, though some may feel she is a little hard on the m.c.p.'s. It is a solemn sociological book which includes four case-histories of such Stygian misery that one rather begins to wonder if sociologists can be happy in their work... must women's lives be dictated by libber-sociologists? Because in that case the housewife is simply jumping out of the frying pan into the fire: she is being manipulated and exhorted to conform to yet another role. Who can conceive of an ideal world full of babies howling for their absent mothers, of dinnerless husbands, and of homes snug as the Augean stables?[3]

Or:

One might expect the author of a book called *Housewife* to wear a flowered pinny and serve home-made cheesecake. Not Ann Oakley, who has written a sociological treatise on the housewife... She sits neat and serious in brown in a William Morris-covered armchair in her neat villa in Ealing and we discuss the husband doing more in the house; or, as her book would have it, the possibility of 'a revolution in the ideology of gender roles current in our culture'.

The Oakleys themselves do not have gender-differentiation problems. Robin Oakley, a university lecturer, does his fair share round the house, shopping, childminding and cleaning...[4]

This point did seem enormously interesting to reviewers. One male journalist, who interviewed me for the *Sydney Morning Herald*, found my conclusion that the abolition of the family was necessary, 'startling':

I... asked Dr Oakley... whether she had meant precisely what she said.

She said no, that the conclusions ought to be read more in a metaphorical sense than a literal, that it was clear that traditional family relationships must be changed but at the moment the primary road to this change appeared to be the long one of education of the young...[5]

Did I really say that? And why was I 'slim, calm and gentle-voiced' in that review too? Or five years later in the *Observer*, 'a mild-mannered sociologist, a happily married mother of three children . . . very far from a ferocious messenger'.[6] It all goes to show how stereotypes enslave; I am not the gun-pulling liberationist of my stereotype, and yes, I did mean that last chapter as metaphor. I meant: we must find a way not to stereotype each other, not to force each other into roles we don't like and haven't chosen. We must be together because we can give each other love and support, which is not of a predetermined role-differentiated kind. The family should liberate, not imprison its members. Everybody in it should feel they are better off with it than without it, and not only because they aren't brave enough to face the big, bad world alone.

Speaking for myself (for that is all I can confidently do) I would say I don't like being a wife, I don't like being a housewife and I don't like being a mother. But I love Robin and I love our children; it is, indeed, the achievement of this 'family' that I prize most of all in my life, far above and beyond all my other achievements. It is odd that this simple biological happening adds up to so much: one doesn't even need an intellect to produce a family, one doesn't even need to appreciate the Marxist analysis of women's household labour to feel that the reproduction of the world is worth a hell of a lot in the way of inconvenience and deprivation.

The bad moments are, as Adrienne Rich says,[7] inseparably joined with the good. Would I feel about my adolescent son as I do now if I hadn't hated his guts at age two? If I hadn't wanted to throw him out of the window when he was eight weeks old and wouldn't burp at 3 am, would I gaze at him with such admiration now? If I hadn't hated Robin vitriolically for his lack of understanding of my 'housewife's depression', piled all his books in a ghastly heap in the middle of the room and broken a fair amount of crockery (including a cast-iron frying-pan) in my effort to vent my feelings, would I feel he is as much of a friend to me as he truly is? If I could not resent the loud-voiced and temperamental demands of my daughters as much as I do my own, would I feel they are my life, my stake in the future in the best possible sense? What I do feel we have all wrought out of these years of trying is a tremendous respect for one another. I don't think any of us maltreats the others in any serious way.

I have considered getting divorced, dividing my family into

two units, changing my name; but I wonder whether any of this would produce a higher degree of liberation than that which we have already managed to possess. I am a member of this second nuclear family as I was a member of my first for powerful historical reasons. Coming from one, I felt impelled to create another. I cannot wipe out that particular historical pattern: all we can do is make this second family different from the first. And that is what we have done. Now, most of the enslavement we feel comes from other people, from their expectations that we will behave in a certain way—that I will be there perspiring by the kitchen stove, that Robin 'minds' me earning more than him, that Laura will suffer from maternal deprivation if I stay away a night, that Emily and I must tear each other's hair out because that is what all mothers and adolescent daughters do. It's easier to think in roles but much lazier. I would like to live on the moon where it doesn't happen, but I have learnt to survive in this culture, so I suppose I'd better stay here.

The War between Love and the Family   I

Throughout the Christmas season, embedded in familial obligations, she continues to ponder deeply on the inequities of sexual
love. Between the stuffed turkey and the warm mince pies, she
pauses and thinks of their (her) dilemma. Despite her intuition
that this dilemma can only have one resolution, the end of the
affair, he did not respond at all kindly to this suggestion; neither,
for that matter, did she. The obsessive allure continues. Tension
is endemic; strain shows in the marks beneath all four of their
eyes.

In her Christmas considerations, she's not sure she gets very
far. She writes a few lines, called 'Abelard in His Telephone
Box':

this is Christmas 1980
a ten pound tree only faintly aromatic
firelight on metallic spheres starkly shining
the fairy squashed nose-to-ceiling
directed at a dangerous angle to wet blue skies

the bounty stretches across the needled carpet
crisp red paper barely concealing corners
of what has been hastily or lovingly chosen
to give pleasure or satisfy convention

the half-tights are filled in an attic cupboard
with bumps and titillating instances

of childhood equipment

the turkey sits complacently
bursting with newly pungent entrails
cats watch angrily through a hole in the roof

everything is ready

or

the scene is set

for the gathering of families
the ritual incantation of sentiment
the correct phrase and semi-affectionate regard
cold cheeks held out for tepid kisses
taut laughter hiding quite venomous disdain
the smile that veils the not-quite-guarded secret...

you are Abelard, I your Heloise

Abelard in his telephone box
warm with the smell of wine and his wife
dropping money
as he drops the words I love you
as the fairy squints on miles of gifts
as the cats covet the stuffed bird
as Christmas is to families in fact

vacuous as the spaces in our hearts
full as the world for those who want it

A man cannot love a woman the way a woman loves a man.
That is one point. She is inclined to think that the strongest,
least ambivalent motivation a man can have is the decision not
to lose what one man of her acquaintance once inadvertently,
but revealingly, called the 'package' of his wife and children. She
cannot identify with that concept. Her child and her child's
father are no package to her. Yet she can see that it must be so
nice for a man to come home at the end of a hard day to a lit,
warm, food-filled house with three people in it who solicitously
oversee the provision of one's comforts, so impossible to
disentangle what she does and is from what they do and are. Yes,
she can see why one would not want to lose that. But, on the
other hand, consider her own position in this love affair. She is

an unequal partner in this relationship. His wife doesn't know about them and he believes she will leave him if she finds out. However, her husband does know and will not 'leave' her because he is not chained to her by the jealousies of romantic sexual love. This means that what her lover and she are able to share together must be determined not so much by what his wife can bear but by what he thinks she can. And, while she is confident that when he says he loves her he means it, and, equally, thinks that his judgment of his wife's level of toleration is probably right, she is bound to protest over and over again that in this arbitration of their meetings by his deceit of his wife she is being subtly but plainly abused. (His wife is too, of course, but that is a different point.)

Is such a woman in such a relationship not only serving her lover's needs but being subservient, too? While one is wholly admirable, the other isn't. In addition, does she forgive him for what he is doing to her, or to the other people she loves?

How can one compare love for a child and love for a man? The little girl looks at her mother with such tired, trusting eyes. Her fever last night has closeted the two of them up together today. Now she has put on her coat and her red boots and is sitting on the swing at the end of the garden wiggling her legs in an effort to propel herself through the air. Her mother sits at the kitchen table and the little girl's red legs catch her eye. (Always in her moments of most focused thought something is distracting her.)

Each time she expects at the next meeting with this man, her lover, a crashing disillusionment. She thinks they will look into each other's eyes and see through the images they hold of one another to the horrible truth at the centre: just two selfish, boring, disenchanted and disenchanting people. They will realize what a romantic fiction it all is; that when they speak of love they mean only the passion of sexual conjugation and the clichéd touch across the candlelit table; that there is relief each time they become 'ordinary' again—wife and husband, but not to each other, mother and father of real children whose parentage divides them. But it doesn't happen. The disillusionment hasn't arrived. The scarring revelation of the first encounter is with them still: nothing he says surprises her; nothing he does seems odd to her. When they have been together she struggles with remembered fragments of their conversation. Was that really what he said or is it only what she thought he might? Did he say that because she asked that question or was it that he read it in her eyes?

'There is one particular thing I don't want you to think,' he said, 'and that is that I am taking advantage of you, because I'm not—no more than you are of me.' No, she doesn't believe he is. But she does understand how she comes to think that, and she has tried to explain it to him. He says they can control their relationship, their emotions, their connectedness: they can confine it to prearranged times (five minutes in a call box, thirty on an office phone) and places (forty hours in a European city, two lined pages of an airmail letter). He says that control is possible because before him looms the awful spectre of losing control. This is what he fears most—the strong, silent man becoming weak, noisily weeping his unbearable love. But he is wrong about thus confining the relationship. They can't. Moreover, why should they? What is there of value in life apart from the breaking down of barriers surrounding the lonely self? We are all alone. But sometimes the fortunate among us are offered the chance of not being so. She wants to say: take this opportunity fully, take it with all its consequences. It will never come your way again.

She supposes that somewhere in the back of his head he knows that their discourse in these past two days has been on two different levels. On one they are a man and a woman enjoying a torrid international love affair—really enjoying its dangerous deceit, the hours prized away from everything else, acting out all the clichés in the most flamboyant settings they can find. How magic was the air on that mountain, the thickly frozen snow holding diamonds of a pale sun; how wonderfully the glassy water lay, benignly blessing the white slopes on which little children in bright blue and red suits learnt to ski; how innocent their laughter as they skidded on the ice and fell, walking back up to the mountain top to catch the train poised there, waiting; how peaceful their coming to rest, sipping cognac and enjoying peace in the midst of war. The war between love and the family.

But the other level they lived on was different altogether. Each of them dropped remarks into the air between them which referred to the possibility of a more permanent arrangement between them. What would he do about his pension if he changed countries? Which of their children would get on—or not—with the others? Did she know there is an English school where he lives? Did she know he would be with her when she died? He couldn't share the housework but he might do the shopping. He would like her to cook him a meal. (She would like him to wash up afterwards.) There is a progression in this dialogue. They did not talk like this three months ago. Either there has to be an end to this relationship or something dramatic has to happen. He, not she, said that. They skirt round the problem, firing out sharp remarks which echo like shots in the air: here today, gone tomorrow, leaving no mark behind them so they can be conveniently disowned. But the bullet holes stare them in the face.

This morning after the day before she watches the two of them together: her husband and her daughter who has spent some of the night with him in his bed. The little girl puts her thumb in her mouth and reaches out to place her other hand, palm outstretched, in his hair. They are symbiotic, he says. When she asks a naive and loaded question (will he ever let her go?) he asks is that her response to watching them together, or is that because she actually has some other arrangement in mind? She says the first: he says no, the second. Fixing her with an unusually firm look, a look she recognizes because it has always in the past preceded his achievement of a goal, he says nothing will ever separate him from this little girl. She is everything to him. And that, he adds, is not purely a statement of intent. It is the truth. No court of law will ever take her away. He would use everything in his power to keep her. For once, her mother will not come first.

He doesn't forget that she loves her too. He even thinks she is necessary to the child's existence. She is not sure about that, but she is sure the child is necessary to hers. She went through an ordeal to bear her. She is part of her. A child is the future. She could never live with the guilt of not putting her first.

It is the reality of the war between love and the family. Not only between a woman's love in a love affair and her love for her family (note the distinction: a family cannot be a love affair), but between a woman's love for her child and her child's father and the structure and conventional sentiments of family life in our culture. Every day is a strain to make emotions acceptable. If we, the women of this culture, can label this or that feeling the way they're supposed to be labelled, then everything will be all right. We watch television and see that we are supposed to feel deeply about the colour of our washing or our lips, that only bad women are not darling household slaves. We understand that women are not acceptable for what they are, but must fit themselves into certain routine shapes: square like a washing machine, round and comfortable like a ball of lemon-scented soap, shapely like an egg-timer measuring the withering away of time. We see this, know it for the lie it is, but stubbornly reach out for its promise of security. If we can be like that we will be all right. If I were a trim, tidy-minded secretary, a vapid, inconsiderate actress, a pugnacious busty politician—if I were an aproned mummy or a smiling wife everything would be fine. We try to adjust the tidal waves inside us. Can we redirect them? If we can't, then there is something wrong with us. We've been wrongly programmed. So it isn't our fault after all.

The Nightmare of a Happy Anniversary

She has a living nightmare, just as someone else once had an important dream. In this nightmare she is doomed for ever to pursue misleading signs in anonymous concrete places. She doesn't know why she is there or if she will ever get out—or why, indeed, she should want to. Her eyes are unseeing and her heart beats like a drum gone mad. Her feet obey peculiar commands: she is a person of 1984, if person is the right word at all.

Here she is searching for the exit or entrance to a multistorey car park. All the cars look the same. The signs 'Way Out', 'Down', 'Lift and Stairs', 'Level 4', are not legible; or they are interchangeable. She doesn't know why she bothers with them. Here she is walking interminably back and forth between the terminals (an intended pun, because what is terminated in them? The end is only the beginning) of the largest, most horrendous airport in the world. Here she is traversing plastic tunnels, ploughing up ramps, pondering on travolators (a true 1984 concept), disappearing round countless corners and all the time she discovers with a child's sense of disappointment that the sign doesn't mean what it says; that brash, brightly yellow conglomeration of letters cruelly promises her a future where there is none. She is fated to spend all the hours of the day and night scanning the black signboards in the arrivals or departures halls of these places (she is never sure who is arriving and who is departing). She watches the white letters roll. Their language she can't fathom but all the same it is music to her ears—a pattern in which she would like to put all her trust. These marks of journeys made, planned, hoped for, hated—these are a sort of religion.

Here we all stand looking upward, praying: has it landed, is it due, expected, delayed? Our eyes are fixed on those little television sets suspended in the air that claim to possess authentic information of a particularly specific and useless kind. And all for the dreadful journey that follows: down unlit motorways with unkind rain beating on the window. We are always going the wrong way and are wrapped in such a fog of confusion and misplaced concentration that we never even see the directions to the place we want to go. This may well be partly because we do not know where that is. Round and round the roundabout. On and off the M3, the M4, the M40. What does it matter? We are all duped citizens of this alienating misleadingly signed and baldly leafless terrain: the world, this country, our only home.

After the journey comes the ghost-inhabited house. In the house they have come to this time nothing works. It's like Doris Lessing's *The Four-Gated City* in which the nuclear holocaust is prefaced by the breakdown of all domestic appliances. Here, now, the bottom drops off the telephone: the line, like so many lines of communication, is really dead. The windows don't open. The radiators are switched either on or off according to some mechanical whim. The one in the sitting room drips like a rotten tap behind the plant that flops its dusty and dying leaves all over the table which is, itself, in the wrong place. It is always too hot or too cold. She can't sleep and she can't stay awake. Is she hungry or is it the pain of love? She can't find herself or him, either.

At different times in these fourteen hours they are locked in a classic domestic scene: either side of the fireplace in armchairs, two sides of the dining table, passing each other in the kitchen, taking turns in the bathroom. He looks tired and seems older. She feels both. He keeps looking at her and saying 'What's wrong?' What is wrong is the world. Not them. They are all right. Or they would be, given the half a chance they will never have.

They have a conversation about reality. What reality? They talk about the fact that they will never and could never have more of a relationship than this. That they, even, do not want it. They say the opposite of all the things they said before, the last time. She says she will never leave her husband, her little, pensive, red-haired daughter. He remarks that it was in a weak moment that he floated the idea of a migration; it is their different countries that divide them more than anything else.

In the car back, in the nightmare returning to the airport that delivered him to her, she tries to explain what she has only recently come to understand, that fantasy is part of reality. Reality is made up, sustained by, fantasy: fantasy feeds off reality. Their child will never be born but exists in their heads. Their marriage is not made in heaven or in a registry office but in the looks that they exchange; in the thoughts they have, in the feelings they confess to—or rather bravely announce to each other. That is the way it should be. And anyway they do not believe in marriage, do they, which just shows you the essentialness and essential absurdity of the dreams we cling to in this ghastly universe.

She no longer knows what she feels about him. He is like the air she breathes and who knows what they feel about that? Seeing him is hell but not seeing him is worse. In the morning, when he discovers that he cannot take a later flight than the one he had booked, his face wears an expression like stone. She cries and he says, 'No man is worth a woman's tears.' It's only later she appreciates the double meaning; but she nods, yes, that's right. Please could someone tell me how to stop the tears? Please, doctor, I have no control over my secretions today. I love you. I need you here I need you here . . .

Is this really the beginning of the end?

Or is it a new beginning?

Nightmares are visions as well. There is no end, only a series of incomplete beginnings.

In the letter she has on her desk that he wrote over Africa four days ago, he tells her of how the morning is chasing him on his long flight across the world: it pursues the aircraft, but never quite catches up, so that dawn is permanently postponed. He says he wouldn't mind having such a night with her. She thinks they've had one. Five whole years of days and nights dwelling on, if not within, each other. It was five years ago exactly that they met. Five years ago they weren't younger, but older; these months of love have been a rejuvenation. She is grateful, and so is he. They wouldn't have been without any of it. But they both would have chosen to avoid this agony of having to end every beginning as soon as it's begun: of having to stop each new opening of the floodgates in its tracks, of having to shut up their feelings in little iron boxes and pretend they are nothing but two ordinary different people living properly in time instead of always on the edge of it.

How many meetings have they managed? Yesterday before their last separation he asked her to count them. How many clutched couples have they been at airports, how many not-so-secret glances at conferences have they exchanged, how many times has there been the euphoria of the expectation and the leaden depression of the only just bearable aftermath? How many times have they made love—apart from all the time? How could she ever believe this relationship was just sex—or just his expert sexual technique? He is only a human being, with the enormous flawed promise of all human beings, the capacity unmatched to the appetite, the eyes fastened on the ever-elusive star. But such joy! A product of the way they are together, a fusion of their minds as well: because of love.

The first of these two nights he wakes, jet-lagged at 2 am, and she is not beside him: where is she? Desperate, he searches the house calling her name. He can't find her. He puts on his clothes and peers out into the still black night. But he has failed to notice her sleeping form hidden in another bed. He sits on the bed and wakes her. 'I couldn't find you,' he says, 'I thought you had gone.' She thinks it is morning and goes back to bed with him. They make love again, as though by such constant conjugation they are able to defend the point they are otherwise always trying to escape, namely that in their multiple divisions they are for ever and at heart united. At 4 am they decide they are hungry and go into the kitchen for tea and cereal. He says he must walk around the streets where she walks because (a) he must know everything about her, and (b) it is 11 am according to (parts of) his body. They await the dawn which does come, now he is no longer in the sky evading it. The sky over England lightens and the birds sing. She goes back to sleep. He walks, then lets himself into the house and climbs into bed beside her. 'I love you,' she says, asleep.

The next night over a planned candlelit dinner she sees in the mirror exactly how it will be twenty-four hours from now.

Another twilight and her alone. She is upset and he is upset and in his jet-lagged fatigue he sleeps again for an hour, waking just as she is ready to sleep, waking again with an erection and another mission to accomplish. So it goes on. They laugh because it *is* bizarre, always trying to match their waking and sleeping but not their enormous desire for, nor their vast sweet knowledge of, one another.

He has brought her a jewel to hang between her breasts, carefully chosen to be the right shape for that place he admires so much. In the darkness he remarks that he can bear the pain of these repetitious departures if she can—only if she can; he says, too, he is falling into pieces, it is all such a mess. At breakfast, she says she would like to love him for ever. 'I love *you* for ever,' he says, 'there is no doubt about that. I will always belong to you, and you to me. Whatever happens.' What he doesn't say is that she is teaching him to recognize the validity and strength of his feelings. This is a most dangerous thing. It is mixed with a retreat into an old problem. 'How do I compare,' she asks, 'with the other women who are, or have been, in your life?' 'Well,' he says, 'you know I can talk to you in a way that I have not been able to talk to any other woman. You are strong. You are not dependent, as other women are. You have self-confidence. I can have an equal relationship with you. And the sex we have together is nothing like the sex I have had with anybody else. But other than that I simply love you. I love you for what you are, for who you are. I cannot say more.' She touches him beneath his dressing gown: 'it's all yours,' he says, 'I am all yours, even if I cannot ever be.'

Who is strong? What *do* you mean?

For the first time in her life she is spending a night alone. There is no one else in the house with her. It is silent around her but still, at this hour, friendly: the circles of light and dark are familiar patterns holding no unknown terrors. Noises form a welcome background to her thoughts; the creak of the pipes, water running in the kitchen, the hiss of the central heating controls, cars outside in the street. This is her house and she does belong here. She sits cross-legged like a schoolgirl on the sofa made up to be a temporary bed for those who still have a schoolgirl's fear of the dark; she sits, in her blue dressing gown with white flowers on the lapels, newly bathed and fed, a glass of brandy in her hand and misery inside her head.

Why has she never learnt to be alone? Or, rather, why does she so much long for aloneness while never having faced the hazard of being alone, the inescapable physical solitude, the absence of another presence to turn to when the branch of a tree scrapes the window as it is doing at this very moment? What is all this talk of liberation for women, of women's inner strength and independence, when this one woman can scarcely gather the courage to face herself alone in the middle of one dark night?

It is a fact that often those experiences and situations that are most needed are not most wanted and vice versa: if desire and benefit could always be matched, conundrums such as the one she is in would not come to plague us as often as they do. In particular tonight she is conscious of two conditions. One is the condition of being loved. The other is the condition of love not making any difference.

Love can't be quantified. But she knows that quantities of it exist and are focused on her, especially tonight. Quite a lot of people might miss her if she died; more than a handful would never ever forget the quixotic quality of life she has; a few would mourn her as part of them for ever. Not everyone alive could say this. Therefore, she is lucky. And she appreciates not only her good fortune but the work she has put into loving other people, believing in *human* connection, in articles of old-fashioned kindness and good faith. They are concerned for her and are with her in their minds, those people out there in the night: her husband bravely facing a family holiday on his own, her female friend with her lover in their lakeside hotel concocting another deception for another deceived wife, her solicitor and his wife who gave her last night's supper of chicken and white wine to block her tears, the man she loves who now must cherish his own fears for her safety and his self-love alone and far away.

But what difference does the difference between the loved and the unloved really make? We each have to face many micro-cosmic nights like this all our lives. Nobody is responsible for us. We are responsible for ourselves. If we can't cope, no one can. She goes back in her heart to the loneliness of her childhood, to that photograph taken one hot and misty summer's day when all the children in the street were lined up playing trains together and only she sat alone, a yard away, staring vaguely into the sun and out of focus. She is out of focus now. No one is looking at her. If no one can see her, will see her for another twenty-four hours, does that mean she doesn't exist? That particular philosophical conundrum which never puzzled her in the past, appears, at this hour of her life, in a different light.

The noises build up into a crescendo inside her head. The tree tries to break the window again. The house is hers no more, but an enemy enveloping her while she is damaged in it, handicapped and chained in irons. Love takes us back to things we didn't know, and it also provokes in us that panic we had when we were born: of separation that never can be breached, of difference that never can be surmounted. What is it adults have learned that little children do not know? Is what replaces innocence worth it—something to be proud of? On a more practical and less obscure level, how will the night be endured? What is at all ennobling about suffering? Why should anyone put up with any of this?

What she wants now is not the reassuring hand of a man or a woman, but the sweet, soft face of a child, luminous eyes lidded in one guarded haven of a night. At this moment she is only sure that parenthood is worth it. Work, sexuality, feminism, poems, parties: these are fictions. But can we as parents make people who are stronger and wiser than ourselves; and if we can't, what is there about life that isn't some form of delusion? Is she mad? Or just silly? Perhaps the unsolved problems really are clearer in the night. One day she'll know.

Family: death of a father

You went into hospital for an operation to relieve the pain; you were going to come home again, but you never did. Did we ever know how much pain you were in? Once you said to me you couldn't bear it any more, but knew you had to, for my mother's sake. She couldn't live without you, or you couldn't live without her, so you had to go on. (And this is love?) Everyone who saw you in those months and weeks could see the pain upon your face, in its lines as much as in its yellowing, sagging, thinning dissipation into death. There were times my mother sent for me: you were asleep, you looked so frail, were scarcely breathing, felt so cold: would you ever wake up again? I saw the scars and the burns of the radiotherapy you'd had that never could have cured the cancer, and didn't even stop the pain. On the way back to my home in the car I was sick at the sight of them. I don't really know what you thought or felt as your dying was in progress, but I've always wanted to tell you what I did. I've always wanted to tell you everything, because you've always been the only person who's ever really listened to me.

First of all I thought: I'm never going to be happy again. I was twenty-eight when I knew you had cancer, twenty-nine when you died. I was supposed to be a mature and independent adult, but I simply thought I couldn't bear to live without knowing that somewhere on this earth you were alive too. I went to my GP and I said I'm afraid of breaking down in front of him. She said you'll need a lot of pills when he's died; I'm only going to give you a few now. They were blue. They were called 'oblivon'. I took them once or twice when I came to visit you; I suppose they thickened the haze through which I viewed you and the awful imminent prospect of your demise; but I never did need those pills after you died.

I thought of your necessity to me despite the fact that a gulf between us had grown over the years. We didn't talk much. Or if we did it was at cross purposes. We felt we didn't understand each other, and we didn't. Gender and generation do divide people (but we didn't think they would divide us, like the psychiatrists who can't recognize or prevent craziness in their own children). I remember one day in particular. You and my mother were coming to supper in our house. She was already there. On the way you had to visit your own mother in the nursing home to which, in desperation, she had been consigned. I was sitting at the dining room table with your two grand-children, aged four and five, when you came in. You stood in the doorway awkwardly. You had on your usual dark grey suit and white shirt and you looked as though you were shrinking from the world inside your clothes. You leant, a little, against the doorpost, with one hand in your pocket. You didn't know what to say and neither did I. We looked at one another like strangers. After you had died I often saw you standing there, not reproachful or resentful particularly, but just a statuesque reminder of my inadequacies as a daughter, of your difficulties as a father, of our complex and enormous love.

If anything in my life has taught me how love can coexist with difference, this is it. There were many things we came to disagree about. Marriage, the position of women, the needs of children, party politics, the cohabitation rule, student radicalism. Yet the basic argument we never had that determined our relationship in the years before your death concerned our significance to one another. You never really could tolerate me as an adult sexual woman, could you? You never wanted me to grow up. A little girl who sat trustingly on your knee was pure and perfect. A woman with a husband and a child was not. I, for my part, had had to insist on my difference from you. It was a condition of my survival as a person. (Now you are dead, I am, of course, free to admit our identity.) I had even written you letters explaining this, putting it in terms of your descent from a pedestal of hero worship, and you said you understood, but did you like it? That is another matter. I do know, because I have been told, how in these years of our non-communication you talked in quite rejecting terms about me to your friends: I was an ungrateful, selfish monster; you weren't going to leave me any money—I didn't deserve a penny; I understood nothing about your position, and not much about anyone else's, either. You hated me with the intensity of one who has to turn away from the pain of love.

When I learnt of your illness, my first impulse was to run and find you in your white hospital bed and put my arms around you and tell you how much I had always loved you and always would. You were a little boy puzzled by his own anger and I a mother who wants to say her love is unconditional and all-surviving. Or was it the other way around? It could have been. It doesn't matter whether I label it filial or maternal or whatever; it was the impulse that counted. And so you opened your eyes to find me there. I did put my arms around you. I stroked your head, your smooth high forehead and the dark still-not-grey hair I had played with as a child, and I did say, 'I love you, I have loved you all the time.' And you looked at me with your gentle dark eyes and you said you knew. You were more awkward than I in this strange encounter between a 28-year-old woman and her 65-year-old dying father; but you glowed with it then and afterwards. It led up to some good conversations in the next few months, by which I mean we really did talk to each other about all the things that mattered. I came to understand my childhood and yours a little better. You came to see what motherhood had meant to me. We both understood how cycles of destructive family relationships can be broken in the next generation, although they sometimes unkindly linger on. You said some things you never would have said had you not known you were dying—and that is how I knew you knew you were.

Publicly, the story went like this: you had what looked like 'dry rot' at the top of your ribs. It was cancer, a six letter word that professors are allowed to use if students can pronounce four letter ones.[1] But it was 'treatable'. This apparently was the word that was used to you by the surgeon as you came round from the anaesthetic. You didn't ask, nobody asked, what it meant. Of course now I see quite clearly that 'treatable' didn't mean 'curable', and I know that both a doctor friend and my mother were told you only had a few months to live. But there was a conspiracy of silence round your condition excluding me. Didn't a daughter have a right to know her father was dying? It may even have been thought I didn't care. Yet through it all you never admitted that people sometimes died of the kind of cancer you had got. You said you were going to get better. You looked forward to the spring when you would plant the seeds that would grow in the summer. You looked forward to the holiday you would take with my mother in the quiet English countryside you loved: you spoke of returning to Greece, all six of us, to the hotel where Robin had so clumsily asked you if it would be all right for us to marry; you looked forward to the book you would write next; to the next political machinations and struggles. These were your public statements. They were backed up by your consciousness of two untoward events and their psychological significance to you. Your mother had eventually died, and it was with her death that the pain of cancer first came to you. You had always said you would never be free of her and this proved it. You were sixty-five and facing retirement. A person like you could never retire, and in the end, of course, you didn't have to. And so you apologized to my mother for your occasional moments of lost control, like the night when the pain was so bad you wept and wanted only to be separated from it, when what you should have done was to have faced it like a man.

I felt angry with the medical profession on your behalf. You didn't seem angry yourself, and I suppose your doctors would say this proves that not everyone who's dying wants to know they are. But you weren't told the whole story, and neither were we. You weren't given the chance to get ready for your death. Or were you really ready anyway? I don't think so. I think if nothing else, you wanted to watch your grandchildren grow up. They did give your life a meaning. You did feel that it was worth having a stake in government and public policy because the world they would live in should be a good one, and it was in your power to help to make it so. I also think you wanted to die with dignity, and, though you did that in my eyes, your dying should have been done much better. Amongst your papers when you died was a yellowed sheet I had given you some fifteen years before on which was inscribed Madame de Sévigné's portrait of life and death: 'To live without growing old, to feel complete and alive to the very end . . . then, when the last hour has come, to find again in the depths of the soul the beliefs of the earliest years, and to fall asleep gently with a strong hope and a firm love for those who live, like us, in the midst of darkness and uncertainty: is not this indeed a fate worthy of envy?' It is, but you weren't quite allowed to manage it.

After the operation you couldn't breathe on your own. They put you on an artificial respirator. By some terrible quirk of fate your granddaughter nearly died that morning too. She had had pyelonephritis (a kidney infection) and was scheduled for an intravenous pyelogram at Great Ormond Street Children's Hospital to make sure there was no real abnormality. In order to have this she had to be injected with iodine dye to which she proved allergic. The doctor inserted a little of the dye into a vein and she blew up before our eyes, constantly sneezing. He ran off at high speed down the corridor for some anti-histamine. After that, proceedings were smooth, but as I held her in my arms full of anti-histamine I thought I nearly lost this child as well: why is everyone I love so fragile?

So it was with Emily, in transit from one hospital to another, that I first saw you on the machine that was prolonging your life. She wanted to see you: my mother and the nurses said no, you can't take a little child like that in there, she'll be horrified. I went and looked and explained to Emily how her grandfather looked. She came in with me and I picked her up and stood by your bed. You opened your eyes and smiled at her and she at you. I am sure it made your dying better. That evening the doctor (another friend of yours) came round to see my mother and me and tell us 'it' was just a matter of time. They were going to take you off the artificial respirator in the morning, so he would like us to be at the hospital then.

We were. But you didn't die. You were semi-conscious. You couldn't speak properly: the respirator had made you sore and you didn't have your dentures in. This was you without your smart clothes, your titles, your important appointments, your department and your international influence. This was you naked and shrivelled and defenceless in a tiny mean hospital room. This was you enjoying the benefits of what you had worked so hard to defend—the British National Health Service. (I'm not saying private medicine would have been better. It wouldn't: only the room might have been bigger.) At one point you asked for a cigarette and the doctor, your friend, an ardent and famous anti-smoker, could at that point only admire your stubbornness (which was part of your splendidly crooked argument that in your case smoking twenty or thirty cigarettes a day for years had not caused cancer of the lung, which was where your cancer had originated). Instead of a cigarette, we gave you a peppermint. You told my mother she should go home and rest. We left you for a couple of hours. When we came back to you you never looked at us again. There were other people there by then: Brian Abel-Smith, your friend and colleague, and Mike Reddin, a junior colleague. Mostly they sat on a bench down the corridor. Mostly my mother and I stayed with you. We didn't talk much but in some odd way the occasion seemed ordinary, routine. I suppose that's because dying in hospital is. I was even aware of thinking, why don't you die? Because that's what you're going to do. You can't do anything else, now. So why are you taking so long to do it? And then I looked at you and thought, if you hurried up and died, I'd never be able to look at you like this again.

Your breathing changed. I actually had already been with someone just before they died—my mother's mother had died in our house, in the middle of my geography homework, of a cerebral haemorrhage when I was eleven. I remembered this laboured breathing from then. My mother turned to me. 'They make an awful noise when they die,' she said, 'the death rattle. I think you'd better go.' She seemed quite calm. I felt rejected, excluded, just as I had done from their relationship all my life. I thought, if I go I'll regret it, because I won't have been brave or loving enough to endure the dying of my father. She doesn't even really want me to go. 'I'll stay,' I said. There was a noise in your throat as you breathed for the last time. A gentle noise: you always were a gentle man, considerate and quiet. And then no noise at all, no movement. One moment I looked at you and knew you were alive; the next you were dead. The difference was impossible to grasp. You looked the same. The dull English sky through the window looked the same. The hospital bustle went on. But nothing was ever going to be the same again. I put my hands over my ears, as though by stopping the sensation of sound I would stop all sensation. I wanted to touch you and I did—your skin was warm, but it did feel lifeless because it was. I wanted to take off the sterile sheets and blankets and look at you and hold you for the first and last time for what you were: the person I most loved in the world, the person who had given me life but had no more life to give.

Your wife and I left the room together. 'He's gone,' she told the others. I didn't know for a moment what she meant. You hadn't gone at all. Not only were you still there, in that little white room, but you would always be there in our heads and in my son and daughter who had your genes inside them. A doctor went in with a stethoscope and came out again looking solemn. A few minutes later Brian, Mike and I went into your room to pack your things. I was crying. You had the sheet over your head but your nose stuck up through it; I wanted to take the sheet off your nose so air could get to it again. One of them pointed out that it was a characteristic of your awkwardness, your rebellion against bureaucracy, that you had died one day into the next tax year. We laughed. We laughed over your dead body? It was the only thing to do: you would have laughed yourself.

As I left the hospital I experienced a strange desire to have another child. According to a psychoanalyst I know who subsequently incorporated my responses to your death in a book she wrote, this is a well-known fantasy. Birth and death are not very far apart. Your death was my birth, in a way. And when you died I wanted you to be born again in me, as another person altogether. The following night my son went to sleep in your bed. He said, this knowing five-year-old, 'You must be lonely, Granny, why don't I come and stay the night with you?' (She wouldn't come and stay with us.) So off he went with his toys and his sweet brown eyes. She rang me up later: 'He's so beautiful, lying there, in that bed, where there was all that pain.' In the morning he wouldn't eat his breakfast until she did, and he insisted on running her bath for her. We were proud of him.

I think children understand more than we do about life and death. We have made a mystery, an alienating medical routine, of death which should be part of life. At your cremation in an unpleasant West London crematorium Emily asked in a loud voice as your coffin slid through the curtains, 'Is that Grandpa in there going to be burnt?' The people who ran this awful place had asked us to choose some music to be played at this point. We selected Wagner's Overture to *The Mastersingers of Nuremberg* because you liked that sort of grandiose sound. You liked the flourish of trumpets, the blare of whole orchestras playing a recognizable tune. It was celebratory, that music. We wanted to celebrate your life as much as mark our sadness at your death. They asked us to bring it on a record. We did. As the coffin moved and Emily asked her question about its destiny, from behind the scenes came the sound of Wagner played at the wrong speed. You would have been amused at that; it seemed as fitting as the original choice, that little human detail of someone not quite managing to get something right, probably because (as you would have said) they were upset about something, their attention was elsewhere: whatever it was about human frailty, you always understood it.

A thanksgiving service was held for you in St Martin-in-the-Fields, Trafalgar Square, on June 6, 1973. A lot of important people came, and so did many unimportant people, students who had met you or read your work and been inspired by you, your presence, or something you'd said. We sang 'Jerusalem' and Brian Abel-Smith read the passage about charity from I Corinthians 13: '... beareth all things, believeth all things, hopeth all things, endureth all things. Charity never faileth...' Richard Crossman (ex-Secretary of State for Social Services) and Wilbur Cohen (ex-Secretary of the United States Department of Health, Education and Welfare) delivered tributes to you. Crossman called you a prophet. 'Richard Titmuss was not like other men. His eyes and his conversation shone with a moral force... He... saw clearly, luminously, consistently, and with a wonderful happiness the vision which deserts most of us pretty often in our lives... A great man has been taken from us.' Wilbur Cohen said you influenced eternity and listed you along with Lloyd George, Sidney and Beatrice Webb, Churchill, Queen Elizabeth I and Seebohm Rowntree as giants of social policy. Trevor Huddleston, Bishop of Stepney, also talked about you. He said you were '*anima naturaliter Christiana*' and that as a bishop of the established Church of England he was proud to be able to point to your character, labour and life as exemplifying the self-giving love of proper Christianity: he said you were used by God, your Creator, to express in a world of appalling inequality and deprivation 'the true end and meaning of human existence'.

˙ Your obituaries used such words as 'pioneer', 'saint', 'poet' and 'metaphysician'. They debated your most important achievements: was it as pensions adviser to the Labour Party, as Deputy Chairman of the Supplementary Benefits Commission, as creator of health and social services for Mauritius, as influential friend of Julius Nyerere, as critic of income tax dodges, as proselytizer of altruism, or as a charismatic teacher that you had achieved the most? Michael Young in the *Observer* said your greatest achievement was that you took your achievements lightly. 'Loaded with fame, he remained the same bright-eyed, thin, inquisitive, nervous, compassionate, incisive, boyish man that he had been in the 1930s.'[2] They referred to the loving support of your wife, support such as is to be found in the lives of all great men.[3] *The Times* said, 'He will be greatly missed by his wife, daughter and friends throughout the world.'[4] David Donnison in *New Society* didn't understand why you were mourned so much until he realized that 'It is for ourselves and our lost youth we grieve.'[5]

I grieved for you not because of your public achievements or my lost youth. To me you weren't a saint; one doesn't need to call you a Christian to see the compassion you had and gave. You were a human being. You were my father, the only one I'll ever have.

SCENE 12

A French Letter

'This hotel is definitely decadent,' she wrote to her lover: 'window boxes of red geraniums barely affixed to the wall, long angled lawns, and in the bedrooms mock chandelier lights and glowering oak cupboards. It is an odd place. A stopping-off point for civilized tourists, a veritable "relais du silence"; an evening out for the locals, whose telephone boxes are inscribed with international dialling codes to the United Kingdom and Germany (but no other countries), and yet who comment with misplaced surprise that the party at the next table "n'est pas français". It is a dormant place. The grey sky, drier than England, covers the grey square round the church. The shops are open, although they look closed; enormous pears, pastries filled with cherries and cream, slim white shoes marked down in the spring sales. There isn't even an air of expectancy about the town, except perhaps in the hotel dining room, where Persil white tablecloths and refractory goblets await an army of gourmet users.

'Just now, when I was out, a young man and a young woman came round the corner together, he on a motorbike, she on one that was motorless, but propelled by her hand on his arm. Neatly, breezily, they semicircled the corner together, as no doubt they had done a thousand times, powered by the same source of energy—his, seeming as though it were the most natural fact in the world, one so unremarkable only an idiot would remark on it. It looked good, I must say. But not natural, for I know it isn't. Is it the same with us? Whose fuel powers me now? Is my hand always metaphorically on your arm?

'At five o'clock on the day you last left me I sat in my car in the greyness of somewhere in London, aware of the dissonant voices of birds, in the rain-soaked trees, cars rushing past, jumbled voices of schoolchildren; and out there, somewhere else in the universe, my dear lover travelling away from me again. There were no tears until on the car radio in Finsbury Park came "Jesu, Joy of Man's Desiring" most radiantly played, forcing the desolation of the moment upon me, the old panic of passion with no object, an unfuelled heart and body.

'I sat there remembering your coming through the Customs Hall just twenty-four hours before. I had tried to pretend you were merely a friend, a good friend but no more than that, with whom I would spend a pleasant evening. From friends, even good friends, one maintains a distance: so it would be with you this time. I kissed you and said yes, I am glad to see you, and drove you to the hotel. It was all perfectly amicable. The sun momentarily shone. So did your face: more brilliantly perhaps than ever. You picked up the discordance in our moods, asked why. I said I am trying not to love you so much, as a way of protecting myself from the misery of our perpetual union. You object, "We must love each other for ever. That is what we have agreed."

'And later I sit remembering your words, marked with your penetrations. I am calm, which isn't usual. I do know I haven't been loved like this before. This isn't better, but it is unique. I am not willing to give it up. I am not, however, willing to give up everything for it. I am trying to recognize that the affair both depends upon a mix of feminism and femininity and surpasses it, so that the contradiction which nourished its conception sustains it. If you select danger whilst conserving convention, so do I. What is there of masculinity and femininity in all this? Only the specificity of organs, the difference in fluids; only the training in control and the disingenuous discharge of tears. We are human beings. It is as human beings that we sit and eat and drink and book rooms in faceless hotels and fix times for talks and meetings; it is as human beings that we lay in that last bed, touching, delighted. "You are beautiful," you said, "especially like that," and, due to an obstacle in my mouth, I couldn't laugh. "I hope you are going to stay away from other men for ever," you murmured as my dark hair dived into the warm water, as the water lapped us both to the sound of the fire alarm going off, inducing in us a frantic but splendid vision of instant immolation.

'On the boat I sent you a message in Morse code. I was desperate; you see, I am always desperate beneath the calm. The amiable radio-operator, who with his own brand of desperation predicted the end of the international telegram service and bemoaned his own tarnished Morse code skills, offered me the use of the ship's telecommunications service for my own illicit purposes and his own comfortable armchair for his. He took in the words I wrote in red on the form and added as I left, seasick and yousick, "I hope it has the desired effect." But despite all I have said we don't know what the desired effect is, do we?

'Some lessons we have learnt. We have learnt our lesson about fantasy, I think: that we must be allowed to dream. Everybody who's really human dreams—but only the inhuman are arrogant enough to act out their dreams. We have learnt the mirage of stereotypes. People's labels for you are not you, any more than theirs for me are either the me I know or the one you do. What vandalizing discourteous lover are you? What innocent victim am I? We are beginning to learn a lesson about the unsolvability of problems. But if we appreciate the impossibility of resolution, our resolve is weak. I don't stop thinking about how to integrate my life with yours and neither are you able to dismiss your unacknowledged hope of a greater union than this. My darling, I love you; here in the arid territory of northern France I love you; in the cobbled streets, in the plastic bars, amongst the graves of men who died unloved, in the clouds that shield me even from a vision of the moon that shines on you. My darling, I have loved you in all the cities where we have been; in all the snows and rains and sunbeams, in all the fields and mountains, lakes and passageways, in all the churches and hotels and baths and beds. My darling, I have loved you at each meeting, at each touch and every kiss, wherever planted, in the utterance of (almost) every word; my darling I am yours for ever, as you are mine.

'But as to what inspired me to such heights of passion I am as ignorant as I was in the beginning. I look around me. I am surrounded by the appurtenances of a not unstressful family life: children's books, shoes, discarded apples, spare knickers. I am getting some enlightenment out of reading a book about the treatment of Chinese women which might explain the still-higher mortality of female babies in that country: "I found her and the baby plugging up the family well."[1] I have just read two newspapers dealing with the life imprisonment of the Yorkshire Ripper, a man who behaved so romantically at home, who always escorted his wife in the dark, who was a loyal son and a trusty friend; a man who killed thirteen women, maimed another seven, and deprived twenty-five children of their mothers, and who, when tired, pinned a notice to his lorry which said (if I remember it correctly), "In this truck is a man whose latent genius if unleashed would rock the nation, whose dynamic energy would overpower those around him: better let him sleep." Yes, indeed. But it is the latent genius, so perceived, of men which constitutes patriarchy. Patriarchy is the structure in which all women, and I mean all, are imprisoned. Of course men are imprisoned in it, too, but revolutions start more easily at the top.

'Your being a man must be one of the things for which I love you. I love you even for the direct emblem of your masculinity, small and shrivelled in the bath, long and firm in me, safe or invaded in beds of various international sorts. Yet I strongly believe that men are enemies of women. Promising sublime intimacy, unequalled passion, amazing security and grace, they nevertheless exploit and injure in a myriad subtle ways. Without men the world would be a better place: softer, kinder, more loving; calmer, quieter, more humane. "A man, who is in general a menace, is supposed to be worth loving as an individual. A masculine body, which is in general dangerous, is supposed to become desirable taken as an individual. Our every day is filled with such schizophrenia." So says Verena Stefan in *Shedding*. The problem about heterosexual love is that "A man can always void his emotional vacuity into the vagina of a woman without his perceiving her as a person, without her essentially being able to defend herself, to escape being dependent on him."[2] Just so. The question is: can love exist without oppression? And, if it can't, who is being oppressed? The question is: why, if my utopia doesn't contain men, are you my utopia?'

The War between Love and the Family   II

At the beginning of her relationship with Jean-Paul Sartre, Simone de Beauvoir made an important decision. Instead of marrying him, she left him in Paris and went to Marseilles to work. Of this decision she remarked, 'In all other cases my resolution coincided with my spontaneous impulse: but not in this. I very strongly wished not to leave Sartre. I chose what was the hardest course for me at that moment in order to safeguard the future.'[1] She chose that course out of respect and love for herself. That kind of regard for themselves and for others of their sex is a state most women find it impossible to achieve. Most do not even seek it.

Our lives are organized around men. As little girls the present or the absent father is the potentate of culture; men belong to the world, they own it, they run it, its representation is in and comes from their heads. Women have difficulty owning even their own wombs, which is important, because within these organs lies their only countervailing kind of power. Although in my own case this contrast between women and men was marked—in my mother's concern for my father's work and welfare and the neatness of the home, and in his concern for the state of this nation and others—even in families with less sexist patterns children pick out the patriarchal formula. Abstracting from the general to the particular, they note that their own parents are unusual; not that the culture is. My mother may work, but mothers don't: my father may clean the kitchen, but fathers shouldn't.[2] As all those women and men who have tried what is optimistically called non-sexist childrearing will know, this leap from the private contract to the public plan is a source of inescapable anguish. (A journalist who interviewed me once about one of my books met Adam and Emily, then five and four, by the garden gate on her way out. 'And what do you want to be when you grow up?' she asked. 'A policeman,' said Adam. 'A nurse,' said Emily.)

Adolescent boys are a distraction to adolescent girls; but boys just slot girls in piecemeal to their lives, measure their intellectual and productive prowess against that of girls, congratulate themselves, and carry on. We must choose, as Simone de Beauvoir did, either to labour for ourselves or in order to catch and hold a man. Marriage for women is almost always a mistake. Married women without paid work are the unhappiest people in the world. But the mental health of men is improved by marriage.[3] Why is this? It's easy to see why. If you're a woman, marriage promises everything and guarantees nothing. It promises undying love, commitment, a snoring body to keep one company at night, dirty socks on the floor and 'pocket money' for ever. The undying love dies and what is left is not enough—for men, that is. As the Arapesh of New Guinea neatly put it, women are of two kinds: 'those which are like big fruit-bats, the bats that nurse their young at only one breast while one breast hangs dry and empty, and which hang up outside the house in the storm and rain; and those like the little gentle bats which live safely in holes in trees, feeding and watching over their young.'[4] Little gentle bats are okay for a while, but they're not very exciting. So men go out in the storm and the rain to see what's around. What they end up with is both kinds of bats: the little unselfish domestic ones and the selfish dry-breasted ones. That way they get the best of both worlds.

But women don't. Women, of both kinds, suffer. As wives we allow ourselves to be harmed by the ravages of our rampaging husbands 'for the sake of the children' or for a still-held hope in a more secure future within marriage than without it. As mistresses (a masculinist word, which is why I use it), we face the mystification of our identity—not only the lies, the secrets and the subterfuges but the quite incorrect representation of ourselves as mistresses of our own lives. There is the feminine mystique and the feminist mystique as well. But the truth is that there are no two kinds of women. I speak as a wife and as a mistress, for that is what all women are. I speak as someone who still feels defined by relationships with men, as is the case for all women in our harsh bisexual ambivalent so-called civilization—defined in babyhood, in childhood, in adolescence, as adults, in old age—perhaps least of all as senescence leaves us in a nearly one-sex world.

When I look around me now, I see a particular instance of this pattern confronting me clearly. Three women I know are wrapped up in the consequence of men's bifurcated mystique of women: the feminine and the feminist. All three women are married and all are mothers. All are in love with another woman's husband.

The first woman's lover lives with his wife and their children. He is rather a flamboyant lying character. Neither of the women in his life quite knows if he's ever telling her the truth. Both are 'desperately' in love with him. One washes his clothes, makes his bed, protects and nourishes him while he works, and waits for his phone calls; the other doesn't wash his clothes, offers him tremendous sexual delights, does him the honour of stressing her own needs, and also waits for his phone calls. Both women are at this moment acutely unhappy because neither of them, not surprisingly, feels they are able to count on the totality of this man's love. However, the fact is that he is probably not easily going to relinquish his marriage, even if it lacks passion. His soft-voiced generous forgiving wife calls forth in him such tides of masculine protectiveness that he is not able simply to turn away from her. She needs cherishing, he says. Cherishing need not be such an honest activity; after all, it is done not purely to serve the cherished, but to swell the head of the person who does the cherishing. Most of the time he has not been willing to give up the passion, either. In his 'mistress' he can both lose and find himself. It is a relationship untrammelled by obligation—or at least not beset by the tiny obligations of ordinary marital living. In his mistress he can forget the past and claim the future: become a better and a different person. How wonderful it has been for him! How convenient! And, occasionally, it has been wonderful and not inconvenient for both women too. Magnanimously, out of the expansiveness generated by his double life, he has been able to present himself to one or the other generously and (temporarily) completely. The rest of the time hasn't been so good. The wife wonders if he really will leave her and thinks she cannot cope at all on her own. The mistress wonders if he really loves her. There are a lot of needs and aspirations and sentiments and considerations mixed up here. But what we see is not two sorts of women involved in two halves of the same man, but the same sort of woman having the same problem with men.

The second woman is married to a gentle, professional man. A few years ago she began to look a little tired and run down. Her face grew lines where there had been none before. The corners of her mouth changed direction. Her clothes were not put on with quite the same degree of care. She confessed one day that she had found herself crying rather a lot recently. For example, she cried yesterday on the train on the way to work. Her GP had given her a number of different kinds of pills to take (the update of the Shakespearean characters stelazine and imipramine). She was going to a therapist once a week. Assuming her to have a satisfactory marriage, and seeing her eyes still sparkle slightly when she talked of work, watching the still-loving glances she cast her family, one supposed it must only be the accumulated strain of managing so well for so long to be so apparently perfect, to be an effortless combination of everyone anyone ever intended women to be, that had led her to begin crying. But the truth was that she had been having an affair with someone else for years. For a while the affair went well, if that is the right phrase to use. It was enormously exciting; sexually it released her for the first time from the feminine inhibitions with which most of us start out. Then she became possessive. Why can't you see me tonight? she would ask. Or, why only two hours, not three? And so on. Nothing was enough. And so he stopped it (the way only men can) because he couldn't take the strain and his wife knew about it and grew upset. And then, guess what, they found they couldn't live without one another (to use the well-worn phrase, which, like most such phrases, hides the fact that it's scarcely ever true). So they got together again. This time she'd learnt her lesson. Enjoy what you've got and ask for no more; after all she didn't intend to leave her husband, did she, so why did she want him to leave his wife? Years passed, not uneventfully. They built up a protective wall of deceit, protecting both her husband and his wife from the truth about their feelings for one another. And then the crisis came. He left them both to set up house with another woman altogether. No, he was utterly at a loss to explain what had happened or why it had happened. No, this new woman was not more beautiful or more thoughtful or more nourishing than the other two; just different, that's all. No, he didn't want to talk about it. He didn't want to face facts or feelings of any kind with anyone.

Hence the tired looks and the pills and the crying. The discarded mistress goes to bed early every night but remains ever hopeful. She says: I didn't know what life was about until I met X. It is in these past years that I have found myself. But I found myself with him: with his hands, with his body, with his mind, with his vision of me. Now he has gone I have lost myself. I can't get him back, but I must get myself back. I don't know how to do that. Would it be easier if I could give up hope? Each time the phone rings I think it's him. Is it better to keep this hope, thus to retain one fragment of him in my life, or is it better to cut him out entirely and return to the blurred mundanity of middle-aged suburban marriage without even the fillip of an evening out with my lover now and then?

The third woman, who is in a not dissimilar situation herself, analyses the distress of the other two, one of whom is a feminist, the other of whom is not. The paradox is, feminism doesn't make any difference. All three women are equally upset, equally desperate. All three men involved have double vision. All seek the conveniences of marriage and the freedom of the sexual chase. All three women want sexual joy and security to be combined in the same person: their image of men is an integrated one. Therefore the desires of men and women are incompatible. Not because the man's desire is for the woman and the woman's desire is for the desire of the man, but because women can't find in men whole human beings, and the whole human beings women are are not what men have been led to believe they want.

The other problem is that men's double image of women becomes the mirror image women see when we look at ourselves. It is difficult for the jilted mistress not to hate the protected wife, for the abused wife not to want to harm the beloved mistress. Patriarchy presumes that women will be untruthful, that they won't, and can't, trust each other; that the motive of their relationships with one another is always men. Watch the 'bitchiness' of teenage girls together: see how they stick to one another like syrupy leeches and then come unstuck, draw blood. This is how they have seen their mothers behave. It is clever to make pointed and salacious remarks about other women. It is clever to attract and reject, be jealous, spiteful and seek revenge. There is nothing clever about affection and honesty and trust. The only news is bad news.

Feminists know that we women should put each other first. And that is what, in many ways, we do. Our best and closest friends are women. We believe that unless women can count on the help of their female friends, then there is indeed absolutely no prospect for women's liberation.

But it isn't easy, because women can be their own worst enemies. The wife who is lied to can't help but see the subject of her husband's lying as a caricature of the woman she would like to be. She is living out the feminine mystique and so she sees her husband as pursuing the feminist one. She sees the other woman as strong, stronger even than her husband. This other woman, her unrealized and unrealizable ambition for herself, is the vessel of all the strength that is needed to tear husband and wife apart. She becomes the scapegoat, the source and cause of all alarms and discomforts. Her human frailty goes unheeded: even her own need for love and support, which makes her vulnerable, seems a strength, because it is such a threat to the enclosed pseudo-harbour of the family. Conversely, the woman who is in love not with *her* husband but with *a* husband sets up a portrait of the little wife at home, tidy, frightened, dependent, meekly protesting with an armoury of feminine wiles, peering nervously over the enormous hedge of her children's supposed need for the symbolic presence of a father in their home to the disastrous utopia beyond. It isn't solely the solicitous attentions of men we seek but that religion, the family. There is nothing so sacred as a happy family. But is there such a thing as a happy family? If all unhappy families are unhappy in their own way, then it is doubtful that a single formula exists for the opposite state.

A historian friend of mine remarked the other day that, as a foreigner in this society, it had taken him by surprise to see how deeply embedded were the values of the established church in the lives and minds of people who apparently had no formal affiliation to it. There can be no firmer proof of this than that the family has become *the* repository of religious values, a religion apart. Families, however they originate, are not sustained by love, by enjoyment, by relaxation, by passion. They are sustained by commitment and decision and loyalty hard-gathered from the once-good times; they are powered by an ascetic code of conduct in which future welfare is placed above present happiness to the extent of totally denying it as a consideration. Families are nothing other than the idolatry of duty.

CHRONOLOGY 29–33

If my aspirations had been for a husband, a house and two babies by the age of twenty-five, by the time I was thirty they were rather different. Indeed, under the influence of feminism, with the seeds of a new self-confidence and simply because the children grew older and went to school, I might have echoed Dora Russell's words to her mother from Peking that two babies and three books by my thirtieth birthday enabled me to feel I had done rather well.[1]

There isn't any doubt that the books did more for my self-esteem than the babies did. Understanding intellectually why this should have been so has never prevented me feeling angry about it. I agree with Adrienne Rich when she says she can't work out whether the experience of motherhood under patriarchy is finally radicalizing or conservatizing.[2] Bearing children demands a certain obedience to the social order into which they're born; we have to adopt a stance towards such concepts/ institutions as the family, school, security. But it also puts us in touch with the 'bitter bedrock truth' of the way things are: the seductive, amazing and heart-splitting beings that we all start out as; the social double bind of idealized and disadvantaged motherhood. If we don't choose revolution, we must subvert our anger to preserve sanity (both ours and theirs). What happened to me was that I didn't think of the babies as a struggle, of motherhood as the problem I had to solve; I thought, instead, of putting my energies into the only kind of work our culture accepts as work—the masculine solution I had earlier spurned. My work turned me into a radical, but turning to work was at the time merely a conservative act.

My Ph.D., which took four and a half years from start to finish, was accomplished largely in the evenings and at weekends during the six (later nine) hours a week when we hired a series of decrepit ladies to watch Adam and Emily downstairs while I ruminated upstairs. One of them, a Mrs Stewart, lied about her age and at four thirty when I came downstairs to take over, was already fixing her hat in front of the mirror. The next, a Mary Hill, was lacking most of her internal organs, and was consequently always catching the children's ailments. She gave up on medical advice, but at least she did take the children to the park a few times first.

My first book, *Sex, Gender and Society*, was written in six weeks during the university vacation, and the publisher, a gaunt chauvinist, thought it had suffered from this tight schedule, and was surprised when it sold in quite large quantities. That same summer, and most significantly, Robin finished his own Ph.D. after years in which I, like a good wife, had organized the house and children so he had time to work. (That taught us both a lesson.) We had settled down into some sort of routine. In 1973 Adam was five and Emily was four and they went to the same forward-looking primary school on a council estate and an access road to a motorway. Not an ideal setting: I used to worry a lot about speeding cars and, later, lead pollution, when it became fashionable. Nobody who hasn't had children can possibly understand the parental crisis that occurs when those hours from nine to three thirty are free for the first time. On the one hand it's liberation, but, on the other hand, what is one going to *do* with all that time? On Emily's first full day at school I was there, waiting, half an hour early at the school gates. In the morning she hadn't even bothered to say goodbye. Her maturity was a constant source of amazement. At three, in the nursery class, she had come home and said, 'A big boy talked to me at school. He said, "You're on the wrong lavatory. These are the boys' lavatories and those are the girls' lavatories." I said, "Thank you for telling me."' It seemed to us that our children knew everything and in particular things that adults spend a long time working out. One day Robin took five-year-old Adam out and bought him some new Lego. When they came home, the conversation went like this:

Ann: 'Your Daddy spoils you.'

Adam: 'Yes, he does spoil me.'

Ann: 'Do I?'

Adam: 'No, not so much.'

Ann: 'But I love you as much as he does.'

Adam: 'Yes, you love me a lot. Daddy doesn't love me as much as you do.'

Ann: 'Why not?'

Adam: 'Because ladies love children more.'

Ann: 'Why do they?'

Adam: (*rather crossly*) 'Because they're *ladies*.'

Ann: 'But what is it about their being ladies that makes them do that?'

Adam: 'They grow the seed of the babies inside them, so they love them more.'

Would he offer such a diagnosis of the inequalities of parenthood now? Probably not, but I would—indeed have done in a way.

Since I didn't like routine, I never seriously contemplated a teaching job. I had enjoyed interviewing women for the housework study and felt my naughty curiosity about other people's lives could be renamed a skill. I decided to do more research. Out of the housework study and my own experience came a conclusion that isn't original now, although it was then, that it is first-time motherhood which forces women to confront the real feminine dilemma. Before that, and as I had done in my early housewife-undergraduate days, you can pretend you're equal. Once there's a baby to care for, you can't. I designed a simple study of first-time motherhood and applied to the Social Science Research Council for money to do it. The application was initially deferred, and then accepted, once I had agreed to make some minor changes to it—although I heard quite recently that in deciding to give me money the Committee commented on the harsh way I treated my husband as a reason for not giving me the grant that they would have quite liked to take into account.

In order to do this study I had to gain entry into the medical world. I needed the names of pregnant women to interview, I needed access to their case notes, and I had decided I needed personally to witness the whole repertoire of staff-patient interaction in obstetrics. The first eminent professor of obstetrics I consulted about possible access to his hospital was most unhelpful. I suppose there is no reason why eminent obstetricians should willingly allow someone like myself to observe their doings and misdoings. When I visited the next one I wore a suit and a wedding ring and talked like a conventional respectable married lady. He decided to let me in. On my first day there I went to his room and he gave me a white coat to wear 'to make the patients more comfortable'. Almost casually he told me that a Caesarean section was scheduled for eleven and it might be a good idea if I went to watch it. In retrospect, I think this was a test which he expected me to fail by falling unconscious on the floor, whereafter he would be able legitimately to exclude me from the hospital. In fact what appalled me was the way the patient, an obese black mother of three, was treated, once the general anaesthetic had taken effect. In the first place the staff made abusive remarks about her, and in the second place the door of the operating theatre opened and in poured a crowd of students, about whose presence the patient had clearly not been consulted.

I spent about a year in that hospital, and I learnt a lot. One thing I learnt that took me some time to recognize was my own ambition to be a doctor. (This is one suggestion that has been made about all medical sociologists; that in order to defuse their criticism of medicine they should all receive the medical training they undoubtedly at heart want.) Not for the first time I wondered about my education. Why had medicine never been suggested to me as a possible career? Why, to do a medical training, does one need to excel in science and mathematics, when the art of communicating with patients demands none of this? I learnt a lot of lessons about the profound miseducation of obstetricians and gynaecologists.[3] Most are educated to believe that diagnosis and treatment require a paternalistic surveillance of a territory and an experience which is entirely foreign to them. Although, and because, women outnumber men in the total health care labour force, male doctoring is ultimately about control over women, and this is nowhere more true than in the domain of reproduction. I saw daily evidence of this in the time I spent in the hospital, but I also learnt another lesson I didn't entirely want to learn—that doctors are human beings too.

Sociologists call this a methodological problem inherent in the process of participant observation research—it's called 'going native'. In the appropriate jargon, 'The attempt to integrate oneself in the field is not without negative consequences. The problem here has to do with over-empathizing with one group's perspective in the setting. This can result in the observer's uncritical acceptance of, or identification with, that viewpoint to the exclusion of others.'[4] In other words, what happened was that at three forty-five after two hours of a busy antenatal clinic I too would sigh with the doctors as we jointly peered into the corridor and saw, still waiting, another row of abdomens. We wanted our tea. Or at two in the morning I wanted someone to get in there quickly and do a forceps delivery so I could (like them) go home to bed. I came to understand something of the pressures obstetricians are under. While I think this has certainly helped my views on the current state of the maternity services to be accepted by doctors as reasonable, I did at one stage have to make a deliberate attempt to extricate myself from the medical viewpoint and remind myself that patients are people too.

The first woman I saw having a 'normal' delivery in this research gave me quite a shock. She had had an epidural anaesthetic, which meant one wire up her back and another one taped to a vein in her hand; she was attached to a machine which monitored the baby's heart and her contractions, which meant two more wires up her vagina. Her face showed no expression at all. She was just lying there. She looked like part of the machinery. When a midwife or a doctor entered the room, they paid more attention to the technology than to her. In fact, she didn't seem to be a terribly important part of the whole business at all. While this wasn't my memory of having a baby, it wasn't entirely out of tune with the first birth I had experienced, seven years before. I suspected that the attitudes I had objected to in 1967 were those that brought about this present situation. I think I was right.

What started out as a narrowly sociological study of the transition to motherhood became increasingly a study of medical attitudes and behaviour. I became more and more interested in the relations between medical care and social action, and have since then continued to be, seeing medicine as (amongst other things) an absolutely key institution in the social control of women in the twentieth century in all sorts of ways.

One side effect of this change of focus was that friends and colleagues, and even the doctors I followed around with notebook and stopwatch hidden in the pocket of my white coat, began to suggest that, so intense was my involvement in the whole research project, I was bound to carry the strategy of participant observation to its logical conclusion by becoming pregnant again myself. I objected that I had more control over my own life and impulses than that. Why should professional women get their public and private lives confused? What were feminism and the liberation of women all about, if not the practical control of fertility and the damming of irrational desires to introduce more babies into an already ghastly world?

I became pregnant again for the third time in 1974, for the fourth time in 1975 and for the fifth time in 1976. Only one child survived. But so did I, which in 1974 and 1977 seemed unlikely.

The summer of 1974 felt like a rational time to me. My father's death the previous year had, as I have already said, inspired the desire for another child, but I had always had that anyway. I didn't like being a nuclear family of two children (boy and girl in that order, as in the cereal packet norm). I had been so tired, so 'depressed', when Adam and Emily were little that I felt I had missed important parts of their babyhood. I felt I hadn't had the experience of bringing up one child. Perhaps I thought this important because I had been an only child, and proper motherhood properly accomplished would for me have to include a repetition of this experience. The decision to have a third child was one with which Robin concurred, although not very enthusiastically; he was worried, I suppose, that I would become 'depressed' again. But he knew I was serious, and he knew what a lot of people in my social circle didn't—and don't—recognize, that feminism and motherhood are only contradictory aims because of contradictions imposed on women by their culture. Feminists must break this code. They must re-establish reproduction as authentic and unalienated labour. That is what I wanted to do—on a minimal personal level—in 1974.

Looking carefully at my interviewing schedule, I could see that the only reasonable time to give birth was July 1975.

Accordingly, in October I took my temperature for a few days in the middle of the cycle and conceived, with implantation of the ovum occurring during an interview about my most recent book on the *Jimmy Young Show*. It seemed a sensible way to behave. Why shouldn't babies be thus calculated if they would ultimately be loved? I wasn't really surprised when the plan worked. However, I did feel enormously stressed at the time and it was, looking back on it, a completely idiotic idea. I began to bleed. At first just a little, followed by a few days' respite, and then I had a short late period. I visited an obnoxious pharmacist on the North Circular Road who had a good line in abortion clinics and who told me my pregnancy test was just below positive and that I should return in a few days, which I did, achieving to my great distress exactly the same result again. He warned me, this obnoxious man, that the pregnancy might not be a normal one. I disregarded his warning but visited my GP's surgery, where I was examined by a lady doctor with long purple fingernails who said that because I'd had two normal pregnancies, this one was probably normal as well. She dispatched yet more urine for an NHS pregnancy test: the NHS tester rang her up and said he'd never seen anything like it; my specimen had yielded two positive and three negative results. I came home and thought about it and descended into hysteria. What was going wrong with my splendid plans? Why didn't I know what was going on inside my body? Rather more immediately, why wasn't anyone taking my (by now very real) worries seriously?

By phoning the GP who had attended Emily's birth, I obtained an appointment with a gynaecologist in a different hospital from the one I was researching. This man most slowly and deliberately examined me and the evidence and a few days later beamed and said, 'Hallo, love,[5] this is nice and straight-forward, the HCG levels are normal and everything's okay.' A few days later I returned to see him after a weekend of pain and bleeding. I thought I was having a miscarriage. I had never had one before and therefore didn't know what they felt like. The pain was rather one-sided, and I mentioned this, but nobody took much notice. A threatened abortion was diagnosed and I was admitted to hospital. During the next few days I peed endlessly into containers which were duly transported to the laboratory and analysed. I was told that unless the results were clearly negative, I would be kept in bed until the bleeding stopped—for the whole of the rest of the nine months if necessary.

Eventually a senior registrar whom I had followed around at the research hospital appeared on the scene. I trembled at the sight of him, since I had noticed that the internal examinations he carried out made women much more uncomfortable than those carried out by the other twenty-five doctors in my study. It all began to feel like something out of that film *Hospital* in which patients (and doctors) keep dying in corridors and nothing happens that isn't some form of medical mistake. I asked this terrifying individual not to put his hands on or in me, but I did ask him to come back and see me once the ritual of the ward round was over. I had decided that it was necessary for me to plead for the termination of this pregnancy in order to get someone to investigate the scenario inside me at all. I said, 'I want an abortion, please.' The registrar consulted the consultant who agreed. Coming round from the anaesthetic after the D and C, I asked the first person I saw, who happened to be a nurse, what had transpired. 'Oh, we're not allowed to tell you,' she said, 'but sometimes these things are for the best.' Later a young doctor informed me that they didn't get 'much of anything' out of my uterus and that I must therefore have miscarried without noticing. I told him that I wasn't in the habit of dropping fetuses without noticing, and went home feeling sore and confused.

Five days later I was buying socks for the children in Marks and Spencer's when I felt a bit faint. I went home and found I had started bleeding again. It was our tenth wedding anniversary. The children were singing in a carol concert at school that evening. I ate a handful of valium and sang 'Hark the Herald Angels Sing' along with everyone else. Then I went back to hospital and fell asleep instantly, oddly reassured by being in hospital again, a place where curable conditions were supposedly cured (although I had begun to wonder whether my own condition *was* curable).

The next day I saw the consultant, who said he would like to do a laparoscopy in the next day or two. This would mean an inch-long split in my naval and would enable him to rule out (or in) most of the various possibilities. Before this second operation I was confronted at breakfast time with another doctor bearing the usual consent form. He asked me to agree to sterilization, since, he said, it would be a convenient time to sterilize me and, in any case, I had had my two children (my boy and my girl), hadn't I? I said I don't want to be sterilized, thank you.

When the consultant did his laparoscopy I was ten weeks pregnant. He found a ruptured tubal pregnancy. The tube had evidently ruptured two weeks earlier during my weekend in pain and I had been haemorrhaging internally since then. Two pints of blood were extracted from my abdomen, along with some thriving placental tissue (but no fetus: that apparently had disappeared earlier) and my left fallopian tube. The consultant kindly left me my ovary. He later generously admitted that another day or two would have been too late, and he didn't know how I had managed to stagger about with all that blood floating around inside me; that all the hormone levels since the very first ones had been characteristic of a normal pregnancy, and that in fifteen years of ectopic pregnancies at that hospital no such levels had ever been shown; that every blood test done on me had indicated the kind of respectable haemoglobin levels that proved health not illness. In short, he almost apologized for only just saving me from death.

I did actually feel grateful to him, and I didn't actually blame him at the time for failing to make the right diagnosis earlier. I was concerned then only about one thing, and that was getting out of hospital as soon as possible. Christmas was imminent, and my children were not allowed into hospital to see me at all, a rule which healthy patients ignored by slinking off to the main hospital lobby when the staff weren't looking and having powerful illicit assignations with their little loved ones. But when I came round from the anaesthetic, I found blood from a plastic bag dripping into me, and when it had finished dripping some other bag full of liquid was put up there instead. I was not allowed to eat or get out of bed. I knew if I was to get out of hospital in time for Christmas I had to prove myself capable of instant recovery. So I engaged in a series of attempts to establish this, beginning with accidentally severing the second drip and moving on to decorating the ward Christmas tree, a task which nearly made me faint. A friend came to see me and brought me brandy, which helped. I asked Robin to bring in all the children's Christmas presents so I could wrap them up and install some in stockings ready for the great day. For hours my bed was littered with toys and books and children's clothes and Christmas paper. The young doctor passed by and said he'd take his unwrapped, if I liked. A great deal of jocularity thronged the air, along with the faint smell of pine combating the scents of hospital. The consultant visited, pressed my large vertical abdominal incision and said, 'Super'. I said, like a supplicant child, 'Can I go home soon, please?' He said, 'How are they managing without you at home?' I said, in carefully modulated married tones, 'I've got a fantastic husband, he's been doing everything for three weeks.' 'Hmmm,' he said. 'Wednesday would be about right.' Wednesday was Christmas Day. I got hold of a nurse after the consultant had swept out of the ward with his entourage and asked her if I'd said the wrong thing. 'Oh no,' she said, 'He'd keep you longer if you'd said they couldn't manage without you.' She looked at my notes. 'I think you'll be all right. He's written "? discharge Tuesday".'

I became totally obsessed with the exact day and hour of my departure, no doubt partly as an escape from thinking other thoughts and not only because ward life was so terrible—I came to enjoy its sisterly camaraderie, if not the food or the nursing rituals. But the task of negotiating discharge is a well-known part of the patient career as studied by me and people like me;[6] 'getting out' of hospital is like being released from any total institution—it's a restoration of the self, and, unless one has completely given oneself up for lost, it's bound to count.

On Tuesday, Christmas Eve, anxiety mounted and no doctor could be found to pronounce me fit for release. They all seemed to be at parties. Around three the consultant strode in, leaned heavily on my wound, asked me if it hurt (no, I lied) and said, 'Okay, come back on Friday to have the stitches out.' Robin arrived to see me a few minutes later, but without my clothes, since he didn't know I was going home. (Why *is* it that patients have to stay in hospital while their clothes go home?) I leapt into the car in my dressing gown and arrived home in time for the second half of the Christmas carol service from King's College, Cambridge, which I listened to in mild ecstasy with both children sitting on my stitches.

It is truly shocking to discover that bodies can play such nasty tricks as mine played on me in 1974. My main reaction was a feeling of intense personal failure, and I wrote long letters to my friends about how even feminists can mourn the passing of their fallopian tubes. I gazed at my marked abdomen and unhealed scars with dismay. I cried eventually not for myself but for the baby who had briefly grown and quickly died inside me.

The consultant, to whom I returned for a check-up some weeks later, said no cause had been found for my misplaced pregnancy. He said he thought I should be able to conceive again quite easily if I wanted to. I wanted to, but couldn't face the challenge. I lost a lot of weight over the next few months and buried myself in work. I continued to use the old and trusted cap (or rather its nth replacement).

One evening, some months later, I was watching one of my interviewees courageously give birth to her first son when I felt quite sick and had to leave the delivery room abruptly. Thus I came to be appalled for the second time at the way events could take place inside me without my consent.

On this occasion I resolved that there would be no misdiagnosis, no errors or confusions. Slightly more than a week after the missed period I was in the ultrasound department of the hospital where I was doing my research (an appointment I negotiated for myself behind the scenes). Twins were diagnosed. Twins in the uterus. I made rather a business in public of the notion of adjusting to this unplanned pregnancy, yet secretly I was pleased. I began to wander into Mothercare again, and happily returned for repeat ultrasounds at seven, nine and eleven weeks (I think I was caught in a hospital research project, which probably serves me right). This pregnancy happened almost exactly a year after the ectopic. I lay in bed on Christmas morning 1975 remembering the disasters of Christmas 1974, watching Adam and Emily opening their presents, and thinking, self-indulgently, next year there'll be another baby too. (One of the twins had disappeared on the subsequent ultrasounds, as apparently is quite often the case.)[7] Then I got up to pee, and bled into the lavatory bowl. I managed to get through Christmas Day and Boxing Day and the day after that with lots of vodka and alcohol of various other kinds (it's what they use to stop premature labour I told myself). I considered it a temporary problem, one that would pass. I certainly didn't contemplate calling a doctor.

In the middle of the night on December 27 I woke up with contractions. I lay there for a while crying, then woke Robin. I said, 'I'm losing this baby too. I don't want to go into hospital again. If people should have babies at home, they should have miscarriages there as well.' We lay there wide-awake in the darkness with my uterus contracting away. It was like watching my father die: there came a point when I just wanted it to be over. But it seemed to go on for hours and it hurt unbearably, unlike the birth of a real baby. Perhaps because of this, and perhaps because we lost confidence in ourselves and nature, we did telephone the doctor. In due time one unknown to us arrived, asked me two or three questions in an uninterested fashion, felt my pulse, and said I had to go to hospital. He rang the hospital and then rang his wife and was having an animated conversation with her about this and that when I went to the lavatory and passed the fetus, complete in its grey-blue gestation sac, and suspended, nearly bloodless, between my legs on the end of a six-inch strip of umbilical cord. It hung there, evidence of death, swaying slightly, but descending no further. I looked at it in horror. It was an alien object. I was terrified of it. I screamed. Robin came in. He called the doctor. The doctor said I should go and lie down. I said, 'How can I go and lie down with this thing hanging here?' He said sourly, 'What do you want me to do? I can't pull on the cord, you might start bleeding heavily. We must just wait for the placenta.' I said, 'Well, can't you even cut the cord?' 'I don't think I've got any scissors,' he said.

In the end he did cut the cord. I lay down and waited for the ambulance men to transport me to hospital. We rushed through the night with lights flashing and bells ringing. I took the fetus with me to hospital in a yoghurt carton. The pathology report when it came some weeks later said, 'Fresh female fetus weighing 13.43 gm. Lungs weight 0.3 gm. Development consistent with about ten weeks menstrual age. No malformations seen. Placenta weight 28.8 gm with 9.5 cm of paracentral umbilical cord.'

Knowing the sex of this baby enabled me to mourn it more precisely and more effectively. Whatever sex means, it is a predictor of gender and thus of character. In addition, I had wanted a daughter (though I hadn't worked out why). This time the death of the child was my first and only concern. I became quite cross with people who dismissed it as 'just a miscarriage'. No human being can be that. I derived great hope from the fact that this baby had to fight to be conceived—through layers of rubber and spermicide, and facing the obstacle of one blind alley. I entered into an entirely private decision that the only way out of this muddle was to have a proper baby properly without benefit of medical technology, or, at least, without its possible hazards in the early stages of pregnancy. At the beginning of June 1976 we arranged for Adam and Emily to go and stay with Robin's mother for the weekend. Robin and I went to the Cotswolds, to the Lamb Inn in the small village of Shipton-under-Wychwood. Laura was conceived there on June 4 and was born in London 265 days later.

The day after she was born I lifted her out of her perspex cradle, tightly wrapped and already milky. I sat up in bed and propped her against my knees. I knew then what I hadn't known in 1967, that mothers have no instant bonds with their babies and have to fall in love. This moment was my own falling in love: I looked at her and she looked at me with her amazed blue newborn eyes. She was a pretty baby with a translucent skin and soft pale hair sitting like a crown on her head. She was physically exactly what I had desired: a large healthy girl with different hair and eye colouring from the other two. (Brown gets boring.) Moreover the signals of her temperament I had picked up so far were pleasant; she was very alert but in a calm fashion, born with the clear intention of taking life at her own pace.

The next day I dressed her in ten-year-old baby clothes and a new white shawl and we all took her home in the spring sunlight to a room full of flowers and welcoming pictures painted by her brother and sister (then aged just ten and nearly nine). I laid her in a borrowed basket on a pink flowered sheet I had made, under a coloured blanket crocheted by a friend. She slept and woke and looked with interest around her and at her admiring father, siblings and visitors, and drank my milk tidily and with relish and slept again. Robin looked after me devotedly, bringing me delicious meals and insisting, from the very start, on changing the overflowing nappies breastfed babies tend to produce. Adam and Emily held Laura carefully, watched the midwives bath her, and told me how babies ought to be looked after. Everything was perfect. All the traumas of 1974 and 1975 had been overcome. I thought of Laura as my last child and was glad I had done it right at last. She wasn't a medical triumph, but a personal one, which is, I think, how parenthood should be.

One evening when Laura was a few weeks old I was feeding her in bed when I was suddenly overtaken by a horrible premonition that our good fortune, our state of familial bliss, was soon to be eclipsed by some awful event. It can't last, I said to myself. Was this the dreaded postnatal depression? Or the puritan suspicion that luck only lasts by being earned, and happiness is a commodity which is spread thinly and harms people if they have too much of it? I went downstairs and told Robin that something terrible was about to happen. I don't think he believed me.

About this time I began to notice a sore place on my tongue. It hurt when I ate apples and when I stuck it out and looked at it in the mirror, it was bumpy and irregular-looking along one side. I consulted *Black's Medical Dictionary*: 'Tongue, diseases of'. Among the statements made in this section were the following: 'Growths upon the lips and tongue may be simple warts, or cysts . . . but the commonest tumour of these parts is cancer. It seldom appears before the age of forty, and is much more common in men than in women . . . The glands in the front and sides of the neck in such cases become early the seat of secondary malignant growths; and as the foul state of the interior of the mouth, after such a tumour ulcerates, causes much interference with the general health, the duration of life is not long, being placed by authorities upon the subject at little over a year after the tumour first appears . . . '[8] I told a friend I had cancer of the tongue and she did tell me I had postnatal depression.

In the course of time, in fact when Laura was about seven weeks old, I went for a routine dental appointment. Almost casually I mentioned the state of my tongue to my dentist. He peered at it. 'It's not cancer, is it?' I joked. 'You think it's about to drop off, do you?' he quipped back. He did think I ought to have it looked at 'just in case'.

Two days later I spent several ghastly hours at a grey institution called the Eastman Dental Hospital, accompanied by the breastfeeding Laura, having my mouth looked at, photographed, X-rayed, prodded and ultimately biopsied. The man who decided on the biopsy told me a long and convoluted story about his sister-in-law who'd had a mastectomy and outlived her surgeon who died shortly afterwards of a quite unexpected heart attack. I was advised to return five days later for the result of the biopsy.

The morning I was due to get the result I awoke to a room flooded with sunlight. Pink and white blossom was visible through the window, and the birds were singing. I picked up Laura, who was also singing, to feed her, and with a sense of relief realized that I was, at least, alive now.

When we got to the hospital the consultant I had seen briefly on my first visit came out to conduct me personally into his consulting room. He began to ask Robin to come too, but, on spying the baby in the carry-cot, said no, perhaps he had better wait. Behind the closed door the consultant waited for me to settle myself in the dental chair. He stood, his back against the window, a few paces away from me, in his neat dark blue suit. 'Most of the area we biopsied was all right,' he said, carefully, 'but a little bit in the middle was invasive.'

It would be trite to say I won't ever forget that moment. I won't; my mouth, centre of the universe, was dry as a desert, the palms of my hands ran like rivers, my legs turned to lead. But what I most remember is the terrible jumble of thoughts, questions and fears in my head. The first thought I had was that I was immensely glad that I had had three children. The second thought I had was to wonder why nobody except me could use the word 'cancer'. The third thought was to wonder if I was brave enough to ask the many questions to which I only wanted the right answers.

The consultant dealt with some of the unaskable questions for me. He said it was a very early tumour and the chances of successful treatment were high. He said he wanted me to go immediately to another hospital where a plan of treatment would be decided on. He said I shouldn't let my condition affect my life; that I should just carry on with my normal activities. He smiled encouragingly. It was a quick interview, and through it I was possessed by outward calm fired by an inward sense of total disbelief.

The next hospital turned out to be the one where my father had, five years earlier, had his own cancer diagnosed, and the consultant I was 'under' there was the same one as had kept the truth about his condition from him, which didn't help. During the obligatory wait, I retired to a spare examining cubicle to feed Laura and heard a doctor and patient in the next cubicle having a discussion full of clichés and avoidances about what was obviously the patient's own malignant disease. I looked down at my lovely suckling child and wondered how the milk continued to flow into her, whether it, too, was malignant, how she would grow up without a mother and how I could ever sensibly agree to die and leave her in a motherless state.

The cancer specialist, a famous, clever and totally impersonal man, looked in the envelope I had brought with me from the dental hospital, and into my mouth and spent a long time feeling my neck. 'How much do you smoke?' he asked. 'I've never smoked,' I said. There was a woman in a white coat standing next to him who was apparently a radiotherapist. He began to talk to her about how many of my heavily filled teeth it would be necessary to extract, about the techniques it would be necessary to use to deliver the appropriate dose of radiation to the affected area, and about the desirability of applying more radiation to my head and neck after this initial treatment. It was a highly technical discussion. It didn't appear to concern me at all. Neither of them said anything to me. I began to cry. How could I, who felt so healthy, be so ill? What was this nightmare? How could I have grown the beautiful Laura and a tumour as well? They must have got it wrong, got my notes muddled up with someone else's.

The consultant asked, 'Why are you crying? The treatment won't affect your appearance,' he said, as though that were the only thing that mattered. I asked what the prognosis was—that was the word I used, since I suppose I felt as euphemistic as they did at that point. He paused to think. 'Good,' he said, guardedly. I left the clinic with Robin and the radiotherapist who was to arrange for the dental extraction. She said my first task was to wean the baby. I replied that I didn't want to wean the baby unless there was good evidence that continuing to breastfeed would make a significant difference to the chance of successful treatment. She said no such evidence existed, and that if I was lucky my milk would last the week I would have to be in hospital and separated from Laura. I began to see a little light at the

end of the tunnel. Going on with breastfeeding was tremendously important to me because I thought that if I could sustain
Laura I might have a chance of sustaining myself; and I
think the radiotherapist, who was herself a mother, understood
that.

The six teeth were extracted several days later in the hospital's
dental department with intravenous valium, and the whole
exercise scheduled to fit in with Laura's feeding times. The worst
bit was the journey home in the car, when Laura cried and I cried
because the local anaesthetic was wearing off and the pain of my
amputated gums was intense. The dentist who took out the teeth
was also very kind. He told me this bit would hurt the most (it
did). He told me I would be able to have false teeth one day to
replace the lost ones. He visited me when I entered the cancer
ward ten days later to have the tumour treated with an implant of
radioactive wires. My tongue was slit open, these wires, which
were made of a substance called iridium and had to be ordered
'hot' from a nuclear plant, were inserted, the tongue was sewn
up, and threads attached to the wires extruded from my mouth
and were taped to my chin. It didn't actually hurt very much
then, since the effect of the radiation was to kill the tissue in the
immediate area. I was even expected to eat hospital mince and
parsnips with the wires in place. I realized how radioactive I was
when I saw the radioactivity sign on my door and when, shortly
after the operation, I was taken to be X-rayed, and a nuclear
physicist appeared, calculator in hand, to work out exactly how
many hours the wires would need to be in position to kill the
tumour. He stood in the doorway very obviously keeping his
distance from me.

I missed Laura very much indeed; because of the radiation, I
was allowed no contact with her at all. After admitting me to
hospital, Robin wheeled her round the streets of Victoria and he
found himself crying, which was not a usual activity for him. He
told me some time later that he really thought I was going to die,
and he really felt for the first time truly responsible for one of his
children. Laura had bottles for my four radioactive days, but
disliked them so much she would only take two or three ounces
at a time. She therefore needed feeding every two hours or so and
put on exactly half an ounce in weight altogether, which was
very considerate of her, because I didn't want her to starve, but

nor did I want her to thrive on anyone else's milk. Adam and
Emily *were* allowed into hospital to see me this time. They were
told they could run in and hold my hand briefly, but that was all.
It was a very tense time for all of us, although not without its
humorous aspects, as when I fought to acquire a breastpump to
deal with engorged breasts (a *breastpump* on a *cancer* ward?) and
then I couldn't make it work because I'd never seen one before.

A few days after my return home dozens of raw ulcers appeared
all round my mouth. These were radiation burns, and I would
have liked to have been told about them in advance. I could eat
only babyfood and I made my own meals along with Laura's in
the liquidizer. I woke all through the night with a very painful
dry mouth and for a while spoke only when I had to,
communicating with Robin and the children via a series of
grunts and gestures—it's interesting how few words are really
necessary when it hurts to pronounce them. It was eventually
decided by means of an internal battle within the hospital
hierarchy that I would receive no extra radiotherapy to my head
and neck as an outpatient, as had been suggested; it was hoped
that the treatment I had been given would be all that was
needed.

Illness is either a visitation from the Divine for personal wrong-
doing, or it is a condition of human beings with a specific
physical cause. Or it is a process set in train by an unquiet
mixture of forces in the head as well as the body, outside the
person as well as in: and whether one includes the gods or not is
neither here nor there. In these years from 1974 to 1977 when
my body played tricks on me, I continually sought an explana-
tion of why I had become ill, and a ready-made set of
explanations is, after all, one reason why people hold on to a
religious faith. Why *had* all these things happened to me? People
who knew me watched with morbid amazement and when
eventually I got cancer many of them were plunged from disbelief
into a gloomy speculation of their own prospects ('There but for
the grace of God . . . '). I wanted to, and did, identify a specific
cause for each event. The ectopic pregnancy, I concluded, was
brought about by the stress of the Jimmy Young interview; the
miscarriage by a late unintended conception and faulty implantation; the cancer by a fifteen-year history of peppermint-sucking

and the temporary alteration in my body's immunological defences occasioned by pregnancy. I was, in other words, just unlucky to have been so unlucky three times in rapid succession. The intermission provided by Laura's perfect (i.e., medically uncomplicated) gestation and birth proved the point about luck: it wasn't that my body had altogether given up on me.

The explanations I selected (which had a certain amount of evidence in their favour)[9] of course did not exonerate me from personal responsibility. That wasn't their aim. If *I* had caused the problem—by agreeing to an unimportant interview, by sucking mints—I wanted to know, because only then would I be able to stop it happening again. In some sense, these episodes would thus have become more acceptable to me: they would have become part of the pattern of belief and experience that constituted myself. It isn't that suffering is ennobling, but that understanding breeds greater charity towards oneself, others and the future. Locked in angry or violent despair, one is robbed of action; nothing more can be made of one's life.

Health, as Illich says, is a personal responsibility and a task in which self-awareness aids success. But such a claim goes against the grain of the growing medicalization of life in our so-called 'advanced' society. It was not coincidence that one of the books I took with me into hospital in 1974 was Illich's *Medical Nemesis* which I had been asked to review for some journal or other. 'The medical establishment', I read on the first page of its introduction, 'has become a major threat to health.'[10] Now, having just been saved from death by the medical establishment, I found that hard to take. I decided Illich hadn't ever been dangerously ill; that *Medical Nemesis* was the healthy person's bible. Yet I did and do agree with his point. The point is that we have lost the balance between taking responsibility for our own health and assigning it to others. Anyone who becomes ill and who thinks about it must oscillate between the self-blame which is one version of personal responsibility on the one hand, and medical conspiracy theory on the other: that doctors should have prevented one from being ill, or at least rescued one from sickness speedily and wholly. I can see now how both I as a patient and my doctors concurred in the same abject model of social relations during my illnesses. I was the body that had gone wrong; they were the deified mechanics who would put it right.

It was not their role to receive the information I offered them about the workings of my body or psyche, as it was not theirs to impart much of their 'knowledge' to me. It's odd how even someone who has watched and analysed and understood and criticized this pattern still replicates it herself. In part this is because in times of crisis old habits die hard. In part it is because old habits never really die at all, they merely have to compete with new ones.

In the case of cancer, equality of communication between doctor and patient is notoriously difficult. When I first became a cancer patient it wasn't obvious to me why this should be so. Evidently not everyone who has cancer dies of it. Evidently there are other illnesses such as multiple sclerosis that are just as horrifying, if not sometimes more so, in their effects. So why should cancer have this special place: why should it evoke such unbearable emotions, such visions of disaster?

Cancer is a metaphor for proliferation, uncontrolled growth. Cancer means forces out of control. 'Cancer patients are lied to, not just because the disease is (or is thought to be) a death sentence, but because it is felt to be obscene—in the original meaning of that word: ill-omened, abominable, repugnant to the senses.'[11] So says Susan Sontag in *Illness as Metaphor*. She observes that the social treatment of cancer is paralleled by that meted out to TB in the nineteenth century. Both cancer and TB have been seen as diseases of passion—TB as caused by too much, cancer as the result of too little, as an affliction of sexually repressed unspontaneous people. As passion is a threat to economic and social stability, so cancer is a metaphor for all real and imagined disorders of civilization; civilization out of control is cancerous: cancer is nature beyond redemption by human means. It is significant that a masculine military rhetoric abounds in describing and treating cancer: hence the word 'invasive'; hence the importance of the body's 'defences'; hence the notion of 'bombarding' tumours with toxic rays; hence the very aim of 'killing' the cancer cells. It's horrid enough to discover one is growing an uncontrollable growth without having all the other rubbish to do with mythologies of cancer to deal with as well. But it helps to recognize the existence of the mythologies, and there were times when I wished the people around me could realize the power of these mythologies too—

especially those people whose response to my illness was to avoid me like a leper or to expect me to look, and be, radically different overnight merely because of a one-centimetre-wide problem on the right side of my tongue.

In John Berger's moving story of a country doctor, A *Fortunate Man*, Dr John Sassall puts a syringe deep into a man's chest: 'There was little question of pain, but it made the man feel bad: the man tried to explain his revulsion: "That's where I live, where you're putting that needle in." "I know," Sassall said, "I know what it feels like. I can't bear anything done near my eyes . . . that's where I live, just under and behind my eyes."'[12] I felt the same way about my mouth. To have a cancer in that particular place was a direct attack (to use the military language) on my identity. Given the importance of words in my work I needed my mouth, not primarily to speak but to think in words, to write. It was where I lived. It was the source of my vitality, my creativity; and I suppose here my stunted career as a flautist was not unimportant. (I had played the flute avidly between the ages of fourteen and twenty.) My mouth was also, and despite my GP's protestations about the tongue not being a sexual organ, a site of my sexuality. Because of this, one of the first things Robin did when the diagnosis of cancer was made was to kiss me.

When Bertrand Russell lay in bed in China recovering from a severe bout of double pneumonia, he realized he had been close to death. 'Lying in my bed feeling that I was not going to die', he wrote, 'was surprisingly delightful. I had always imagined until then that I was fundamentally pessimistic and did not greatly value being alive. I discovered that in this I had been completely mistaken, and that life was infinitely sweet to me . . . I have known ever since that at bottom I am glad to be alive.'[13] I myself wrote, instead of (at that time) an autobiography, an article for the *British Medical Journal* called 'Living in the Present: a confrontation with cancer',[14] in which I said something of the same kind. I did, indeed, realize in 1977 that being alive is very precious. It wasn't that death frightened me. It didn't and doesn't do so. I feel no terror at the thought of actually dying, or of what might lie in store for me once I'm dead. But if you're dead you can't do or be anything any more: you can't smell the blossom or the baby-shit, feel the wind, taste garlic, touch a child's cheek; you can't write books or poems or get nervous before giving a lecture, you can't cry, and you certainly can't smile. In the face of death there is no aversion to feeling too much. Hell is not being able to feel anything at all.

I also, however, became aware in 1977 that the way I had been living my life was not altogether a good way. I had been used to spending a lot of time thinking about the past or planning for the future, and not nearly enough time enjoying the present. For example, I did at times experience the usual conflict between work and motherhood, but this was always set in the context of the long-term harm that might be done to my children through my work, and not in the context of the short-term harm that could be done to me by depriving myself of them. The motto 'living in the present' expressed for me both a profound awareness of the pleasure that is to be experienced in the present moment, and a way round the cancer statistics. When my condition was diagnosed I knew nothing about cancer of the tongue (except what I had gleaned from the outdated *Black's Medical Dictionary*), and I didn't begin to want to find out about it until the treatment was over. Then Robin and I (plus Laura) went to the local library and looked up 'cancer' in the *Encyclopedia Britannica*, a naive and not very helpful act. I subsequently read in the library of the Office of Population Censuses and Surveys in Holborn a more informative report on oral cancer which told me that 54 per cent of women with cancer of the tongue die within five years.[15] (It was with difficulty that I realized my own chances of dying were exactly the same *after* reading the report as before reading it.) Cancer of the tongue is not common among women, nor is it a common cause of female deaths. There are 0.28 cases of cancer of the tongue for every 100,000 women aged fifteen to forty-four. Cancer of the tongue accounted for 3 per cent of female cancer deaths in 1979; one hundred and fifty women died of it. There is the same uneven distribution of life chances for oral cancer as for most illnesses: if you're going to have it, it's best to be a man or a married woman in Social Class II. 'Living in the present' was a way to say: we could all die of anything at any moment—the message that the dental surgeon at the Eastman Dental Hospital had been trying to give me before my diagnosis. For example, there were four and a half times as many deaths from suicide as from oral cancer in England and Wales in 1979.[16]

Taking it like a Woman

I had many letters in response to my *B.M.J.* piece. They came from Canada, Czechoslovakia, England, Greece, Holland, Hungary, India, Israel, Scotland, Switzerland and the USA. A medical practitioner in Madras, India, wrote, 'If I were your doctor, I would have told you all about cancer.' He went on to say, reassuringly, that birth and death are two sides of the same coin: two stages in a cycle: that everyone exists in everyone else, and therefore 'you are never born and will never die'. A radiotherapist in Harrogate just wrote to wish me 'all the luck in the world'. A doctor in Birmingham said he was having the article photocopied to give to all his students; a GP in Scotland wondered whether non-communication between doctor and patient wasn't something to do with the authoritarianism of a state health service. Some discussed the philosophical meaning of that phrase 'living in the present', noting that it is a recurrent theme in the reflections of ill people. One letter asked why it is so difficult to live in the present. This letter-writer went on, 'When that question is alive in me, then I am more alive and closer to living in the present. When I forget the question, or imagine that I have found the answer, the quality of present-ness disappears and when I next am more aware I realize I have been lost to dreams, fears, hopes . . . To be able to live in the present—to discover who I am (perhaps it is the same)—that is miraculous.' It eventually became clear to me that living in the present does have to do with knowing who one is, but that it also has to do with appreciating that timelessness denied by the modern world in its preoccupation with superficial change and senescence; with making a friend of eternity. Eternity was defined by someone a long time ago as holding and possessing 'the whole fullness of life in one moment, here and now, past and present and to come'.[17] For most of us there are moments when we do feel timeless. Those are the moments in which we feel we are truly alive, but they are rare.

Romance of the Rose: with an inexcusable scent of death

The air is pure and seems full of doves. The country is flat, occupied by rectangular out-of-season flower fields, ordered testimony to a population of unimaginative minds. Stalwart healthy children on bicycles pass. There is the odd car, the odd man messing around with his plants. Every half mile or so a house appears and each gleams immaculately, complacently, with lace-curtained windows overseeing domains of cropped lawns dotted with red flowers and little functionless windmills hardly turning in the still air.

They walk in the middle of the road between the flowing hedgerows and aiming for the sea. But where is the sea? There are none of the usual signs pointing to it—no breath of salt streaming over this field rather than that one. This is a directionless country. Does it mirror their own directionless state? They ask the children on their bicycles and one of the old men. Finally the ground turns to sand; on the flatness is superimposed the rise and fall of pale yellow sand-dunes sprouting tufts of grass and promising a different world beyond. They take off their shoes. They are released. They feel as though they have escaped from all their problems; here on the sand-dunes they can be young and free and no one will hold their dream against them; there is no one to hold it up to the light and inspect it for holes, no one looming in the doorway to recite tales of disease and domesticity, doom and dreadful responsibility; the sun shines only on them, the bell tolls nowhere for everybody else.

Creamy waves curl up at the brink of a deep sandy shore. Into

the sea they go, clothed and loudly joyful. The warm waves lap
their legs and spray their faces. The ocean is a marvel, wide and
silver and full of promises. The ocean is in their kisses, the sting
and the promise mixed, peace profound and elemental rage,
calm and terror joined. Love mature becomes an infant's passion,
attitudes and gestures learnt in universities disembark on the sea-
shore; they hold on in desperation to the passing moment, to
each other, coated in the salty sea, and each other's bodies, wet
and dishevelled; to each other's thoughts and feelings like
antique possessions, hard-bargained for but gained with honour
and kept in a polished state for ever. They run laughing along
the edge of the tide as it floods their toes, sharing a scenario from
the distant twentieth-century media world—all those unsubtle
images of strong suntanned men and slim long-haired girls in
their imputed conjugation of foam-topped waves and oceanic
rhythms. But the difference is that this is real. This is the
original from which all the copies have been made.

In the city later that week he tries to buy her a rose. One red
rose. But the flower-sellers for which the place is famous will not
sell him one: only ten. He doesn't want ten. Various passing
individuals, including a man in a lorry, become embroiled in the
argument and understand very well the logic of his (her) desire,
but it almost appears as if the government has made a law
forbidding the sale of single red roses. Nothing, as these passers-
by understand, makes sense to lovers except love.

This is a beautiful city, but they hardly notice it, taking from it
only what they desire: its cerebral but exotic atmosphere as
subliminal refreshment, food and wine to revitalize themselves
more directly. From these days together they finally grasp the
notion that they cannot afford to turn their back on this
relationship. With this most certain and sudden knowledge they
come to a decision: they decide that they cannot stop loving
each other, that they will not stop loving each other, that they
must believe in the future without knowing at all what it will be
like.

She experiences a change in her thinking about him, about
the two of them. She knows it is pointless to resist what he does
for her. The person she is when she's with him is someone she
hasn't met for a long time. But it doesn't matter. She will happily
greet this other person and establish some mode of cohabitation

with her. This resolution is aided by the fact that she has discovered she can even give public professional performances with him beside her. There is no contradiction here. He makes her feel strong. It isn't, as she once thought, that he ambiguously allows her to be dependent on him while loving her fake aura of independence. It is that she is capable both of being who she is and of loving him; there is no identity-merging going on after all. She has found, not lost, herself in love.

Which is not to say that the romantic rainbows surrounding their relationship have been dispersed: on the contrary, the colours glow yet more fiercely now. When they stand looking at the sea together lines from Lamartine's 'Le Lac' pour into her head: those 1817 perorations to the tubercular Julie:

> O temps, suspends ton vol! et vous, heures propices,
>   Suspendez votre cours!
> Laissez-nous savourer les rapides délices
>   Des plus beaux de nos jours![1]

—along with injunctions to the wind, the reeds, the trees, the rocks, the stars and the scents embalming the air to know such love abounds and believe in its curative beneficence. Nevertheless, what has happened now for them is that romanticism and pragmatism have joined hands. The two themes aren't fighting with one another any more. It's possible to recite Lamartine along with conference programmes and speeches about this and that. Life is a whole. They are whole together.

On their last day, they take a taxi to another town bereft of all conference colleagues. There they find a hotel in whose lobby sits imperviously a majestic grey-haired woman at a table draped in a marvellously coloured rug and crowned with flowers. She is a version of the Madame in Dickens's *A Tale of Two Cities*, who knits impassively throughout the French Revolution. This Madame in another land books rooms and exchanges any currency of travellers' cheques (with extremely mean exchange rates) and runs the entire world from her lavish vantage point: she is king, queen, prime minister, pope and insurgent revolutionary rolled into one. The hotel lobby where she sits is a vast room crammed with many gaudily wrapped tables, leather brass-studded sofas, mahogany-framed pictures and obese white cats, purring. The room overflows with great bowls of roses and carnations and chrysanthemums and every other bloom in all sorts of colours. It is a festival to celebrate something—the stable economy of the country, the immortality of love, the brevity of life.

After booking a room he voices his recurrent request: one red rose. Madame X mutters in their own language to a younger, more twentieth-century-looking woman and to an apparently deaf centenarian behind the key desk. A smile creeps unwillingly over at least one face. The younger woman selects a rose carefully from an abundant bowl and gives it to him—and he gives it to the woman with whom he has some sort of ill-defined affiliation.

She carries the rose up to their room, which is at the top of this weird building. There is a hole in the ceiling. Out of another hole in the wall stick naked electric wires. The beds are covered in clean white sheets and green-flowered duvets. The window is open, and sunless air from the canal, currently grey and motionless, blows in, disturbing the eternal lace curtains. Whatever its imperfections, the room is perfect. Moving the beds together, they lie down to make love for the last time. Since they know no one here and will never come here again, they feel there are no rules; they abide by none. She is bleeding. He bleeds with her, is covered in her blood; it streaks his chest, his arms, his legs, his hands, his penis; it lies in pools beneath them: he even wonders if she is losing their baby and is prepared, most rashly and most wrongly, to promise her another, some day.

It is late when they finally sleep. By then even the exuberant teenagers on their bicycles chatting on bridges have quietened down. Their last hours are occupied by a discussion of the details of a research project she may do one day and which he happens to think important. Then he sleeps, unmoving like a child, his face turned to her as to the sun. She watches him sleep. She watches him board his plane five hours later. She doesn't feel the desperation of loss this time. It's another kind of desperation she feels.

The War between Love and the Family III

We have been married for eighteen years. Our relationship is a source of puzzlement to many people, who are divided into two camps, one of which cannot believe that a man finds any advantage in living with me, while the other can't see why I should live with a man. There are more people in the first camp than the second, I think.

The answer to both questions can be couched in historic or pragmatic terms. As I have said I—and you—were children of our time. At that time, the time we met in the early 1960s, marriage automatically marked adulthood. Both of us wanted to have children, and said we were impressed by the inferior status and rights of children born outside marriage. A main motive on my part for marrying was to change my name. These considerations account for the decision we took in 1964 to marry one another. They do not account for why we are still married or, more important, are still living together.

The continuation of the legal state of matrimony can be dealt with in a sentence. We would have got divorced a long time ago if British law allowed one to divorce simply because one no longer wants to be married (but it doesn't). Neither of us believes in marriage as an institution. In this we differ from most other people in this society: national divorce statistics are no indication of a widespread disillusionment with marriage, for, although divorce rates are rising almost epidemically, some 50–80 per cent of divorced British couples re-enter the marital state. However, it is interesting that among women (but not among men) the length of the previous marriage is inversely related to the chances of remarriage.[1] This is one among many items of evidence suggesting that faith in marriage as the proper way to live remains, but men and women actually find it very difficult to live happily with one another.

We haven't found it easy. One of my first memories of my relationship with you is of you taking me to Cambridge to meet two friends of yours, Peter and Barbara Russell, who, you said, represented the kind of couple you wanted us to be. I recall their enormous double bed, and that we slept on their kitchen floor. A year later Peter walked into our own nuptial flat in Oxford weeping, saying, 'Barbara's left me for another man.' Barbara said she hadn't ever loved Peter, really. (They are now both quite happy with other people, but only Peter has remarried.)

The question is: in what way do we manage still to live with one another, have we managed to do so for so long? To begin at the end and work backwards, and to begin with a part of our relationship that is both not important and extremely so, the situation in 1982 is as follows:

Employment Both currently employed full-time, one on a short-term research contract, one in a supposedly secure teaching position.

Money Annual incomes roughly equal.

Childcare You do three weekdays and I do two; I do more of the weekends than you do.

Cleaning the house I do this, on Fridays, in a hurry,* but you wash the kitchen floor when our feet stick to it.

---

* There is, of course, much more to the history of my involvement in housework than this. I began in the classic mould of the houseproud housewife with severe obsessional tendencies absorbed in childhood in the normal manner. The state of our marital home reflected the state of my mind, and vice versa. It was only when I did my survey of housewives' attitudes to housework in 1969–73 that I began to understand what was going on. During this period, and for most of the subsequent eight years, I hired an assortment of other people for several hours per week to do some of the housework. These were usually women with classic obsessional tendencies themselves, which is why the arrangement worked so well (although I learned not to disclose it in women's liberation groups). The years of not being wholly responsible for the cleanliness and the tidiness of the home have had a deep psychological effect. I am now (I think) able to regard housework as just another task to be done. From the point of view of my own liberation I wish, perversely, to do it myself at least for a time in order to prove this point to my own satisfaction. This fact arouses a fair amount of guilt in Robin.

Cooking On your childcare days you cook, on mine I do (and also at weekends).

Washing up We have a dishwasher. Our son and elder daughter are supposed to take turns unloading it (how it gets loaded is nobody's business).

Food shopping You do this, weekly.

Clothes shopping I do this, for four of us.

Washing I do this as a form of therapy late at night.

Ironing My task, but it isn't therapy.

Mending clothes I do this, but it often takes years.

Money management You do this, and I make your task more difficult by not filling in the stubs of cheques and losing Barclaycard forms in the traditional feminine manner.

Mending machines etc. Amazingly, you do this (with displays of bad temper). Our son (amazingly) washes our two usually non-functioning cars when he wants more pocket money.

Gardening Some years I am intensely interested in gardening, other years not. You have a more stable attitude. Our son cuts the grass.

Animals We keep these to a minimum, but expect a visit from the RSPCA any day.

Social Life There's not a lot of it about.

As a researcher who has studied intensively the way couples organize their households, I would find the above information very difficult to classify. Is it evidence of 'joint' or 'segregated' roles?[2] It must be joint, surely, because childcare is shared. But, on the other hand, why does she do more of the inside feminine tasks (washing and ironing, for example) while he is the household and car mechanic, aided in a most undisguised sexist way by the son of the household? Why does he manage the money although she earns it? I would need more information on some items. For example, it would be of interest to know that this couple have separate bedrooms and fairly separate social lives (in so far as they have social lives at all). Is this the deciding factor that turns their role-relationship into a segregated one? Another striking fact is that there must be a lot of strain in this household because, unlike the great majority of 'dual-career families', there is no paid domestic help at all—despite the fact that the household contains one pre-school child and two not particularly helpful adolescents.

During a conversation which took place in August 1981 the following additional historical data were supplied which address other problems of the relationship as well:

Him: 'It's ridiculous to suppose that our relationship was free from sexism in the beginning. Of course it wasn't. But it never occurred to me that you'd be somebody who permanently wouldn't pursue an occupation or a career. It didn't *occur* to me.'

Her: 'But it did occur to you, because when Adam and Emily were little, I didn't "work".'

Him: 'Yes. But the only question was when you were going to go back to work. The model that I accepted then was the two-stage model with an interruption.'

Her: 'I didn't see you as somebody who valued me for my work as well. On my side, I saw *you* primarily as someone who was going to be a secure and reliable husband and father...'

Him: '...who would be involved in the care and rearing of the children.'

Her: 'Yes. I thought you'd never let me down.'

Him: 'Part of the package... A lot of sexist men are like that. Remember what we're talking about. You asked me in what way did I see our relationship at the beginning. Stick to the point. Many many men are honest and reliable, but they're sexist.'

Her: 'I saw you as somebody who'd look after me. I thought I needed looking after... I think our relationship was very sexist at the beginning, but it wasn't sexist purely in terms of your expecting me to stay at home or my expecting you to support me. It was sexist in emotional terms.'

Him: 'You mean dependence.'

Her: 'Yes. We expected it to be a relationship in which I was emotionally dependent on you, and you had some kind of collective image of your wife and children as people who needed to be protected.'

Him: 'Pussy and her babies.'

Her: 'That's right.'

Extract from letter 8.8.64 from Him in Novi Pazar, Yugoslavia, to Her in Acton, London:

'I am sitting at an old wooden table on an old wooden bench under what must be an ancient tree. In front there is a little Byzantine church of brown-tinted limestone, bright in the sun, surrounded by short grass and hard ground, which stretches about thirty yards out to a red-tiled stone wall about as tall as a man. Beyond are trees and fields and rounded forested low mountains. A black-dressed, black-hooded nun is dragging a hosepipe across the grass to water some yellow flowers. I sit here imagining in the peace and fresh warmth that you are beside me . . .'

Letter 15.8.71 from Her to Him in Ealing, London:
'Dear Dr Oakley (to be). Please put your beautiful smelly feet in this bed, and think about the future. It will not all be nights of coping with aching work-harassed wives, german-measled sons and dreaming daughters: some of it will be different. The important thing is to remember what is important. We love you with your dribbled jerseys, pseudo-halitosis, unswerving calm and incipient thesis: long live your dual/triple roles. Go to sleep thinking about chocolate pudding: rivers and island beds. Think what a contribution you have made to the world in your children and keeping me, for what I am worth, sane for seven years.'

Her: 'I think you still have that image we had at the beginning, to some extent.'

Him: 'No, it's nothing like that. No, you and the children have now to be separate entities. Because you are a separate and autonomous person—now.'

Her: 'But I'm still someone who needs to be protected and helped and supported?'

Him: 'Not in that sort of way.'

Her: 'Have you ever regretted marrying me?'

Him: 'No. Right? Any more heavy questions?'

Her: 'Why don't you regret having married me?'

Him: 'Why the hell should I? It's a silly question to ask of someone who feels basically happy and in favour of a relationship and satisfied with a relationship, do you regret marrying me? It's like saying do you regret having children. Because I have no reason to do that. Do I regret *marrying* you? Yes, I would say in a very *specific* sense, I would say I regretted marrying you, in that I regret having been constrained to marry you in terms of a legal marriage. I would much rather it was a free contractual relationship. But that's not the point you're after, is it?'

Her: 'No, what I'm after is do you regret having lived with me for eighteen years and having had three children with me?'

Him: 'Not in the slightest. The last eighteen years have been terrific.'

Her: 'But a lot of people looking at it from the outside would wonder whether it really could be so for you, because in terms of what other men have achieved, you've obviously lost out because of me.'

Him: 'Yes, but I don't sit around judging myself in terms of what other men have achieved. It may be of interest to me what other men have achieved, but that doesn't necessarily produce any standard of what I think is good or satisfying. I go by my own feelings and my own standards. Basically, I think most men lead grossly impoverished lives, certainly compared to mine, in terms of what I see as a good life.'

Her: 'What's a good life?'

Him: 'One in which people are closely in touch with other people and with their children, and do work which is intrinsically satisfying to them. I think most people fall down so badly. Most men have *no* relationship with their children, virtually no relationship with their wives, very superficial relationships with the adults they work with, thoroughly alienated work lives.'

Her: 'And you don't have any of that?'

Him: 'I don't feel I have an alienated work life, no. I feel I have a very close relationship with my children. And in terms of my own capacities and needs, a close and very rewarding relationship with you. But you have different expectations of the relationship. So I'm always aware of the possibility—the constant reality—of it being somehow viewed by you as a relationship that's inadequate in fundamental ways.'

Her: 'In what ways do you think I think it's inadequate?'

Him: 'Because it doesn't sufficiently meet certain needs that you have; your needs for intuitive understanding of your feelings and those needs, for predicting them, and being quickly responsive to them. And by implication because I'm slower than you and sometimes seem to irritate and annoy and dissatisfy you, drive you either to feelings of desperation or to trying to meet these needs in relationships with other people. I think people like you and me should be able to have good relationships and meet needs in each other, but to expect that marriage can be an institution that can totally provide for one another I now realize is very inhumane.'

Her: 'Why did you actually want a wife like me?'

Him: 'Well, I didn't quite know what I was getting! No, I wasn't aware, and this is a characteristic of my life—that I go into situations because they look interesting and exciting and I'm not capable of seeing . . . '

Her: 'So I looked interesting and exciting?'

Him: 'You made me feel good. I felt there was a tremendous amount of potential. You were very vital. You were full of interest and excitement and life.'

Her: 'Were?'

Him: 'Then—I'm talking about then, when I met you.'

Her: 'How do you see me now?'

Him: 'Much the same!'

Her: 'You'd rather have had your children with me than with anybody else?'

Him: 'I find it unbelievable that I would have had them with anybody else. I have absolutely tremendous faith and trust and love for them. I regard you all as the centre of my life. I don't know what I'd do without all of you.'

As the poet said:

. . . In order to arrive there . . .
In order to arrive at what you do not know
You must go by a way which is the way of ignorance.
In order to possess what you do not possess
You must go by the way of dispossession.
In order to arrive at what you are not
You must go through the way in which you are not.
And what you do not know is the only thing you know
And what you own is what you do not own
And where you are is where you are not.[3]

The formula changed. But it changed only gradually, and it changed only because I changed and because I wanted our relationship to change, which bears out the truth of the statement that the vested interests of all men are inevitably in the continuation of patriarchy.

Certain moments stand out: the day, when on the way to Sainsbury's, I went into a jewellers' and sold my wedding ring (I only got £4 for it because they said there was no market in second-hand wedding rings, because there is no market in second-hand marriage); the day I learnt to look at the children's window from the train on the way home from the library, and not to go home until their blind was down, so disturbing did they (initially) find the re-emergence of their mother at the end of a day when their father had been taking care of them; the day when you held our third child in your arms and said, 'I want to look after this baby, I don't want to put her in a creche.' Such trivia are only interesting to those who believe in conquering unfair tradition and see that it is a matter, not of grandiloquent statements, but of practical day-to-day details.

I don't believe we have conquered sexism, do you? We haven't found a solution, but we have arrived at a resolution. To be practical for a moment: I don't believe that anybody else is going to do as much for my children as you are. And you understand that nobody can offer your children as much as I can. My work, my freedom, is based on your willingness to relieve me of some of my oppression. Your capacity to work and your freedom are reduced but also enriched by this. So far, the services we have rendered each other far outweigh the disservices.

One might ask, why does sexism matter? Why do I want you to be fair to me, and why have you responded? Why do I go on and on about it? Why have you listened, are you still listening? I don't answer questions like that because I query the terms in which they're put. But if anyone wants an answer it is that sexism matters in the same way as slavery mattered. I'm not going to be any more philosophically sophisticated than that, at this particular moment in the history of gender.

Appendix: the disservices

A Things that annoy you about me

My driving cars very fast.
Not being able to talk as much to me as you would like; not

having enough time with me.

My not bringing hot-water bottles downstairs.

That I'm almost always right when we have a disagreement; my capacity to understand situations and have foresight.

When you like fresh air in a car and I want to keep warm.

That I'm so bloody efficient and good at everything (e.g. cooking and writing); you say you're like the moth at the light: I've got an awful lot of things that you want, that attract you. You're mesmerized.

The mess my room is usually in.

That I sometimes overreact to offhand remarks of yours.

My not sleeping.

Having problems about using the telephone because I am.

My eating puddings with a fork.

My leaving my coat in the hall while telling the children to hang theirs up (N.B. I'm getting better at this).

My insisting that you should write down things about me that annoy you.

My squeezing the toothpaste tube from the top.

PS. This is an open-ended list. I might start something new tomorrow that will annoy you.

B *Things that annoy me about you*

The noise you make when you eat.

Selective deafness: or only hearing what *other* people say.

Your terrible memory: having to make lists all the time and then forgetting them.

The way you sit with one knee on the floor.

Complaining to the children about their behaviour instead of *discussing* it with them.

Your wearing pyjamas.

The way you watch television standing in the doorway.

The way in which, on the rare occasions when I watch television, you talk all the time.

Your passivity in the face of imminent disaster (N.B. You're getting better about this).

Your always coming back to fetch something you've forgotten when you go out.

Bananas in brandy.

Your problems in thinking and planning ahead.

Your fussing about the way I squeeze the toothpaste tube.
PS. I don't think this an open-ended list.

To summarize: I don't believe it really is a war we are fighting any more.

But neither do we, nor should we, dwell in total harmony and peace. I'm not likely to give you the chance to do that, am I?

Reminders of the
Unmentionable

I am resentful of the fact that on such a bright, hopeful, sunny day it is my task not to enjoy it but to visit the cancer clinic.

Walking to the hospital is not itself an unpleasant task. I pass Big Ben, the Houses of Parliament, St Margaret's, Westminster, tourists in groups rubbing their cold hands and surveying each glossy chauffeur-driven car for its quite possibly titillating contents. There are crocodiles of schoolchildren too, looking pale and undernourished, but impressed by this temporary redefinition of what education means. I notice for the first time (why the first?) the statue of Emmeline Pankhurst in the little park by the river Thames. By the time I reach the flower stall where loving and unloving visitors buy overpriced daffodils, I feel sick: I just want it to be over. I want to be coming out of the hospital, not going into it. But will I be? I always think there is a possibility I will never come out of those doors again. Now, this is obviously silly. I feel well. There is nothing wrong with me that time and experience won't cure.

I visit the ladies on the way up to the clinic, because I know the wait will be a long one. I open the door on a lady who didn't lock it, who is busy rearranging an enormous number of underclothes, including some particularly enclosing tights. Turning into the clinic, which is on the second floor, I am confronted by just exactly what I feared: rows and rows of drab people, mostly old, mostly with yellow faces and clothes drooping loosely off them. They sit there with such resignation.

I hand my card to the receptionist, who is happily not the bossy one, the one who makes me feel like a naughty child (a feeling that comes easily to me in such places). I sit down and try not to observe the moment when my notes are taken off by the officious nurse who weighs us in case we are wasting away to nothing and haven't noticed. Ten minutes later, 'Shoes off, please,' she says, 'and your jacket.' 'Why?' I say. 'Because that's the rule.' 'I've been coming here for four years, and I've never been asked to do that before,' I say. 'What goes for one, goes for all,' she reprimands. All I'm interested in is not doing what I'm told and retaining some self-respect in this un-self-respecting situation.

Five minutes later the nurse passes me taking a bundle of notes into one of the two large rooms either side of the waiting room which house those kings, the doctors, presiding in their stiff white coats over pages of stiff white notes, turning their eyes and minds and hands and instruments from time to time to us, their captive subjects, who only sit and wait. The whole system took me some time to fathom. The first conspiracy against the patients is that the doctors never come on time and are constantly leaving to do other things. The second is that it doesn't matter when your appointment is, you get processed in the order in which you come. The third is that you can never tell when you're going to be summoned to the regal presence—you can't even tell from watching and counting the people there before you, for only some need couches to be examined and some can be done on chairs; it depends on where you had (have) cancer as to when you will go in, and *that* you can't tell from just looking at people. So, whatever one does while waiting is liable to be interrupted within a few minutes or after a few hours. It's like childrearing; the constant possibility of interruptions saps the concentration, to the point where the mind altogether loses its capacity to focus itself.

One of the doctors has just pranced past me. He has a fat bulbous face and fishy eyes and straw-coloured hair. His white coat is a bit long (his legs are a bit short). He wears it tightly buttoned, like his face. He thinks he is important. When he walks past us he doesn't look at us because that, too, is against the rules. The officious weighing nurse stops to tie the shoelaces of a man who is too weak to tie his own. That reminds me of the time when someone just fell forward and died in this clinic while waiting to see the doctor. That is the logical conclusion of the system: you make the patients wait so long that they give up and die and then you don't have to see them after all.

I arrived here at eleven fifteen. It is now twelve o'clock. Why don't we all get up and leave? A powerful fantasy: if all the patients got up and silently trooped out, off to do better things, to give their flowers back to the flower-seller, to catch a plane to Shanghai, to have another baby, to eat a very large rump steak, to take a boat ride down the Thames, what would the doctors do then, poor things? Yet we don't do it, and we won't. I hear a woman behind me say to the next one, 'You could go to sleep here.' The other says, in return, 'I didn't sleep at all last night.' 'I know the feeling well,' the first one says. The conversation becomes more precise. It's about cysts and X-rays. I hope they both survive. I hope we all do. That is, of course, why we don't leave. We have this suspicion that we need the doctors—that there are things they can do to us that will make the boat ride, the rump steak, and the vistas of unvisited places, just that little bit more likely.

A blind man walks past. A woman with an artificial leg is weighed (I notice the nurse didn't tell her to take that off). There are not so many people left here now. Do they all have tongues to be examined? I am hungry. I want a cup of coffee. I want to go home. Most of all I want to go home. Perhaps the doctors have gone home? I'm sure I will see a new young man today, one whose professional role is not yet comfortable to him. Shall I put him at his ease? Patients have surreptitious forms of power. Oh God (who can't help me), I only want it to be over. A nurse in a blue maternity dress has lost a patient. A defaulter! In a few minutes I am going to default, too. I shall tell everyone I've been for my check-up and I won't have been. No one will ever know the difference.

Twelve sixteen. Why am I the only one who looks impatient? It is at this point that I always think they've lost my notes. When I went for my first postnatal examination in 1967 I waited three hours and they had lost my notes; they told me to eat plenty of spinach instead. (I'd better warn the new young doctor about my dirty tongue. The children have flu and I've had a bad night. Otherwise he might think the whole thing's gone rotten on him.)

Twelve twenty-six. This time last week I was in ecstasy. Now I am in agony. Perhaps it would be better if neither of these states occurred. The man next to me is smoking. He reminds me of my father and my father's last request. We all choose our own poison. An atmosphere of quiet has descended on the clinic. I think they're going to lock us up until tomorrow.

Twelve fifty. The nurse occupying the doorway to the right-hand room calls out 'Mrs Oakley'. As usual, I look round for my mother-in-law. I am directed to the usual narrow cubicle. 'Sit on the red chair,' she says, as she always does. I take my coat off and my book out of my bag (*Professional or Public Health* by Raymond Illsley). However, I am only two pages into 'Medicine as a system of social control' when a young man comes up behind me and into the room. 'Hallo,' he says, and smiles. I smile back. 'How are you?' he asks with deep meaning. 'Fine,' I say, 'how are you?' A little disconcerted, he transfers his eyes to my notes. 'Was it last time you came,' he asks, 'or the time before, that I read your article?' I am sufficiently taken aback by this to attempt to read the label on his coat. A Dr Pickering. 'Well, it was published a long time ago,' I said. 'That's right, I was most impressed by it.' What happens now? Do we move on to the unequal part of our relationship? I decide not yet, savour the moment. 'I had a lot of letters in response to that piece,' I offer. 'Who from?' he responds eagerly. 'From radiotherapists, GPs, some from patients.' 'What did they say?' he pursues. 'They said,' I enunciate carefully, 'that they thought I was right, that doctors find it hard to talk about cancer. As hard or harder than patients do.' 'I'm sure that's right.' He smiles again. 'Why is it, do you think?' 'For all of us,' I tell him, 'cancer is such a terrible word. And people do die of it.' 'But they also die of other things, for instance chronic heart disease,' he points out, not believing his own point. 'When you say' (I hardly let him finish his sentence, so keen am I to make the observation) 'that one out of five people dies of cancer, that sounds awful, but when you say four out of five don't, that sounds much better.' 'The old statistics thing,' he counters, wanting to agree with me.

He looks at me like a statistic, then. He moves his facing chair closer to mine so my legs are between his own and in this clinically intimate position examines my neck, mildly, pausing over the slight protuberance that has been there since my neck was first examined in 1977. 'That's okay,' he remarks, not casually. I warn him about my dirty tongue. 'I'm probably getting flu myself,' I say, 'you ought to stay away from me, but you can't do that, can you?' He laughs and puts on what I always think of incorrectly as the miner's lamp these doctors wear, consisting of a mirror stuck on a broad rubber band encircling the medical head and designed to reflect a light behind the patient into the patient's mouth, thus illuminating all its dreadful crevices. Dr Pickering peers into my mouth and asks me to stick my tongue out, an act that remains faintly painful and which I have sometimes committed in anger, but not now. Next he places a rubber condom on his finger and runs it gently along the side of my tongue. I try to keep my tongue relaxed, knowing that if I stiffen it in the places where the biopsy was done and where the wires went in and out it could feel maliciously angular to him. 'That's fine,' he says, again. He himself has visibly relaxed. 'How long is it since you were treated?' 'Four years,' I say. 'That makes it pretty unlikely that. . . ' he leaves the sentence uncompleted, 'doesn't it?' 'Yes,' I say, 'I don't think about it all the time any more. I did at first.' 'I bet you did,' he says.

We talk about the attitudes of people who have cancer. He tells me that even some 'intelligent' people don't want to know. They don't, according to him, want to confront the problem. I tell him I can't understand that. I think, but do not say, that he will be a good doctor one day. 'When do you want me to come again?' I ask, finally, feeling anxious to conclude the encounter, now that the important business has been transacted. 'Six months,' he says.

The panic, which was really only momentary, has receded. *Why* did I panic? I can't remember. I fly speedily down the stairs and out of the hospital into the burning white light of the day. Until my reprieve, I saw the houses and the streets and parks and people and, yes, even the flowers, in monochrome; now they are outrageously coloured, like a Gauguin painting.

SCENE 14

Movements in the Clouds

It is winter again. Is it the winter of their discontent?

She returns to the snow-filled city where once they met, not to meet him but to give some lectures. There are golden buildings here that she didn't notice before, rectangular against dancing snowflakes. The snow is everywhere. It glistens, rises, shakes into a fine powder, forms cruel icicles that hang like a greasy fringe over the tops of the windows. It is piled in the streets and on the coloured roofs: it is ploughed out of the way by persistent gentlemen wearing earmuffs in yellow machines. When you go out here, you wear a lot of clothes, but, even so, the snow and the ice cling to you in frozen lumps, won't leave you alone.

The lectures go well. People seem to be pleased with her. They are serious and nod in agreement. Even the criticism is passed in a muted and courteous way. The culture, being a formal one, throws up a series of social engagements in which one scarcely dare relax for fear of getting something wrong. She is introduced to the Prime Minister, and doesn't know what to do with the cocktail sticks with which the sausages are speared at the reception in the Government's festal suite. She discovers that the people she meets don't understand the meaning of certain key words in her vocabulary. She meets a cheerful iron woman from Moscow and tells her something about her own country she doesn't already know. Her sisters say to her, if you can't answer a question at the conference, just say you're a witch. Witch-like, she is, for a change, in control. She, too, is strong. On the frozen sea with a friend she begins to learn to ski for the first time; moving not so slowly along, getting used to two-metre-long feet, seeing the way the skis cut neat tracks in the still-falling snow.

On her way home she stops off in another country to meet him. This new airport—new to her and also new in a more general sense—is almost deserted when she arrives: and he is not there to meet her. He arrives a few minutes later, and as he bends to kiss her, she senses in him a fire of anger against her and their situation that masquerades as love, as pleasure to see her, as desire to touch and enter her and claim her body as his again.

'I don't want to go on being obsessed with you like this,' he says. 'I can't work, and I must work, you must help me. We have to reduce the intensity of our feelings for one another. I can't go on spending so much time and energy running around looking for telephones to ring you, arranging professional meetings to facilitate ours. We can't live without one another; but we can't live with one another either. Think of our children, our different countries.' But then again, 'I love you. I want to be able to love you for ever. One day I shall live with you, we will live together. I want you to marry me: we shall give each other gold rings and promises, and the snowflakes will fall like confetti on our heads.'

The next morning she gives him a letter in which she states what could be seen as an ultimatum. The letter is about lying. 'Lying is done with words, and also with silence . . . In speaking of lies, we come inevitably to the subject of truth. There is nothing simple or easy about this idea. There is no "the truth", "a truth"—truth is not one thing, or even a system. It is an increasing complexity. The pattern of the carpet is a surface. When we look closely, or when we become weavers, we learn of the tiny multiple threads unseen in the overall pattern, the knots on the underside of the carpet.

'That is why the effort to speak honestly is so important. Lies are usually attempts to make everything simpler—for the liar— than it really is, or ought to be.

'In lying to others we end up lying to ourselves. We deny the importance of an event, or a person, and thus deprive ourselves of a part of our lives.'[1]

For some years now he has lied about her, deceived his wife into believing the relationship is over. Well, it certainly isn't news to her that he is full of contradictions, too. It isn't news that he can lie so effectively to one woman and conceal nothing from another; that he resents the fascination the second woman holds for him while, at the same time, wanting it to endure untarnished, always.

She has decided that at this meeting she will not allow any negative experience to mar the few hours they have together. They have had a bad time, recently. They have had some bad telephone conversations and she once stood there with a bottle of pills in one hand and the telephone in the other trying to make him understand how his definition of the situation—the need to pit passion against domesticity, the need to lie in order to delve further into the truth—was destroying all of them: him, his wife, her, their relationship, her family. So now, sitting next to him, or walking along with him or lying beside him, she will not allow desperation and anger to move to the fore. But he will. He is determined. He tries a series of strategies to provoke her, beginning with 'How can I ever trust you, knowing you may have had other lovers, besides me?'—hardly an original or particular question. And eventually she is provoked by him into being a little upset. She falls silent across the table in the restaurant, and he does too, not looking at her. The flame of the candle flickers unkindly on his face, etching its sullenness, its coldness, the hard lines of an unreceptive country. 'I hate women. I hate all women. I'm glad I hate women,' he says. 'Women aren't worth loving or respecting. They're only worth exploiting. They don't deserve the truth.' 'Well,' she says, after some reflection, 'what man, properly brought up, does not hate women? The art of survival lies in the transcendence of gender. That is the lesson the two of us are only able to learn from each other. That is the essential fascination: our hatred of the other sex as a class, our raging infantile self-love, which we find mirrored in the other, for at heart what we each love in the other is what we each love in ourselves.'

Exhausted, they fall asleep enclosed in each other's arms. A noise wakes her. Someone screaming. Her. She is shaking. She didn't know it was she who screamed, nor why she did so; it wasn't a dream, or a nightmare, just a single high tense note arising out of the black void of sleep. He is terrified. He wants to protect her and save her from every awful fate, from the voice of her unconscious that shrieks the truth, from every sort of human or natural holocaust (and coming suddenly out of sleep himself, he cannot immediately tell the difference). His arms around her express what words cannot—or what he cannot express in words. She is a rose enfolded in an iron lung, a secret locked away from the world.

The next day they fly together crisply through the blue sky above a white fleecy field of clouds. This is the first time they have actually sat together on an aeroplane—a momentous occasion. On the way to the plane he keeps asking people to make sure they have actually been allocated seats together: 4A and 4C but whatever happened, he asks the stewardess, to 4B? 'I don't know,' she responds, and smiles. They touch as the plane takes off and points its firm line upwards. There are movements in the clouds as the plane passes through them.

Outside the airport where they are to change planes and go in opposite directions, they stand looking at the grey sky, grey landscape, icy sea. His country. She opens her coat and her blouse and he bends down and takes one breast in his mouth, then the other: he is both son and lover, extracting from her every drop of nourishment she is able to give. As he does that, she sees behind him over a low, gently curved mountain outside the city far away the sun rapidly and generously burst out of ashen clouds.

What is the meaning of passion, anyway?

The sun is setting on his country. A strip of pink joins the low mountains to the white basin of the sky. She sits watching and waiting in the airport lounge for her own departure. She reads a book, *Mirror Writing*:

> This caused me to reflect on the whole notion of continuous identity and to wonder why we accept so readily the Freudian belief that identity does not change significantly in adult life. Our lives change, our situations, our luck—do we bring essentially the same 'character', the same 'personality' to new situations, or do external changes break up and reform our fluid 'selves' as stones and boulders divert a stream of water?[2]

In front of her on the aircraft there is an unaccompanied child, about eight, with a white face. He crayons determinedly throughout the voyage, belongs to no one.

After the plane has landed, she turns to look back down the runway. Another plane is lowering itself out of the blackness like a triangular glowworm, following exactly the same path to the terminal building, but with a number of minor variations induced by human whims, if not errors, and invisible to the naked but incurious eye.

In the Heat of the Day

In the mornings she feels quite calm. The stalks of corn line up across the newly sown field by the side of the house, their creamy tops creating a disturbance in a solid line of green. In front of the house stands a tall cypress tree like a flagpost. Across the road are fields of tobacco and more corn (the corn is mostly used for fattening the livers of geese), and then the haze-hung violet of mountains inserts itself between the fertile land and the changing sky, this morning silver instead of blue, with a sharp wind in place of yesterday's deadening heat. To the back of the house is a dark forest. On the other side a farm, where a loudmouthed farmer daily berates his cows, moving the animals with red flags along the main road to and from their pasture. He keeps a score of noisy geese and chickens as well, and there are times when his garden is full of people shouting to one another in a broad regional accent, unrecognizable as classroom French; the animals shout, too, in choruses paced to fit the times and places of nature—dawn, sunset, the first falling of the dew, the quick drenching of the landscape by sudden storms, that makes the cows especially bray in an elemental panic.

A mouse scurries up the kitchen wall. Flies, mosquitoes, moths and sundry other bits of wildlife dash around in the sky and in the upper halves of the stone-floored rooms. It is peaceful. The telephone will not ring. The postman will not come. Friends will not call; the television will not project its tawdry soul into the room. This is a protected place. It is an atom of rural France with its twentieth-century modalities still comfortingly suggestive of much older peasant habits. Medieval shepherds' families in Montaillou, a village not so far from here, never washed: a strong odour was a good sign, a sign of humanity. De-lousing was a companionable act; lovers did it, so did the priests. Wetnurses became stoutfaced farmers' wives; children often died but not without being first treasured and later mourned. Time was marked visually, aurally, or simply physiologically: after sunset, at the hour of the first sleep, when the cock has crowed three times. Weeks and the lunar month didn't matter very much; the 'half year' meant the important change from winter to summer pasturage. Geography was not a question of North or South but of beyond the mountains; towards the sea. The peasants appreciated beauty but it was, most surprisingly, human beauty they liked, for nature presented them with too many problems. Morality corresponded only vaguely to the tenets of Catholicism. Guillaume Bayard, a magistrate of Sabarthès, slept with two pairs of sisters. They were called Gaude, Blanche, Emersende and Arnaude.

'How could you sleep with two sisters?' he was asked.

'If I had slept with women close to me in blood, I would have committed a shameful act. But with two sisters! No, really. It's of no importance. Mere trifles.'[1]

The farmer who calls today (to repair the plumbing—one of his wells has dried up) looks as though, except for his rattling Peugeot, he could have come from any century. He is an inheritor of the native practices of this place. (His name, Recurt, is that of a village ten kilometres away.) His brown face speaks not of a wisdom forged by a life close to nature but of an enclosed attitude: this is how life is, how human beings are, how can it be any other way? Indeed, how can it? The rural rituals have a quietening influence. The sun induces a slowed-down mind. On the surface the woman in the rented farm house begins to relax; she doesn't rush around any more making lists of things never to be forgotten, emitting instructions in the terse Morse code of her stressed domestic voice. But underneath the battle rages. Underneath she is nearer to, not further away from, the crisis; and when the sun goes in and the cornfields drip with black dew, and huge beetles hurl themselves at the primitive electric lights, and enormous moths with red painted wings affix themselves unwelcomed to the flowered walls, and the cicadas hum with their degenerate frenzy, she knows that she is being taken over by the problem, the problem that can so well be named but is so irremediably without solution.

Love pulls, in every direction. Back into the past, now in this moment, forward into the plausible and glistening moments of the future. Love fights the morality of a belief in autonomy, the particular autonomy of women. Loyalty, duty, and an other-oriented compassion mock the paltry pretence of love: what is love? It could be a primitive puzzle: two men, one woman, or, even, two men and two women. It is the puzzle of pleasing dependence on the one hand and bravery to make one's way alone on the other. It is the security of habit versus enormous risks: the safe squat home facing the limitless, swallowing, exciting ocean. It is love of one kind and love of another. It is a love of all kinds. The pale ingenuous face of a child, the strength of one coming into adulthood: their nexus of needs. It is his love for her: proud and fierce and unaccepting, and hers for him: flattered, strong and resentful. It is their familiar married love as well, and familiarity doesn't only breed contempt, it breeds peace. Isn't peace what she wants? What the world needs!

It is the morning again, but it was the night; a night of sleeplessness, of terror. Falling quickly into a brandy-soaked sleep she wakes, alert, at three o'clock. She opens the shutters and looks out into the coalblack night—not a star, not the slightest hope for the sun tomorrow in sight. She feels breathless, as though she is suffocating. Going back to bed she leaves the shutters open to move air around the room. She breathes deeply, and tries to clear her mind of the obstinate circular thoughts that occupy it. But her mind, like the night, remains clouded.

The little girl wakes, is hot, complains of pain. She sits on the blue plastic pot and there are little white worms in her shit. She doesn't see them, only says, 'Is it morning, can I read? I want to read in bed with Mum.' Mum is reading a silly book about a Chicago adolescent called *Endless Love*. She's glad to finish it, but, the little girl sleeping again, she finds not even this bad literary product can put her to sleep. She lies with the light on, listening. Breathing sounds; something in the field outside? Are there foxes in the wood? Or other dreadful animals passing through the cornfields at night? The worms, a common enough childish ailment, seem intensely significant. They stand for decay, a rotting death that starts inside and then creeps out, signalling the body's invasion. She shudders to think that human beings can harbour such parasites, even though she knows that their bodies and minds are open house to all sorts of parasites, all the time.

At six thirty she gives up the effort to sleep. She opens the wooden door and looks out across the field with the cypress tree in it to the road and beyond, to the mountains. The sky is grey. It is raining slightly, although warm. The mountains can't be seen behind a thin screen of mist. The grass and trees and shrubs are lush and dark, dripping jungle fluids. The concrete path is darkened for two-thirds of its length with soaked-up rain. At its edge lies a mahogany red beetle, two to three inches long, on its back clawing the air with six slightly furry limbs. Its eyes are black eggs on stalks. As it gesticulates at the morning it moves slowly along, an inch every five minutes or so, making a scrunching sound against the concrete. The rain falls in its unearthly eyes. It has got stuck in a dip in the path, a half-inch-wide line along the border. The only progress it makes is to edge further up this indentation. Nothing it does will turn it on its front and set it free.

The cockerels and the chickens begin to chatter. The birds are already doing so. Cars begin to pass more frequently on the road in front of the house, headlights on, speeding to and from the south, to and from work. The house itself is absolutely silent except for the occasional hum of electricity.

The beetle's movements grow weaker now. At times there are no movements at all, then they start, uncoordinated. The black eyes seem to look into her own, beseeching. Wildly, the limbs move again; another inch, still on its slimy back. What fate condemns this beetle to die like this? What fate makes sure she doesn't sleep, is crowded with terror, with thoughts of her own execution? Perhaps that's what the beetle is committing— beetle-cide. Perhaps in a depressed, absent-minded mood it fell into this mistaken crevice, a half-willed act. Perhaps it doesn't really want to live; perhaps those eyes are saying, 'You and I are in the same boat. Animals decayed by time, parasites and circumstance. The only difference is that you think—have thought—yourself greater than I, being so-called human, having supposedly a helpful intelligence.'

She picks up a black twig from the grass and pokes it at the beetle, prising it over on to its stomach. Its back gleams blackly. It is completely stunned, doesn't move. Then slowly it begins to flex its limbs and it moves round in a circle, as though testing itself and its territory. It arches its back, dances a little. Is it happy to be saved?

Rain falls more heavily now, large splashes making darker circles on the concrete path and channels through the grass and trees. There is no end to the life of the countryside. Beetles and raindrops fall back into the rhythm of things, alive or dead, it matters not so much at all. But human life? The life of one conflicted urban woman in the twentieth century?

I love you, she said, whoever you are and whoever I am. Life is only as good as you make it. I can't make it good any more.

In the end no man was enough. In the end no child could patch the yawning blackness in her head. In the end no one else was a reason for living: faith had to come from within, but within was no faith. So she finally took responsibility for her own life in a way that she always knew she would—being in the end just another woman: having lain there and shed over her chosen grave the hope that one day such acts of violence would be transcended, that women one day would feel enabled to rise above the problems, would find and hold the key to the conflicts of love or whatever it is that tears them apart and rots even their living flesh, would open their eyes and see a better world which made sense to them, of which they could make sense, so that they themselves would do the overcoming, no longer being overcome by it.

Every day in England and Wales eleven people take their own lives; suicides represent something under 1 per cent of total deaths each year, and the rates have been increasing over the last five years.[2]

Suicide may be defined as 'self-killing deriving from one's inability or refusal to accept the terms of the human condition'. Suicide is therefore largely rational: 'the real problem is life itself'.[3] Suicide is self-hate. Suicide is a feminine answer, a cultural solution. Against all the evidence—of their own creative power, of their sensitivity and genius—women feel they are worthless creatures. There is no doubt that in Western culture women think this more than men. Equally, there is no doubt that they try suicide more often, less often meaning to succeed than men, but sometimes succeeding when they mean to fail.[4] No one who hasn't contemplated suicide can understand the source or torture of the desire. It is, above all, a desire to escape. 'I've had enough.' Enough of what? Of feeling, of remorse, of self-hatred, of guilt, of depression, of midnight sweats and early-morning panics; I am tired of waiting for the sun to rise, for the wet fields to let the sun succour them, for things to be all right. Suicide is a way of clearing the head. Antonin Artaud, who lived mostly in lunatic asylums, remarked, 'If I commit suicide, it will not be to destroy myself but to put myself back together again.'[5] Or, as a French student said in protest against the Biafran war, 'I'm against war, violence, and the destructive folly of men [and women]... If I die, do not weep. I have done it because I could not adapt myself to this world.'[6]

It's also true that suicide is a great passion, like love. In both, as our cultural mentor Freud said, the ego becomes overwhelmed by the object. A Polish girl, finding herself in the grip of an unhappy love affair, swallowed a five-inch brass cross, one hundred and one pins, two rosary beads, twenty nails and seven window bolts, amongst other things.[7] That seems a little extreme, if not painful, but there is no end to human inventiveness even *at* the end.

Sylvia Plath's last poems record the dreadful disillusionment and hatred one feels for oneself at the moment when suicide is seriously contemplated:

The hills step off into whiteness.
People or stars
Regard me sadly, I disappoint them

—a poem completed two weeks before she died. She regarded herself at this point as powered only by the biological mechanics of her body, as in another poem, 'Paralytic':

My god the iron lung

That loves me, pumps
My two
Dust bags in and out
Will not

Let me relapse

but they did. In her last poem, 'Edge', she describes the dead
woman as perfected—only in death, because it abolishes the
object that is hated, can perfection lie.[8]

Note on the Ultimate Contradiction

Well, it is, isn't it?

It's the contradiction between a woman wanting to live and a woman not being able to bear it any more. Between the insult of having disease take you over and decide things for you, and insisting on your own right to determine your exit from the world. What could be more contradictory?

Think about it: most of the important bits of human life are built around one contradiction or another.

Flaubert wrote a letter to Louise Colet explaining that he could never see a cradle without thinking of a grave.[1]

In the *Forty-Seventh Annual Report of the Local Government Board 1917–18* it is written that 'a life saved is but a death postponed'.[2]

If people grew throughout their lives at the same rate as they do during the latter part of their sojourn in the womb, each of us would weigh two trillion times as much as the earth does.[3]

In a patriarchal and patrilineal society, children only belong to men because women tell men they provided the sperm to start them off, but who actually did so must remain, to all men, a matter of conjecture. Moreover, frightened slaves are not in the best position to be counted on to tell the truth. Moreover, it is extremely important that men can identify children as their legal and social possessions.

A baby is salvation and damnation. Out of that utter dependence is bred utter resentment; babies are the most-loved and most-hated people of all. The cry that never stops in the night that's never over turns the beloved pearl-soft face into a white skull round a square black hole and the well-integrated housewife (and her husband if he is there) into a violent screaming wreck. Yet they forgive us. Children store up treasures for the future but not memories to hold against us; in this is hope.

A love affair between a man and a woman, which seems in the golden splendour of its initial heat destined to outlive Armageddon, is by nature evanescent; the flames eventually are dwarfed, the coals lose their glow, each spark becomes more and more solitary. 'So you no longer play tennis, no longer move from place to place in the summer, no longer understand what use you can make of the sight of the Andes or the columns of Luxor.'[4] But tell that to the united couple and you will hear incredulous laughter.

Men and women believe that they are one another's best friends. But who, in the act of dying, remembers an orgasm of twenty years ago, or is thankful for a thousand sinks of dirty dishes washed by one of the opposite sex?

And, talking of explosions, consider this: that the nuclear catastrophe when it comes will not come upon us out of the blue at all. It will be a consequence of a million other disasters, trivial mistakes we all, in our time, have made. These constitute the real tragedy.

Why, then, should the wish to live and the wish to die be seen as opposed? They are both solutions. Everything that is negative is also positive and goodness has its blackened other face. The eternal is soon over. Life is a fatal illness; love between man and woman doesn't last. Some of the most important kinds of knowledge are the subject of mere guesswork. Forgiveness cancels out anger. Remember that.

In these ways there is nothing odd about women—nothing inhuman about them. All human beings are in the same leaky boat. There is nothing odd about the woman who is 'she' in this book, either. I have used her as a paradigm of all the contradictions to which modern woman is exposed. She is a literary device, fictional in her own manner. In addition a man like that—so magical and so beastly—has to be an invention; who could possibly imagine that he was real? I can't do better than quote from a very intelligent and amusing novel by Nancy Thayer on the trials of step-parenthood:

Last night I dreamed a beautiful and erotic dream. I went into a house, and there was Count Dracula, very aristocratic and handsome and mysterious. I fell in love with him and embraced him: merely embraced him, we did not kiss. I yearned to be with him, he was so tempting, and yet I knew everything about him was dangerous and wrong, and yet that only made him more attractive. I finally left his house, to walk in a garden, to think, to try to decide whether I would choose to live with him, really live with him or not. There were heavy moral and religious questions involved, I knew. I had to do serious thinking, but underneath it all . . . I was so happy, so exquisitely happy.

I wonder who Dracula is for me. Help, Freud.[5]

Fortunately, Freud isn't available for consultation. (How much would he charge, if he were?) My story, which I have also recited in this book, has lessons of its own.

Remember Me

◯

This ending was actually her first choice.

Actually, there were four possible solutions to the affair and the problems it posed or re-evoked, viz:

death—physical, of one or both
death—of the relationship
life—living together
life—living apart

It is interesting that she only ever saw one pathway to the first solution—her own death. She did not particularly feel she wanted to kill him. (Although at moments when things were very difficult she would mentally line the whole of his family unit up against a grey brick wall and shoot them neatly one by one.) It is interesting, too, that despite her playing at times over the years with the idea of terminating the relationship, she only seriously felt this threat emanating from him; that is, she could make a decision *intellectually* to withdraw from the relationship, but only he could do so effectively (effectively for whom?) *emotionally*. He seemed to her to be the one with the power to turn away, with the capacity to reject love and its embodiment. She was right about this, for the facile resolution of problems by denial is, and has been, a most significant strand in the historical articulation of patriarchy.

And so it was important that this particular truth become not only clear to her, but perceived by her as a viable basis operationally for her emergence from the affair (as a newly or partially autonomous person).

'Well,' she said, greeting him for the nth time, 'how are you?' He
looked surprised, not expecting to be answerable as to the
niceties of his state of health; expecting to be told rather than
asked, as had been customary in their relationship, as was
customary in the relationship between men like him and women
like her (women of the sort he believed she was). 'What's the
matter?' he asked suspiciously, not quite understanding what he
might have to be suspicious about. She shrugged the question
off. He turned to look at her as she drove away from the airport.
Slightly suntanned from her recent holiday, auburn hair longer
on her shoulders, fingers naked of rings curled casually round the
steering wheel. She had, he thought, a hard edge to her that she
hadn't had before: an invisible film of metal separated her from
him. 'I don't like your mood,' he said, churlishly.

'Don't think I've become hard,' she replied. 'That's only how
you have been trained to see it and I to act it. What I have
become is tired. I am tired not of you or of love, but of what you
and love do to me.'

'What do I do?' he asked.

'You say one thing and mean another, or mean something you
can't say. You pretend to be overendowed with the ability to act
while cowering passively in the shadow of your dilemma: your
family or love? Her, or me? You glorify "control"—no tears,
statements of feeling, dependence, need or weakness—when you
cannot even recognize what it is you want to control or why. You
cope by closing your eyes. But I do not want to love a man who
doesn't see that he's blind.

'Shall I give you,' she went on, 'a history of our relationship in
a nutshell?' (How could he refuse such a generous offer?) 'There
you were at a certain stage in your life, however many years ago,
looking for some excitement. There I was, in a not dissimilar
position. The sun was shining. The flowers were blooming. We
fell in love. Through separation we kept up the magic for a long
time; each was for the other an escape, a vision of pure
happiness. You lied in order to maintain our relationship, while I
told the truth in order to do so. Eventually I objected to being
lied about (perhaps you objected to being told the truth about).
Eventually you started to tell your wife the truth, and then,

seeing her reaction, hastily stopped and began to lie again. "The relationship is over," you said. If she believed you, it was because she wanted to. I do not think you are an especially good liar, though I appreciate that being a liar has been quite important to the furtherance of your professional career, given that the reputation of ambitious men is considerably enhanced by having a wife and children at home and a mistress in every port. Am I being unkind? You must understand that I am an oppressed person, whereas you are not.

'After some years of this, during which we continued to meet, continued to experience one another with much passion and— dare I say it—understanding, someone else told your wife "the truth" for the second time, i.e. that her husband was in love and in constant contact with "that woman". Angry, she turned against you. Temporarily. And then (from what precise motive I do not know) hurled herself back at you, children cleanly dressed and expectantly in tow: "Look at us, how we have been wronged," she cried, "do us the honour of making us a proper family again!"

'If I remember correctly, I was abroad when you went back to her. I only knew because when I rang the telephone number of the flat where you were supposed to be staying there was no answer. You were "at home" watching the World Cup on television (no doubt with your dog on one side and your wife on the other). Sitting on the grimy floor of a German telephone box at 3 am one night I came to bemoan the fact that so much of significance in my life had been lived in telephone boxes. It was also there that I finally knew a man like you can't be saved. You had betrayed me (my trust in you) but much more important you had betrayed yourself. Not in going back—oh no; for who am I to condemn someone I love to living alone, to living apart from their children? Not for going back did I despise you, but for not seeing what it meant to go back, what it would mean for your wife and children, what a fictitious promise it would be for them, what it would mean for me, for me and you.

'I threw away your ring. Yes, you had given me a ring. One day it disappeared out of my bedroom window, soaring like a bird into someone's unpruned roses. Mentally I threw you away too. And diligently, by stages and by stealth, you crept back again, reinserting yourself in my heart and my life. "I'll lie again," you said. "Anything to keep this relationship going. I can't get you out of my mind or my life."

'But you did try, didn't you? You even brandished some theories in front of me about "changing the relationship". I never knew what you meant, except that for some extraordinary reason you chose to believe in a theory and not in me, or in us.

'Shall I tell you something I've never told you before? You have no courage. And you have no courage because you run away from everything that is real and difficult. You want love without commitment, joy without pain, loyalty without intimacy, privilege without responsibility.

'Yes, I know you love me. I know this isn't just any relationship. But I am not just anybody, despite the way I may have felt (been made to feel) sometimes. If you won't fight with me, I won't fight against you. To put it plainly, I won't be lied about any more under any circumstances—not because I regard it as my right to interfere with your conduct of your life—I don't—but because in lying about me you move further and further away from knowing what it is you feel, or who you are, or that you might, in fact, behind that stiff and incurious façade, actually be a person who can love himself and hence be worth loving.'

When he had left she felt relieved. She felt she had reclaimed and not lost a part of herself, whilst remaining grateful to him for the way he had loved her, without which she would never have stood and faced herself.

'Remember me,' she would have said to him, had she given herself or him the chance, 'remember my voice as it first spoke to you, my arms as they first enfolded you, my breasts as we first kissed, my tears as they first anointed you, my cries as you were first stirred by them. What happened in the beginning happened in the end. We never lost the sweetness, never would have done. Remember all the countries, all the cities, all the places, all the exotic and ordinary airs; the English flowers and smooth lake of the first spring; the strawberries on the harbour steps of the first northern summer; the bleached lunar landscape of the third winter; all the music we heard and made, all the harvested fields and unclimbed mountains of our wanderings. Remember us. Our conjugations and conversations, our hesitations and deliberations, our pleasure, our pain, our power and our glory.

'What has been should not be regretted. The proper use of memory is for liberation—from false hopes of the future as well as from enslavement to past actions and desires. Did we love or only desire? Don't let your memory rewrite the past. Remember me.'

CHRONOLOGY 33–38

These are years of retrenchment rather than advance. Age doesn't always wither, but nor does it rejuvenate; I am aware of the passing of time, yet feel that time 'stands still'. Time is my enemy. To relinquish my grandiose and not-so-grandiose plans even temporarily in order to sleep is hard. For years I have only been able to sleep if there is no clock or watch in the room; only if there is no mechanical measuring of time visibly in progress do I feel free to waste it in sleep.

After Laura's birth and the diagnosis and treatment of cancer, I retreated into domesticity. The most interesting aspect of this move was that I still bore the burden of three misconceptions: that domesticity and the public world are for women opposed fields of labour, that illness is a punishment for misdeeds of one kind or another, and that the greatest misdeed of all for women is infidelity to marriage and motherhood. I therefore resigned from every committee I was on, and determined, as soon as my current research project was completed, to have a period without a full-time job. I started knitting. We moved house. I painted walls, made curtains (the right way up this time), settled the two older children into a new school, and fiercely resisted all Laura's attempts to wean herself from the breast (until at fourteen months she climbed down off my lap one day, said 'No,' and walked politely away).

In order to justify this volte face, I used the argument that the diagnosis of severe illness had enabled me to distinguish the important from the unimportant business. But was that really it? Certainly I believed that if I had only a few years of life left I would rather spend them with my children than sorting out worthy from unworthy research applications or arbitrating the funds of this or that committee. Yet I think now, looking back, that my new devotion to knitting had a different significance. Even a pessimist could see that I was likely to survive for some time; the extremity of my own reaction merely matched those of others, for whom cancer posed a metaphorical threat to life. More relevantly, I had reached that point in my life—my public work-life—where the next logical step was in a direction that I did not want to take. It was logical now for me to seek and accept (if I could find it) an academic position with more administrative responsibility, more duties to do with overseeing the work of other people rather than doing my own, a higher status, more so-called 'security'. To continue to work in the way I had been doing—that is, carrying out, and writing about, 'small-scale' research—was a negation of the accepted career pattern. One moved on to bigger things. Although I did not (do not) really want to do anything else (apart from writing publishable novels), I was (am) a woman in a man's world. There is only one concept of 'a career' in this world, and that is loaded in terms of increasing power to manipulate the lives of other people, and increasing financial reward commensurate with this form of highly regarded power. Women lack an equivalent model. For them, the problem, since the present social structure was established in the eighteenth and nineteenth centuries, has always been to reconcile the conflicting demands of home and work in such a way that they appear to be conforming either to the feminine housewife model or to the male career model. An acceptable alternative pattern has yet to be established—either for women or for men.

If I have any regrets about the way I have spent the last five years, I would say this: that I have sadly not been able totally to preserve that insight born of illness which I called 'living in the present'. I did preserve it for a time. For several years I was able to savour life in small measures, drop by drop, without giving much thought to the ocean into which the drops fall, behind and ahead of the present moment. I would wake in the morning glad to be alive. I could spend time contemplating a sunset, knowing that there would never be another the same. I prized safety and calm, and even the setbacks had their advertised silver lining.

The insomnia that had plagued me since adolescence temporarily abated; sleep was something to be welcomed, not resisted. Yet this was life-in-aspic; a condition quite out of tune with my character. Perhaps it suited an uncertainty about survival, but it did not really suit a situation in which survival had occurred, as I began to confront the question: what next? In the two years following Laura's birth I completed my analysis of the Transition to Motherhood material, submitted my final report to the SSRC, and put together two books—*Becoming A Mother* (renamed *From Here to Maternity* when it came out in paperback) and *Women Confined*. In 1975 I had met at a conference in Warwick an enthusiastic young epidemiologist who, in 1977, was given the task of setting up a new research unit in Britain, the National Perinatal Epidemiology Unit. This unit was intended to 'conduct epidemiological research in the perinatal field with a view to providing information which can promote effective use of resources in the perinatal health services'.[1] Among the six core staff positions listed in the unit's contract with the Department of Health was one for a social scientist. It seemed plain to many people that this job might suit me, and since there weren't at that time vast numbers of people in Britain who could call themselves social scientists and had carried out research in the perinatal field, I was under a certain amount of pressure to apply for the job. Negotiations went on for some months and resulted in my being appointed as a kind of (very) part-time consultant who would be responsible for the social science side of the unit's work in an interim period before the full-time position could be filled by a less experienced person. Once this person had been found, (and I had finished the women's studies textbook I wrote in my 'consultancy' year), I secured a grant to carry out some research on the history of antenatal care, also at the unit. For at the same time as wanting to participate in the development of that organization, I wanted to feel I was retaining my freedom. One guiding nightmare of my life has been the routine 'office' job—having to go to a certain place at a certain time each day every day year in year out as Kafka described it.[2] I am willing to forgo quite a lot in order to have my freedom from such tyranny. This is obviously a form of maladjustment to ordinary life on my part.

I did very much want to be associated with the unit. This was a new desire for me, since I had never before seen myself in terms of any institutional affiliation. But I saw the unit as a place where important social and medical questions to do with childbirth might be united, and where the usual split between clinical practice and social issues would not be permitted to reign supreme. I had a vision—and so did the enthusiastic epidemiologist, Iain Chalmers, who has since become a close friend and to whom I now give presents of feminist science fiction books in order to sustain this vision, which does, of course, have to compete with numerous constraining realities. These include what powerful people think such a unit ought to be doing; how many square metres of office space we are allowed to snatch from the laboratory in which the 'more important' kind of scientific research is done; and the financial cutbacks imposed as a consequence of there not being enough money to go round—or, rather, because perinatal research is a mean, dwarflike activity according to a scale of values in which military expenditure and big business are at the top, and finding out what is really good for people's health and welfare is at the bottom.

'I am listening tonight to bells that have rung for hundreds of years at Oxford. I can't help wondering why it is so difficult for us to learn from our history . . . human beings are not free to design life just as they would wish it, but they are not powerless, either.'[3] It is strange to be in Oxford again, in the building right next door to Somerville College where I arrived so full of youthful enthusiasms two decades before. Occasionally now I wander in there and see its lit windows and sloping lawns as an escape from, not a promise of, life. I went there only yesterday, as a matter of fact. Out of the back gate of the hospital, round into Little Clarendon Street, into Somerville through the new graduate block. I stood in the middle of the snow-covered grass, seeing paths like tattered seams cut across the layer of white, bent figures walking crisply, passing archways and uncurtained orange windows.

The new library doesn't smell like the old one: I stand by Darwin's *Origin of the Species* and take down the volume next to it, the little-heard-of *Expression of Emotion*. It doesn't feel the same. Two decades ago I sought enlightenment, an education, the story book romance of marriage. Now I know education only props up a sexist and classist state, that the purest enlightenment is to be found in untrammelled revolutionary politics, that marriage as an institution merely liberates women from the pseudo fear of being excluded from it. I have achieved all of what I dreamed about, twenty years ago. Successful work—even a degree of international repute; love, friendship, marriage, motherhood. And yet, and still, I am not satisfied.

The American photographer Diana Michener felt that the only answer to the anarchic situation in her head was to be alone and confront it. So she demanded four weeks to herself, sent her children off with their father, and rented an empty and remote farmhouse on Prince Edward Island. For three nights and two days after arriving there she lay in bed. On the third morning she woke up laughing—at herself, with affection, for the first time. She got out of bed, found her camera, set the self-timer, got back into bed again, and re-enacted her getting up.[4]

What do I want that I don't have? This isn't what I ask myself, in fact. I would merely like to feel remotely satisfied with the way my life has gone. I am tired of feeling *dissatisfied*, that there is always some other grand project to be done, that choices were made that were perhaps not the right choices, that certain options are no longer open to me because I am not eighteen and malleable in all directions. What I most of all want that I don't have is something very fundamental and very surprising: I want a concept of myself. Yes, I know I am Ann Oakley (Oakley's my name, not just his), the author of six books, Wellcome Research Fellow at the NPEU, Honorary Research Officer in the Department of Sociology, Bedford College, etc.: I know I am the mother of three children and friend to various adults in my social network, that I remain the daughter of my parents, too; but who is that person? Or, rather, is she worth knowing?

It is as much of a mistake to believe in the independent woman as it is to believe in the independent man. But a balance must be struck between our own personal strength and autonomy on the one hand and our personal connectedness with others on the other. The balance is hard to achieve. Calling oneself a feminist, or writing six books, or having six children: these are not in themselves answers.

Consider the second of these: the writing of books. Is this an achievement? Why do people write? Is writing easy? If it's easy, then it's hardly an achievement. If it's difficult, then I'm a masochist. This is what Thomas Mann says about writing in *Tonio Kröger*: the urge to write is a curse born early in one's life 'by your feeling yourself set apart, in a curious sort of opposition to the nice, regular people; there is a gulf of ironic sensibility, of knowledge, scepticism, disagreement, between you and the others; it grows deeper and deeper, you realize that you are alone.' This may very well be why women have made literature a field of their own. 'I could not live in any of the worlds offered to me,' says Anais Nin, 'I believe one writes because one has to create a world in which one can live.'[5] Just so. I write in order to live, to have a world in which to live. There are many ways to put this. I could say that I don't know what I think until I see it written down. This is true, but it misses the basic point. Writing has nothing to do with the ease or difficulty of that particular task. It has to do with the psychological importance of the written self-created world. From this point of view, whether the written world is fictional or non-fictional matters not at all. All writing is a matter of new arrangements of words, and thus of new forms. All writing is an invitation to the imagination.

I do, in fact, find it hard to write. I can only write under certain very specific conditions. If I can hear music of any kind I can't write. I need a pen in my hand (not a typewriter on my desk). I need not to feel hungry, tired, or in pain. If the telephone is within view it distracts me. I must have a window out of which to gaze 'lost' in thought. If I know I'm going to be interrupted, no words will come into my head. It is obvious that these conditions don't exist very often, and so in that sense writing is difficult—but it's also difficult in the good times, when the conditions are right. Then I struggle. It is always a struggle. But, like childbirth, the product seems to me more worthwhile than any other that might be conceived, and that is why I go on.

The only way to stop writing would be to find the 'real' world a more comfortable place. But I find it less and less comfortable as time goes on. I suppress but acknowledge the imminent prospect of a nuclear holocaust. Masculine politics is in any case a most disturbing enterprise. The major institutions of British society (and those of other countries) remain male-dominated in ideology and practice. Life doesn't get better for women; economic recession and the belief that we're all liberated now have made it marginally worse. No one has produced a satisfactory formula for combining love and the family. We look to passion for our salvation from life's little squabbles and irritations and then are drowned in it—unsalvageable except by appeals to all those tenets of conscience and duty we threw out long ago, along with the rest of the repressive morality of the postwar years.

It seems to me I've come a long way, but not nearly far enough. For example, I am still afraid of the telephone; I'm extremely nervous with an audience of more than one and find it difficult to say anything sensible in meetings. (Television and radio don't count: here I am, because, I suppose, in a one-to-one situation, usually less nervous than the person who is interviewing me.) I can't cope with public speaking, except by having every word (including the spontaneous jokes) written down— and in moments of complete desperation taking advice of whoever it was who said, just imagine all those important people entirely naked. I live in fear of getting lost and not being able to find myself, which is why I have nightmares regularly and carry large maps of one-way systems in my car. I have all sorts of stupid phobias about being late, offending people, creating the wrong impression, saying what I mean, believing that anyone believes in me. I depend on others for certain essential services like keeping my finances straight and my car in working order. 'How can you be a feminist', says my fifteen-year-old son, 'when you always get me to check your tyres for you?' I can, but I admit it's difficult.

It's impossible to say exactly what I dreamed about. I dreamed of a dead baby, a baby whom I never saw, whom the world kept from me, like an identity I've never been able to claim. I dreamed of a breast swollen and dripping with milk and no one there to receive this nourishment. That baby was female: and as quickly as she was given to me, she departed from me. And then, suddenly, I had given birth to a well-covered boy, so well-covered that he not only weighed ten pounds twelve ounces but was born wearing a green knitted woollen suit. I found this boy upside down on the edge of a bed, screaming, and having fallen out of his basket. I picked him up, he ceased crying. He looked at me with a mature look. His hair was black, his eyes blue. I felt he could be a friend. I held him between my hands and studied him.

But I was possessed by panic. I knew I had four children and that I should tell my mother about these children. I sat by the telephone trying to do just that. Yet I couldn't remember the last baby's weight—despite knowing it—and I realized my mother would ask that, and if I couldn't tell her, she'd be disappointed. There is a law in operation 'that mothers and daughters could not teach each other, could not inherit, could not relate. They must continually react against each other, generation against generation.'[6]

Behind the fireplace in our sitting-room I discovered a secret compartment. A small, exquisitely equipped flat completely hidden from the world. It had a thick brown carpet and a split level oven (not something I have consciously ever wanted) and a small sunny greenhouse protruding from the back. There I was in it, on my own. I felt whole. I felt whole because I was alone and missed no one, mourned no one, except, in a dull ache somewhere, that daughter of mine who had died. Though in the dream she had died because of the obscure cruelty of medical staff, I knew that she had really died because I had made the wrong choice about the circumstances in which she should be born. If I had given birth to her in the right place, she would be here now, and I would know what kind of person she was. But aside from this sadness, I sat comfortably enclosed in my secret compartment. The sun shone. Everything was tidy. Nothing needed doing. I could just exist in a state of total equilibrium, calm, unmoving, like a stuffed animal.

With the exception of a disembodied voice, the second baby was the only male in my dream. It is interesting that he was born fully clothed, ready for life, quite self-contained. Nothing vulnerable about him. He wouldn't be a victim or expend his energies in silly activities as I had done. All I had to do, I knew, was stand by and watch him grow. He would be tall and strong and emotionally composed. But the stronger he got the weaker I would become.

The daughter who died was called Donna. When I telephoned the special care baby unit a man said in a cold voice, 'Donna's fine.' I knew he was lying, because men don't tell us the truth about ourselves. In fact, now I remember, yes I did see her, I was allowed to bring her home with me just before she died. She was the size of a four-year-old. She sat up in her cot and she vomited huge ears of yellow corn. Clearly she was dying. All her insides were coming out. I could do nothing but stand by and hold her hot wet head and stroke her back and try to comfort her.

The only association I have with the name 'Donna' is with a Yiddish musical theatre song Joan Baez sang in the 1960s:

On a wagon bound for market
Lies a calf with a mournful eye.
High above him there's a swallow
Flying freely through the sky.

How the winds are laughing;
They laugh with all their might,
Laugh and laugh the whole day through
And half the summer's night.
Dona, dona, dona, dona . . .

'Stop complaining', says the farmer,
'Who told you a calf to be?
Why don't you have wings to fly with
Like that swallow so proud and free?'

Calves are easily bound and slaughtered
Never knowing the reason why,
But whoever treasures freedom
Like a swallow has learned to fly.

Women: what revolution?

It's well known among those who read the feminist literature that, if women are going to experience a revolution, it will be the longest revolution of all.[1] I don't want to end this book by discussing the causes and cures of women's oppression, by referring in detail to the debate between Marxist and radical feminist modes of analysis: the place for that is elsewhere. But I do want to address myself to the problem that this book raises more questions than it answers. The questions I began with were:

what makes a feminist?
what is a feminist?
what sense does feminism make of a society organized in
    terms of sexual difference and the family?
what is heterosexual love?
in what ways should we allow our mortality to condition
    our lives?

The themes wrapped up in these questions can be put in terms of opposites:

love and the family
dependency and autonomy
emotion and intellect
sacrifice and protest
depression and ecstasy

If you arrange them this way, they become *human* issues, the unresolved problems of the *human* condition.

However, they are also women's problems, and it is with women that I'm most concerned. Why? I've explained why—the answer's a historical one. Feminists, like women, are not born but made. I can't speak for all feminists, nor do I really approve of the attempt to work out which social factors turn some women one way and others another. But in my own life I can see the significance of some factors, viz:

> being born to parents who did not in their own personalities conform to conventional gender role stereotypes (though they did in their roles);
> perceiving the difficult reality, for my mother, of a traditional marriage;
> having a close intellectual and emotional relationship with my father;
> imbibing in childhood and adolescence the theory and sentiments of socialism, i.e. a moral condemnation of social and economic inequality;
> receiving conflicting expectations from both my parents and my formal education that I would fulfil myself as a woman (by marrying and bearing children and caring for them myself), but would also achieve a brilliantly successful career (in the masculine manner).

When I say I'm a feminist, what do I mean? I mean that I believe that women are an oppressed social group, a group of people sharing a common exclusion from full participation in certain key social institutions (and being over-represented in others). Women in Britain in the 1980s are still subject to the awful soul-destroying tyranny of being told the meaning of their lives by others in terms which are not theirs.

Feminism means being more involved on a political level with the situation of women than with that of any other minority or majority group (which immediately makes much of what goes under the heading of 'politics' uninteresting to feminists). To be a feminist means putting women first. The meaning of such questions as 'What about men?' is a meaning invented by other people: as my friend Dale Spender has said, who says we should lead meaningful lives, thus defined?[2]

Much of this book has been about men. Is this not in itself a most objectionable contradiction? I think it is, but that it also must be understood as a cultural product. One of women's difficulties with each other is that they take each other for granted. All women are feminists at heart. In their psychology lies a great love for women as a class. But it's interred beneath a mound of rubbish. Personally, I could not make sense of my life without the support, fidelity and love of women—not in a general sense but in the very specific sense of there being in my life a number of women who are important to me, to whom I can turn at any moment with any problem and to whom I offer (I hope) the same service. It is most important to me to try never to let women down—although clearly I am bound to fail, often. It is important to me to promote a feeling of self-esteem, power and control in women whenever I can, and to look for that gift for myself. I am not naive enough to believe that all women are my sisters (except in a metatheoretical sense): but I do *want* them to be. I am always hurt by the most minor cruelty perpetrated towards me by a woman, whereas I long ago gave up my faith in the loyalty and commitment of men as a class.

But if women cease to be the problem, because one sees both how women are constructed out of the problems and how they must repudiate them for advances to be made, then men, somewhat inevitably, become the problem instead. We come upon the paradox Sheila Rowbotham has described as 'ecstatic subjugation'. How can women love men without being oppressed in, and by means of, this love and that which is, or is not, given in return?

A few feminists I know declare a hatred of men. I myself feel that, sometimes. To see groups of dark-suited, busy, pugnacious and self-important men at conferences, in the street, in hotel lounges, sitting lined up on an aircraft being served drinks by lipsticked stewardesses, is to be made most sharply aware that it is men who rule the world and that men, by virtue of their brotherhood, remove themselves from the possibility of knowing what women's real interests are. I don't want anything to do with these men. If any one of them makes any kind of sexual overture to me, my anger can't be borne: it makes an impotent, inarticulate wreck of me. In part this anger comes from being an outsider. Men rarely have that experience. If they are outnumbered temporarily by women, then at least they are on top.

I begin with Robin Morgan's remark about men's misuse of women in pornography: 'man-hater as I am, I love men too much to believe that they really want to do that to us.'[3] I understand that male chauvinism is as much a social product as feminism. The men who strut and expound their ideas at conferences and in governments, and who equate feminism with a personal attack on their genitals, can't admit the possibility of error, of weakness, of self-doubt, on the subject of their masculinity. To be right and strong is so much a part of being male that men may only cry or give themselves up to listening to others by abrogating their maleness. Now, this isn't such an awful step to take, but they don't know it.

I'm not claiming actually to understand men. The three main male figures in this book are oddly unreal: idealized, I think; I don't believe I've portrayed them at all clearly. There is nothing I can do about this, because ultimately I suppose it is true to say they aren't real to me. In short, I think it's hard to be a man. I wouldn't want to be one. I'd rather be a woman, even if I am oppressed. I'd willingly give up all sorts of power to have some of the experiences I've had that are only possible because I'm a woman.

But the question, for many women, is not, how can men be loved, but how can such love be stopped?

Maggie Scarf set out to write a book about women and depression and found herself writing a book about women instead. She discovered two recurrent motifs in the histories of depressed women: women's struggle to liberate themselves from thraldom to magical figures in the past, and the effort to develop an autonomous sense of self, 'that inner confidence that one will be able to survive on one's own inner resources'.[4] There was no escaping the fact that women's lives tend to be characterized by important business untransacted. So long as men at any level continue to represent answers to women's problems, they will be the problem, a cause of untransacted business. But how do we rid ourselves of the imagery, of the powerful wish to belong to someone other than ourselves?

Miriam Berg in Marge Piercy's *Small Changes* has a sexual relationship that is extremely pleasurable to her with a withdrawn intellectual commune-dweller called Jackson. However, she feels that in the process he is 'having' her, not 'knowing' her:

That scared her, but part of her rose up from under and flowed with it. Caught, hooked, tangled with him. Something in her said, This is how it is supposed to be. This is a man. This is loving. His possessing was a current that seemed to require from her only that she let go, then she would be held firmly in him without tension, without decision... It was a deep image present from earliest adolescence of the strong man who would want her, who would find her, who would carry her off, who would be a world in which she floated, whose being would contain hers.[5]

—much as in the different culture of Britain in the late 1960s and early 1970s Mary Ingham commented that 'Intellectually we demanded to be equals; deep down, emotionally and sexually, we were still looking for the awe-inspiring Mr Right.'[6] Or as the famous Russian feminist and revolutionary, Alexandra Kollontai, discovered to her cost, when she became involved with a married Russian economist called Maslov in 1909; she came across important parallels between the problems of her affair with Maslov and those of a French-born Bolshevik woman called Inessa Armand, who was having an affair with Lenin (who, in the manner of the best male revolutionaries, had a wife at home). In *A Great Love*,[7] Kollontai brings the two relationships together, writing about the unrevolutionary nature of relationships between men and women in revolutionary times. Natasha, the woman in *A Great Love*, struggles with her need for Senya (Lenin-Maslov) while objecting to the patronizing way he treats her, belittling the importance of her work and fitting her into his double life when it suits him. Politics, especially sexual politics, begin at home.

'Being a heterosexual feminist is like being in the resistance in Nazi-occupied Europe when in the daytime you blow up a bridge, in the evening you rush to repair it.'[8] 'The heterosexual couple is the basic unit of the political structure of male supremacy...' 'Penetration is an act of symbolic significance by which the oppressor enters the body of the oppressed. But it is more than a symbol, its function and effect is the punishment and control of women... Every act of penetration for a woman is an invasion which undermines her confidence and saps her strength... So every woman who enjoys penetration bolsters the oppression and reinforces the class power of men.'[9]

Germaine Greer didn't make herself popular with radical feminists by saying 'a full cunt is better than an empty one';[10] nor, presumably, did Simone de Beauvoir in remarking 'coition with penetration of the vagina does provide pleasure of an undeniably specific kind.'[11] You don't have to reject feminism or espouse unedited Freudianism to agree with both of them. No, the basic issue is this: that sex doesn't have the same meaning for men that it does for women; women don't have the same meaning for men as they do for women; men don't understand gender—or sex.

For the language of penetration can be substituted the language of enclosure; he doesn't penetrate me, I enclose him. But that doesn't overcome the fact that men, in having sex with women, get rid of something (possibly sometimes intending to make a gift of it) while women take men into themselves, cannot have sexual intercourse with men without taking the man into themselves and making themselves vulnerable to whatever he wants to do there or subsequently with this act of always unparalleled intimacy.

In *Sleepless Nights* Elizabeth Hardwick describes Alexander thus:

> A good deal of Alexander's life had been assigned to women. Much of his time had gone into lovemaking. Tonight, October, is our second meeting after a number of years. The last time, a month ago, he had told me that for a long period in his life he made love every night. He sighed, remembering his discipline and fortitude...
>
> Casanova: The great exhilaration to my spirits, greater than all my own pleasure, was the joy of giving pleasure to a woman.
>
> Some reason to doubt the truth of that... Alex's vanity was... trapped in the belief that he had a special power, or perhaps a special duty, to please women... So love was a treadmill, like churchgoing, kept alive by respect for the community. Many have this evangelical view of love-

making: There! I've done it once today and twice the day before yesterday.[12]

Sex doesn't have the same meaning for men as it does for women, and it doesn't do so because personal relationships don't have the same value for the two sexes, and this lack of parity in turn proceeds from the early differentiation of the two sexes into the two genders within the family.

Male-dominated culture has designated as female all labours of emotional connectedness. As I have already said, the greater sensitivity of women means that they possess an enhanced capacity to relate to others and find themselves very often in the position of being the only ones able to carry out this life-saving task. The principal mode of developing this sensitivity in women is the gender-differentiated nuclear family. Women mother. Daughters are transformed into mothers. An autonomous sense of self, a self which exists outside and independently of relationships with others, does not need to develop; there are no factors that encourage it and many that militate against it. Women's sense of identity is thus dangerously bound up from early childhood with the identities of others. Not so for men, who as little boys look into their mothers' faces and see what they learn is not a reflection of their own. Everything conspires to make them learn this lesson, or nearly everything.

So, if it isn't in love that women are lost, it's in the family. The tension between the interests of the family and the interests of women as individuals has been rising for some two centuries. It is not possible for these interests to be reconciled. But I know what path women will choose (be pressured to choose) in the future.

I don't hold out much hope. But it is true that the most important battles are even now being fought, as individual women look at the circumstances of their lives, not just through a glass, darkly, but face to face; and in so looking determine, most bravely, not to be overcome. 'I used to want to lodge in someone's pocket and be able to jump in and out whenever it suited me. Now I go round listening for cries from women who I imagine are locked in others' pockets.'[13]

Looking Out to Sea

We stand together and look at the sea. The sea is pock-marked silver, a second-hand mirror with portions of its sheen erased by the efforts of time, too many people looking into it and seeing the falsity of the smile they have put there, the untarnished horror of the mock grimace, the surprise that is for the mirror's benefit alone. We stand together, you and I, looking. Where the ocean touches the sky a strip of golden light points a finger to the west. The routine grey of the sky allows the light's intrusion; for miles around there is a pale iridescence, weak but benevolent, putting an altogether different interpretation on the weather. The light is either the sun coming or the sun departing. It matters not a great deal which it is.

And on the crimplene surface of the sea the light shines like a sword. Fish swim beneath it; seagulls dip their wings above it. Nothing can be seen out at sea. There are no boats and there is no land. Of course, one knows there is land, somewhere; if one skimmed across that sea in the end one would arrive at some destination which would be more than the black void at the edge of the earth. The earth permits us ordinary mortals no stepping into space. For that an astronautical technology is required. Since the earth isn't flat, there's no hope. One must just go on and on circling the globe for ever.

On the shore the waves break, khaki in their depths, like clotted cream on top. Here comes one now, a big one; out of the mirror it rises, curls, advances, now it crashes with a profusion of creamy foam on the concrete piers and crumpled brown stones, our humble sands washed by the seas of time. The sea's symbolism resides in its kindness and in its unknown enormity. Here, now, the water spreads in rounded fingers out across the beach, each finger edged with white, reaching out as far as it can go. The fingers reach out to the heavy lumps of stinking seaweed, the thick dark ribbons that don't bear too close an inspection. They reach out to the occasional stick of wood, the odd lemonade bottle, to comment upon our unkempt destruction of the sacred natural world. For we are profane. In our tears, in our anger, in our contradictions, in our right to live and our wish to die, we are profane. Don't believe them when they say we are all creatures of God: the only God-like thing about us is our very humanity.

You and I examine our shoes; the sea has made them faintly wet. Walking again, we pass through the metal avenue beneath the west pier. Its groves are green and rotting. Children who are not quite adults and adults who are still children commit all sorts of misdemeanours here. The red sign says danger. The pier meanders in a disorganized fashion out to sea. It is a badly iced birthday cake, a celebration gone wrong. Where once it gleamed whitely and full of sparkle, and laughter sprang from its steamy arcades, and cheap fish was sold in the *News of the World*, and fat people in sagging deckchairs snored in the morning sun, and little children darted shouting in and out of its metal pillars, now the pier has all but given up the ghost. On spreadeagled rusty legs it is making its descent into the welcoming bed of the sea. There are no lights on it, and only the spirits of laughter murmur in its ashen structures. There was life; now it is no more: where has it gone instead? This morning the only vitality remaining lies in the waves breaking on the beaches, in the mighty taut energy of the deep hubris of the sea.

Are you cold? Your splendid face, child-like and woman-like, both, is pinched with lack of sleep, with all you expect of life and cannot quite be sure of getting. There is no certainty in anything. I cannot give you, or anyone, the promise that you can't give me. I can't say sorrow will pass for ever, nor that the conditions under which we now exist won't change. But you know I love you, don't you? And that in such love resides not simply your redemption but my own affirmation. Don't ask what love is. No one will answer you, except the pert seagulls lined up along the pier, the sliver of light in the sky, the rancid salty wind, the waving pink flowers at the bottom of the sea. None of us is an expert in such matters. Don't ponder on the complexity of human relationships, on the masochism of women and the heartlessness of men, on the child's innocence and the adult's wisdom. Female, male, lover, spouse, parent, child: these are names, mere names. Who is mad and who is sane? Who is happy and who despairing? Whose smile upset the mirror so it cracked, who tried to heal it with a glare of terror? The dream and the reality inhabit different heads, or the same. Your nightmare wakes us all. My vision of what is possible in the best of all possible worlds keeps not only me but all of us alive.

Life is worth living. Not because there is nothing else, but because of what we each may give one another; pain, joy, anguish, peace. It's not an easy journey. You may even call it an adventure. It doesn't matter about the problems, the contradictions. In our hearts we understand everything. We understand it's the struggle that counts.

Notes

SCENE 1
A Lake in a London Park, 1975

1 Adrienne Rich, 'When We Dead Awaken: Writing as Re-Vision', in On Lies, Secrets, Silences, Virago, London, 1980, p. 35.
2 Aldous Huxley, Brave New World, Granada, London, 1977, p. 192.

CHRONOLOGY 0–18

1 Richard Titmuss and Kathleen Titmuss, Parents' Revolt, Secker and Warburg, London, 1942.
2 Leonore Davidoff, Jean L'Esperance and Howard Newby, 'Landscape with Figures: home and community in English society', in J. Mitchell and A. Oakley (eds), The Rights and Wrongs of Women, Penguin, Harmondsworth, 1976.
3 Liv Ullman, Changing, Weidenfeld and Nicolson, London, 1977, p. 200.
4 Ann Oakley, paper given at UNITAR conference, 'Creative Women in Changing Societies', Oslo, Norway, July 9–13, 1980.
5 Nancy Chodorow, The Reproduction of Mothering, University of California Press, Berkeley, 1978.
6 Peter Shore, 'In the Room at the Top', in N. MacKenzie et al. (eds), Conviction, MacGibbon and Kee, London, 1958, p. 53.

7 Sheila Rowbotham, *Women, Resistance and Revolution*, Allen Lane, London, 1972.

8 Christopher Driver, 'The Rise and Fall of C.N.D.', *Observer*, March 22, 1964.

9 Kathleen Gough, *When the Saints Go Marching In: An Account of the Ban-the-Bomb Movement in Britain*, Correspondence Pamphlet No. 3, 7737 Mack Avenue, Detroit 14, Michigan, USA, n.d.

10 Sylvia Plath, *The Bell Jar*, Faber and Faber, London, 1963, pp. 240–1.

11 Michael Schofield, *The Sexual Behaviour of Young People*, Penguin, Harmondsworth, 1968.

Family: reflections

1 Or perhaps not; the 'Ballad of Pirate Jenny' in Brecht's *Threepenny Opera* describes a prostitute (alternatively referred to as a kitchen maid) who has the fantasy of annihilating her clients—sailors—in a harbour.

2 Philip Slater, *The Pursuit of Loneliness: American culture at breaking point*, Penguin, Harmondsworth, 1975.

3 J. Sims, 'Song of a Growing Girl', *Views*, n.d., p. 94.

4 Peter Lomas, *The Case for a Personal Psychotherapy*, Oxford University Press, Oxford, 1981.

5 See Ann Oakley, *Subject Women*, Martin Robertson, Oxford, 1981, pp. 323–4.

CHRONOLOGY 18–23 MINUS TWO WEEKS

1 Marcus Aurelius, *Meditations*, Penguin, Harmondsworth, 1963, p. 73.

2 Ved Mehta, *Fly and the Fly Bottle*, Weidenfeld and Nicolson, London, 1963.

3 James Morris, *Oxford*, Faber and Faber, London, 1965, pp. 25–6.

4 See, for instance, Sue Sharpe, *Just Like a Girl: How Girls Learn to be Women*, Penguin, Harmondsworth, 1976.

5 Mary Ingham, *Now We Are Thirty*, Eyre Methuen, London, 1981, pp. 116–17.

Love: irresolution

1 Jean Baker Miller, *Toward a New Psychology of Women*, Beacon Press, Boston, 1976, p. 83.
2 Jessie Bernard, *Women and the Public Interest*, Aldine-Atherton, Chicago, 1971, p. 90.
3 Miller, op. cit., p. 71.
4 David Cooper, *The Death of the Family*, Penguin, Harmondsworth, 1972, p. 41.

CHRONOLOGY 23–29

1 Erving Goffman, *Asylum: Essays on the Social Situation of Patients and Other Inmates*, Anchor Books, New York, 1961.
2 Michael Rosen, 'Pain and Its Relief', in Tim Chard and Martin Richards (eds), *Benefits and Hazards of the New Obstetrics*, William Heinemann, London, 1977.
3 M.H. Klaus and J.H. Kennell, *Maternal-Infant Bonding*, C.V. Mosby, St Louis, 1976, p. 14.
4 Adrienne Rich, *Of Woman Born*, Virago, London, 1977.
5 Ann Oakley, *Women Confined*, Martin Robertson, Oxford, 1980.
6 G.W. Brown and T. Harris, *Social Origins of Depression*, Tavistock, London, 1978.
7 R. Cooperstock and H.L. Lennard, 'Some Social Meanings of Tranquilizer Use', in *Sociology of Health and Illness*, 1979, 1, 3, pp. 331–47.
8 Betty Friedan, *The Feminine Mystique*, Gollancz, London, 1963.
9 Ann Oakley, 'Interviewing Women: a contradiction in terms?' in H. Roberts (ed.), *Doing Feminist Research*, Routledge and Kegan Paul, London, 1981.
10 Brown and Harris, op. cit.
11 Oakley, 1980, op. cit.
12 Robert Blauner, *Alienation and Freedom*, University of Chicago Press, Chicago, 1964.
13 Robin Morgan, 'Introduction: the women's revolution', in R. Morgan (ed.), *Sisterhood Is Powerful*, Vintage Books, New York, 1970, p. xxxvi.

14 Sheila Rowbotham, *Woman's Consciousness, Man's World,* Penguin, Harmondsworth, 1973, p. 38.

Family: a personal declaration

1 J. Cunningham, 'Putting Women in Their Place', *Guardian,* December 9, 1980.
2 F.P. Hosken, 'Female Genital Mutilation in the World Today: a global review', *International Journal of Health Services,* 1981, 11, 3, pp. 415–30.
3 E. Hogg, 'Hands off the Housewife!', *Daily Telegraph,* October 31, 1974.
4 PHS, Times Diary, *The Times,* October 24, 1974.
5 John Allan, 'Abolish the Role of the Housewife in the Family', *Sydney Morning Herald,* February 6, 1975.
6 Janet Watts, 'After the Event', *Observer,* January 20, 1980.
7 Adrienne Rich, *Of Woman Born,* Virago, London, 1977.

Family: death of a father

1 R.M. Titmuss, 'Postscript', in *Social Policy: An Introduction,* Allen and Unwin, London, 1974, p. 145.
2 Michael Young, 'The Professor who had no "O" Levels', *Observer,* April 8, 1973.
3 Lord Collison, 'Professor R.M. Titmuss', *The Times,* April 12, 1973.
4 Obituary, 'Professor R.M. Titmuss: An Outstanding Social Administrator', *The Times,* April 7, 1973.
5 David Donnison, 'Richard Titmuss', *New Society,* April 12, 1973.

SCENE 12
A French Letter

1 M.H. Kingston, *The Woman Warrior,* Pan Books, London, 1981, p. 12.
2 Verena Stefan, *Shedding,* The Women's Press, London, 1979, p. 29.

The War between Love and the Family II

1 Simone de Beauvoir, *All Said and Done*, André Deutsch, London, 1974, p. 20.
2 Walter Mischel, 'A Social-learning View of Sex Differences in Behaviour', in E.E. Maccoby (ed.), *The Development of Sex Differences*, Tavistock, London, 1967.
3 Jessie Bernard, *The Future of Marriage*, Souvenir Press, New York, 1973.
4 Margaret Mead, *Sex and Temperament in Three Primitive Societies*, William Morrow, New York, 1935, p. 102.

CHRONOLOGY 29–33

1 Dora Russell, *The Tamarisk Tree*, Virago, London, 1977, p. 167.
2 Adrienne Rich, 'Motherhood: the Contemporary Emergency and the Quantum Leap', in *On Lies, Secrets, Silences*, Virago, London, 1980.
3 See Diane Scully, *Men Who Control Women's Health*, Houghton Mifflin, Boston, 1980.
4 S.K. Danziger, 'On Doctor Watching', *Urban Life*, 7, 4, 1979, p. 523.
5 Such language is endemic in many obstetricians' communication with their female patients. See Ann Oakley, *Women Confined*, Martin Robertson, Oxford, 1980, Ch.1.
6 See Alan Davis and Gordon Horobin (eds), *Medical Encounters*, Croom Helm, London, 1977.
7 M.J. Bennett, 'Real-time Ultrasound in the Second and Third Trimesters of Pregnancy', in M.J. Bennett and S. Campbell (eds), *Real-time Ultrasound in Obstetrics*, Blackwell Scientific Publications, Oxford, 1980.
8 W.A.R. Thomson, *Black's Medical Dictionary*, Adam and Charles Black, London, 1968, pp. 596–7.
9 For a review of the relationship between stress and the outcome of pregnancy see A. Oakley, A. Macfarlane and I. Chalmers, 'Social Class, Stress and Reproduction', in A.R. Rees and H. Purcell (eds), *Disease and the Environment*, John Wiley, Chichester, 1982; there is no firm evidence linking peppermints with carcinogenicity: however, the number of

years over which the habit was practised is typical of the time interval between the introduction of a specific carcinogen and the induction of cancer: on the immunology of pregnancy and cancer see V.M. Dilman, 'Metabolic Immunodepression which increases the risk of cancer', *Lancet*, December 10, 1977, pp. 1207–9.

10 Ivan Illich, *Medical Nemesis*, Calder and Boyars, London, 1975, p. 11.

11 Susan Sontag, *Illness as Metaphor*, Farrar, Straus and Giroux, New York, 1977, p. 9.

12 John Berger and Jean Mohr, *A Fortunate Man*, Penguin, Harmondsworth, 1969, pp. 49–50.

13 Bertrand Russell, *Autobiography*, Unwin Paperbacks, London, 1978, p. 364.

14 Ann Oakley, 'Living in the Present: a confrontation with cancer', *British Medical Journal*, 1979, 1, pp. 392–4.

15 Office of Population Censuses and Surveys and Cancer Research Campaign, *Cancer Statistics: Incidence, survival and mortality in England and Wales*. Studies on Medical and Population Subjects No.43, HMSO, London, 1981.

16 Office of Population Censuses and Surveys, *Mortality Statistics: Cause 1979*, HMSO, London, 1981.

17 The quotation is from Boethius, who was writing in the sixth century.

SCENE 13
Romance of the Rose: with an inexcusable scent of death

1 A. Lamartine, 'Le Lac', in H.E. Berthon, *Nine French Poets 1820–80*, Macmillan, London, 1957.

The War between Love and the Family   III

1 R. Leete and S. Anthony, 'Divorce and Remarriage: a record linkage study', *Population Trends*, 16, HMSO, London, 1979.

2 Elizabeth Bott, *Family and Social Network*, Tavistock, London, revised ed. 1971.

3 T.S. Eliot, 'East Coker', *The Four Quartets*, Faber and Faber, London, 1959, p.29.

SCENE 14
Movements in the Clouds

1 Adrienne Rich, 'Women and Honor: Some Notes on Lying', in Rich, *On Lies, Secrets, Silences*, Virago, London, 1980, pp.186–8.
2 Elizabeth Wilson, *Mirror Writing*, Virago, London, 1982, p.119.

SCENE 15A
In the Heat of the Day

1 E. Le Roy Ladurie, *Montaillou*, Penguin, Harmondsworth, 1980, p.328.
2 Office of Population Censuses and Surveys, *Mortality Statistics: Cause*, HMSO, London, published annually.
3 R.W. Maris, *Pathways to Suicide*, The Johns Hopkins University Press, Baltimore, Maryland, 1981, p.290.
4 Maris, ibid.
5 Cited in A. Alvarez, *The Savage God*, Penguin, Harmondsworth, 1974, p.153.
6 Cited, ibid. p.68.
7 Cited, ibid., p.145.
8 Sylvia Plath, 'Sheep in the Fog' and 'Paralytic', from *Collected Poems*, Harper and Row, New York, 1981.

Note on the Ultimate Contradiction

1 Cited in Elizabeth Hardwick, *Sleepless Nights*, Virago, London, 1980, p.25.
2 *Forty-Seventh Annual Report of the Local Government Board 1917–18*, HMSO, London, 1918.
3 J. Willocks, 'Some Aspects of Fetal Growth and Function', in R.K. MacDonald, *Scientific Basis of Obstetrics and Gynaecology*, Churchill Livingstone, Edinburgh, second edn 1978, pp. 110–11.
4 Hardwick, op. cit., p.112.
5 Nancy Thayer, *Stepping*, Sphere, London, 1981, p.111.

CHRONOLOGY 33–38

1 House of Commons Official Report (Hansard), July 5, 1978.
2 Franz Kafka, *The Trial*, Penguin, Harmondsworth, 1953.
3 K.K. Hamod, 'Finding New Forms', in S. Ruddick and P. Daniels (eds), *Working It Out*, Pantheon, New York, 1977, p.19.
4 Diana Michener, 'Catching the Sun', in Ruddick and Daniels (eds), op. cit.
5 Anais Nin, *In Favour of the Sensitive Man*, Star, London, 1981, p.12.
6 Marge Piercy, *Small Changes*, Fawcett Crest, New York, 1972, p.138.

Women: what revolution?

1 Juliet Mitchell, 'Women: the Longest Revolution', *New Left Review*, no.40, 1966.
2 Dale Spender, 'Theorising About Theorising', in G. Bowles and R. Duelli-Klein (eds), *Theories of Women's Studies II*, University of California, Berkeley, Women's Studies, 1981.
3 Robin Morgan made this remark in a film about pornography (*Not a Love Story*) made by the Canadian feminist Bonnie Klein (National Film Board of Canada, 1982).
4 Maggie Scarf, *Unfinished Business*, Fontana, London, 1981, p.1.
5 Marge Piercy, *Small Changes*, Fawcett Crest, New York, 1972, pp.190–1.
6 Mary Ingham, *Now We Are Thirty*, Eyre Methuen, London, 1981, p.180.
7 Alexandra Kollontai, *A Great Love*, Virago, London, 1981.
8 Onlywomen Press Ltd, *Love Your Enemy? The debate between heterosexual feminism and political lesbianism*, London, 1981, p.7.
9 Ibid., p.6.
10 Germaine Greer, *The Female Eunuch*, MacGibbon and Kee, London, 1970.
11 Simone de Beauvoir, *All Said and Done*, André Deutsch, London, 1974, p.458.
12 Elizabeth Hardwick, *Sleepless Nights*, Virago, London, 1980, pp.64–6.
13 Liv Ullman, *Changing*, Weidenfeld and Nicholson, London, 1977, p.200.